1 MONTH OF
FREE
READING

at

www.ForgottenBooks.com

By purchasing this book you are eligible for one month membership to ForgottenBooks.com, giving you unlimited access to our entire collection of over 1,000,000 titles via our web site and mobile apps.

To claim your free month visit:

www.forgottenbooks.com/free157483

ISBN 978-0-484-32452-6
PIBN 10157483

EVERYMAN'S LIBRARY
EDITED BY ERNEST RHYS

BIOGRAPHY

4 2/692
6. 4. 44

THE LIFE OF MAZZINI
BY BOLTON KING, M.A.

THE PUBLISHERS OF *EVERYMAN'S LIBRARY* WILL BE PLEASED TO SEND FREELY TO ALL APPLICANTS A LIST OF THE PUBLISHED AND PROJECTED VOLUMES TO BE COMPRISED UNDER THE FOLLOWING THIRTEEN HEADINGS:

TRAVEL ❧ SCIENCE ❧ FICTION
THEOLOGY & PHILOSOPHY
HISTORY ❧ CLASSICAL
FOR YOUNG PEOPLE
ESSAYS ❧ ORATORY
POETRY & DRAMA
BIOGRAPHY
REFERENCE
ROMANCE

IN FOUR STYLES OF BINDING: CLOTH, FLAT BACK, COLOURED TOP; LEATHER, ROUND CORNERS, GILT TOP; LIBRARY BINDING IN CLOTH, & QUARTER PIGSKIN

LONDON: J. M. DENT & SONS, LTD.
NEW YORK: E. P. DUTTON & CO.

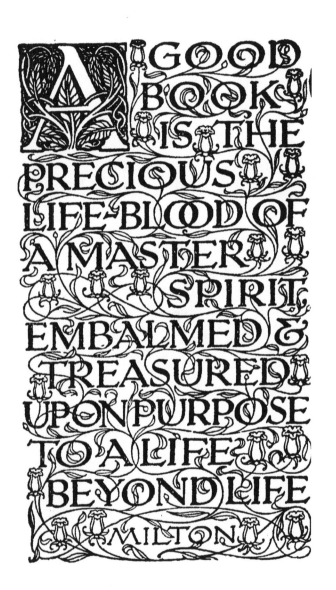

A GOOD BOOK IS THE PRECIOUS LIFE-BLOOD OF A MASTER SPIRIT, EMBALMED & TREASURED UPON PURPOSE TO A LIFE BEYOND LIFE

MILTON

THE LIFE of MAZZINI by BOLTON KING · M·A·

EVERY MAN I WILL GO WITH THEE BE THY GVIDE

IN THY MOST NEED TO GO BY THY SIDE

LONDON: PUBLISHED by J·M·DENT & SONS·LTD AND IN NEW YORK BY E·P·DUTTON & CO

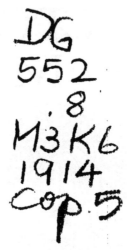
FIRST ISSUE OF THIS EDITION · 1912
REPRINTED · · · 1914

Preface

THIS volume contains a life of Mazzini and a study of his thought. It can hardly be said that any serious attempt has been made either in England or Italy to deal with either. Hence the present volume, however unequal to the subject, may have its use. The thirty years, which have passed since Mazzini's death, make it possible now to place him in his true perspective; and the author trusts that the supreme admiration, which he feels for Mazzini as a man, has not prevented him from viewing the politician with impartiality. There exists abundant matter to allow us to judge Mazzini's political work, and it is unlikely that anything yet to be published will seriously affect our estimate of it. For the personal side of Mazzini's life, the moment is not a very opportune one. Ten years ago it would have been possible to glean reminiscences from many, who are now silent. It has been the author's privilege, however, to obtain invaluable information from two of the very few persons now living, who knew Mazzini intimately. While it is nearly too late for personal reminiscences, it is too early to avail oneself fully of Mazzini's correspondence. A good many of his letters have indeed been published, and I have been able to use a good many unpublished ones, especially his correspondence with Mr and Mrs Peter Taylor, which I have found of the greatest value. But unfortunately only one volume has as yet appeared of the collected edition of his correspondence, and there are still probably many of his letters, which have yet to come to light in Italy.

With regard to the study, which occupies the second part of this volume, the author is very sensible of his limitations in dealing with so vast and complex a system as Mazzini's ethical and political thought. It is his hope that he may do something to stimulate more competent writers to labour in a very fruitful field. He believes that the more Mazzini's thought is disentangled, the more its essential importance will appear.

I have to acknowledge gratefully the kindness of those who have helped me in writing this book. Above all I am indebted to Mr and Mrs W. T. Malleson, to whom I owe the loan of the Peter Taylor correspondence and other invaluable help; to Miss Shaen for letting me see Mazzini's letters to her father, Mr W. Shaen, and the MS. of the "Prayer for the Planters," now first published; to Mr Milner-Gibson Cullum, Miss Dorothea Hickson, Mr Mazzini Stuart, Mr P. S. King, and Miss Galeer for the loan of unpublished letters from Mazzini. I have also to acknowledge my grateful thanks to many others, who have assisted me, among whom I would especially mention Miss Ashurst

Biggs, Signor Mario Borsa, Mr James Bryce, M.P., Mr W. Burnley, Signora Giuditta Casali-Benvenuti (to whom I owe the portrait of her grandmother, Giuditta Sidoli), Mr T. Chambers, Signor Felice Dagnino, Signor G. Gallavresi, Mrs Goodwin, Miss Edith Harvey, Mr H. M. Hyndman, Dr Courtney Kenny, Miss Lucy Martineau, Professor Masson, Mr C. E. Maurice, Mademoiselle Dora Melegari, Mr D. Nathan, Mr T. Okey, Mr Chas. Roberts, Mr J. J. Stansfeld, the Società Editrice Sonzogno (for permission to reproduce some illustrations from Madame White Mario's life of Mazzini) Mr W. R. Thayer, and Mr Remsen Whitehouse.

October 1902.   BOLTON KING.

A reissue of the book has allowed me to revise it in the light of recent publications referring to Mazzini. A good many more of his letters have been printed since 1902 (including a second volume of the *Epistolario*), but with the exception of Mademoiselle Melegari's collection of his letters to her father, they are not important. Nor, with the exception of Signor Cantimori's illuminating *Saggio*, have I found any useful recent studies of his thought. I still adhere to the view that subsequent research will add little to our knowledge of him. I am glad, however, to be able now to take a different view of his connection with the publication of Kossuth's manifesto in 1853, and of Madame Sidoli's mission to Florence in 1833 (see pp. 68 and 169.

BOLTON KING.

WARWICK, *November* 1911.

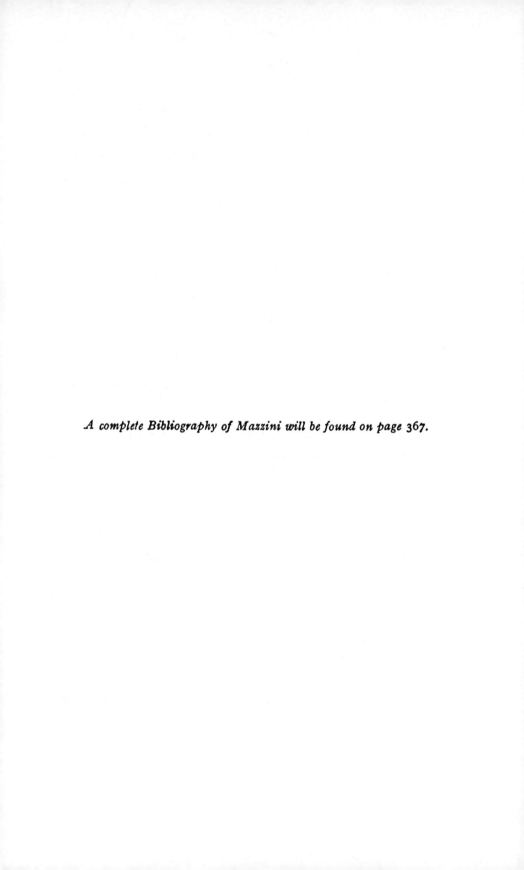

A complete Bibliography of Mazzini will be found on page 367.

Table of Contents

CHAPTER I

THE HOME AT GENOA

1805-1831.   Aetat 0-25

CHAPTER II

YOUNG ITALY ✓

1831-1833.   Aetat 25-27

CHAPTER III

MARSEILLES

1831-1834.   Aetat 25-28

CHAPTER IV

SWITZERLAND

1834-1836.   Aetat 28-31

CHAPTER IX

Mazzini and Cavour

1850-1857.   Aetat 45-52

CHAPTER X

Unity Half Won

1858-1860.   Aetat 53-55

CHAPTER XI

For Venice

1861-1866.   Aetat 56-61

CHAPTER XII

The Last Years

1866-1872.   Aetat 61-66

Table of Contents

CHAPTER XIII

RELIGION

CHAPTER XIV

DUTY

CHAPTER XV

THE STATE

CHAPTER XVI

SOCIAL THEORIES

CHAPTER XVII

NATIONALITY

Table of Contents

"" Where there is no vision, the people perish."

Chapter I

The Home at Genoa

1805-1831. AETAT 0-25

Boyhood and Youth—University Life—Literary Studies—Classicism
and Romanticism—Joins the Carbonari—Arrest and Exile.

JOSEPH MAZZINI was born in the Via Lomellina at
Genoa on June 22, 1805. His father was a doctor
of some repute and Professor of Anatomy at the
University, a democrat in creed and life, who gave
much of his time to unpaid service of the poor; at
home affectionate and loved, though sometimes hard
and imperious. His mother, to whom in after life
he bore a strong resemblance, was a capable and
devoted woman, who had little of the weakness of an
Italian mother, and brought up her children to bear
the brunt of life; with strong interest in the mighty
movements that were remoulding Europe at the time,
a mordant critic of governors and governments inside
the four walls of her house. It was a happy home,
and " Pippo " grew up the darling of his parents and
three sisters, a delicate, sensitive, gentle child, quick
and insistent to learn despite his father's fears for his
health, and giving precocious proof of brilliant talents.
He was nearly nine years old, when the Napoleonic
system was shattered, and the Emperor went to Elba.

Doubtless, Mazzini heard from his father that Napoleon was Italian born and was going to exile in an Italian island.   The shock of the downfall was felt at Genoa, for the proud city, to which Lord William Bentinck had promised in the name of England its ancient independence, learnt that " republics were no longer fashionable," and saw itself helplessly made over to the alien rule of Piedmont.   Bitterly the Genoese chafed at the traffic of their liberties, and we may be sure that there was republican talk in Mazzini's home, which sank into the mind of the thoughtful child. He himself mentions four influences that turned his boyish mind to democracy : his parents' uniform courtesy to every rank of life; the reminiscences of the French republican wars in the talk at home ; some numbers of an old Girondist paper, which his father kept half hidden, for fear of the police, behind his medical books ; and—more than all these, probably— the classics that he read under his Latin tutor.   " The history of Greece and Rome," wrote a fellow-student " the only thing taught us with any care at school was little else than a constant libel upon monarchy and a panegyric upon the democratic form of government."   Like many another boy of his time who had for school exercises to declaim the praises of Cato and the Bruti, he came to regard republics as the appointed homes of virtue.   It was the unintended fruit of the classical training, which the despotic governments of the time fostered to keep their youth innocent of any itch for innovation.

So he lived his quiet, studious home-life, till an incident one day, when he was nearly sixteen, suddenly changed its tenor.   The Carbonaro revolutions of 1820

nd 1821 had ended in deserved collapse ; and the
'iedmontese Liberals, abandoned and defeated, crowded
o Genoa and Sampierdarena, while yet there was time
o escape to Spain. Some had fled penniless, and
Mazzini, walking with his mother, noted their despair-
ng faces, and watched while a collection was made
or them in the streets. Their memory haunted him,
nd with a boy's enthusiasm for his heroes, he longed
o follow them. He neglected his lessons, and sat
moody and absorbed, interested only in gleaning news
f the exiles and learning the history of their defeat.
n his boyish impatience, which came near the truth,
e felt " they might have won, if all had done their
luty," and the thought puzzled and obsessed him.
He insisted on dressing in black, and kept the habit .
o the end of life. He brooded over Foscolo's *Jacopo
Ortis*, till the morbid pessimism of the book wrought
n him, and his mother, apparently with good reason,
eared suicide.

In time he recovered his balance, and went back to
is books with the old zest. He was now studying
medicine, intending to follow his father's profession ;
ut at his first attendance in the operation room he
ainted, and it was clear that he could never be a
urgeon.[1] To his father it must have been a sore
isappointment, but he seems to have at once recog-
ised the inevitable, and allowed the lad to read law.
Mazzini had little heart in his new studies, for the

[1] So Madame Mario, who probably had it from Mazzini's mother, and
Madame Venturi on the authority of a college friend. The memoir by
other fellow-student in *Epistolario di G. Mazzini*, I. xxix. says that he
ought that a doctor was not free to express his opinions for fear of
ending his patients, and that he therefore never studied medicine ; so
Donaver, *Uomini e libri*, 70. But see his *Vita di G. Mazzini*, 13, on
parently good evidence.

arid, perfunctory teaching of law current at the time had
small attraction for one who wanted to know the reason
of things ; but he persevered, and did well in his ex-
aminations, though it is probable that he always gave
a big slice of his time to reading poetry and history.
He was now at the University.   Probably he went
to school, though there is some doubt about it ; at all
events he seems to have escaped the brutality and
bad pedagogy, which generally made school life then
one long misery for a high-principled or sensitive lad.
University life began at an early age in Italy, and
Mazzini had matriculated at Genoa, when he was fourteen.   So far as his fellow-students were concerned, he
was in happy surroundings.   But he was a troublesome
scholar, always ready to rebel against the formalities
that made a big part of University life.   To the last he
refused to attend the compulsory religious observances,
not because he disliked them, but because they were
compulsory ; and the authorities, tolerant for once,
shut their eyes to his insubordination.   The University
of Genoa did not possess a high name for scholarship ;
and at this time it had its special drawbacks, for the
government was scared by the recent revolution, and
fearful that a few hundred lads might shake the pillars
of the state.   No one could matriculate without a
certificate that he had regularly attended church and
confession.   Those, whose parents did not possess a
certain quantity of landed property, had to pass a
stiffer examination, though at the worst, it is probable
not a very prohibitive one.   Lecturers, beadles, porters
all had the cue from government to make life un-
pleasant for the students, and the better professors
dared not be detected in any leniency or considerate-
ness.   Moustaches were forbidden, as a mark of the

HOUSE at GENOA
in which MAZZINI
Was BORN

The Home at Genoa

:volutionary mind, and if any student, greatly daring grew them, he was carried off between two carabineers to a barber's shop.

Mazzini soon became a leader among the clean-living, affectionate, impetuous undergraduates. His appearance was now, as always, very striking ; he had a high and prominent forehead, black, flashing eyes, fine olive features, set in a mass of thick black hair, a grave, serious face, that could look hard at times, but readily melted in the kindliest of smiles. He led a studious, retiring life, fond of gymnastics and fencing, but with small taste for amusements, his cigars and coffee his only indulgences ; his days spent among his books, his evenings with his mother, or in long solitary walks that defied the weather, or in rare and stolen visits to the theatre, which he had to leave after the first act, for the home was rigorously shut at ten. But, though he was slow to make close friendships, he was no misanthrope. He played much on the guitar and sang well to it ; and his musical talents and clever reciting made him in demand among his middle-class and patrician friends. There was none yet of the half-bitter sadness of after life ; he had a shrewd sense of humour, perhaps inherited from his mother ; when warmed by enthusiasm or indignation, he could speak with a fiery eloquence, that was remarkable even among those declamatory Italian youths. " My soul," he wrote afterwards, " was then a smile for all created things, life showed to my virgin fancy as a dream of love, my warmest thoughts were for nature's loveliness and the ideal woman of my youth." He revelled in generous actions, sharing books and money, even clothes, with his poorer friends. But it was sheer

orce of character that gave him his ascendancy over
hem—the loyal, justice-loving nature that made him
hampion of every victim of undergraduate or pro-
essorial spite, the purity of thought, that checked
ach loose or coarse word from those about him.
That clear, high soul, untouched by self, not knowing
ear, passionate for righteousness, gave him even when
ı lad the power that belongs only to the saints of God.

His closest friends were three brothers, Jacopo,
Giovanni, and Agostino Ruffini. Jacopo, the eldest
of the three, had perhaps more influence on Mazzini's
ife than any other man. They were born on the same
lay ; and Jacopo's fine, sensitive, enthusiastic nature
matched well with Mazzini's own. The tragic fate,
hat afterwards brought his life to an early close, only
strengthened the influence ; and the memory of one so
lear, who gave his life for their common cause, remained
ı perennial inspiration to keep his faith alive in years of
weariness and failure. The other brothers had little
of Jacopo's temperament. Giovanni at this time was
ın even-tempered, humourous, brilliant lad ; Agostino
was impressionable, impulsive, shallow, of quick and
rtistic nature. Mazzini's closest companions for some
ears, they proved how little they could rise to his
high level, and they repaid his devotion by a want
f sympathy and an ingratitude, which, in Agostino's
ase at all events, was gross. In later life both
ttained in their small way ; both were deputies in the
Piedmontese parliament, and Giovanni was minister at
aris. They long moved in English society and had
ome reputation there. Agostino, who was for a time
teacher at Edinburgh, is the " Signor Sperano " who
ells the story of *The Poor Clare*, in Mrs Gaskell's

Round the Sofa.   Giovanni, who became as proficien·
in English as in his mother tongue, wrote two notable
but now half-forgotten tales, *Lorenzo Benoni* and *Docto·
Antonio*, which stand among the best second-rate novel·
of his time.

Under Mazzini's lead the group of friends at Geno·
formed a society to study literature and politics an·
smuggle in forbidden books.   Half the masterpiece·
of contemporary European literature came at thi·
time under the censor's ban ; no foreign papers wer·
admitted except two ultra-monarchical French journals
and contraband was a necessity of literary study
Mazzini's strongest interests took him to literature
He read omnivorously in Italian and French an·
English and translations from the German.[1]   Hi·
favourite books, he tells us, were the Bible and Dante
Shakespeare and Byron.   His close knowledge of th·
Gospels comes out in everything he wrote.   He she·
his orthodoxy indeed as soon as ·he began to think
he went sometimes to mass, when a lad, and rea·
Condorcet's *Esquisse* disguised as a missal ; but h·
refused to go to confession as soon as he understoo·
its meaning,—the one thing, apparently, in all his lif·
which pained his mother.   For a short time he wen·
through a phase of scepticism, but the Ruffinis' mothe·
soon rescued him from this, and a deep religious fait·
came to him, to remain the spring of all his life.   Th·
poets he loved best were Dante and Byron, and h·
always remained true to them.   From Dante he learn·
many of the master-ideas of his mind, the conceptio·
of the unity of man and unity of law, the fervid patrio·

[1] He seems never to have learnt to read German easily ; at all even·
he could not do so till comparatively late in life.

sm, the belief in Italy and Rome predestined to be teachers of the world, the faith in Italian Unity, the moral strength that makes life one long fight for good. When only some twenty years old, he wrote an essay on Dante's patriotism, which, however boyish in style, proves his close knowledge of the master. Byron was then at the height of his fame, and then, as always afterwards, Mazzini thought him the greatest of modern English, perhaps of modern European poets. He was "completely fascinated" by Goethe, and would often say that " to pass a day with him or a genius like him would be the fairest day of life." How his admiration for Goethe waned, while that for Byron grew, will be told in another chapter.[1] He read Shakespeare, but always, apparently, with more respect than enjoyment, and Shakespeare too came under the same ban as Goethe. He thought very highly of Schiller, and placed him with Æschylus and Shakespeare, as the third great dramatist of the world. He read a good deal of English literature ; at this time he was a fervent admirer of Scott, but he seems afterwards to have lost his interest in him ; he knew something at least of Wordsworth and Shelley, Burns and Crabbe. Modern French literature, except de Vigny's and some of Victor Hugo's writings, did not now (nor, with the exception of George Sand and Lamennais, at any time), appeal to him, for he disliked the tendencies of French Romanticism, and already there were the beginnings of his life-long prejudice against most things French. Among his modern fellow-countrymen Alfieri and Foscolo were his favourites ; he read Manzoni and Guerrazzi, but largely

---

[1] See pp. 325-327.

to criticise them, though he was ready to do justice to
the strength of both.   He thought Mickiewicz, the
Polish national poet, "the most powerful poetic nature
of the time."   The classics he no doubt read pretty
widely, as every educated lad was then bound to do,
but none seem to have made much impression on him,
except Æschylus, for whom his veneration was unbounded, and Tacitus.   Both now and later he gave
much time to metaphysical and political writers.   He
read something of Hegel, whom he detested for his
political fatalism, of Kant and Fichte ; but the German
who influenced him most was the now-forgotten
Herder.   From him he learned or confirmed his
spiritual conception of life, his belief in immortality,
his theory of the progress of humanity and man's
co-operation in the work of Providence. Among
Italian philosophers he studied Giordano Bruno and
Vico ; he rated the latter at his real worth, and
regarded him as the great luminary of an Italian
school of thought whose continuity he professed to
trace from Pythagoras.   Among political writers
Macchiavelli certainly impressed him most, as a great
Italian patriot, and he excused his morality as a
product of his time.   He seems to have known a
good deal of Voltaire and Rousseau.   Of recent
political writers, he and his circle most read Guizot
and Victor Cousin, whose lectures at this time made
them the mentors of young liberalism ; he records
how the group at Genoa handed on to one another
manuscript copies of the lectures, and found their
inspiration in the men whom they were soon to regard
as traitors.

Now and for long after, literature was the call that

spoke sweetest to Mazzini. Politics and conspiracy were constraining but unwelcomed duties; he gave his love to literature. To be a dramatist or write historical novels was at this time his plan of life. Many a time in later years he was still looking for the day, when Italy would be united and free, and, his political task accomplished, he could give himself to the literary schemes he still cherished,—a history of religious ideas, a popular history of Italy, and the editing of a series of the great dramas of the world. But the burden of his country's woe lay too heavily on him to be long forgotten. It was no time now for Dante studies or play-writing. Sadly and unwillingly he convinced himself that at such a time pure literature was no patriot's first task, that the writer, who would not shirk his duty, must make his work political. Not but what the literary critic still appears on every page; but the whole gist of his teaching is that the value of a book is in proportion to its power to inform the reader's soul to love of country and mankind, and impel him to serve his fellows by political action in the sight of God. He held it wasted effort to do, what Manzoni had tried to do,—to school the individual to a smug life of cloistered virtue, a life which in a vicious or torpid society was impossible to the many. No religion, no morality, he taught, is worth the writer's labours, unless it dedicates men to be workers in the public cause, to hold comfort, and, if need be, home and life itself as cheap, while oppression and wrong are stunting other lives, and men and women round are crying to be freed.

He found his opportunity in the controversy be-

tween Romanticists and Classicists, which then divide
the literary world of Italy into hot factions. Not tha
he held Romanticism to be any final or faultless forn
of literature. But when a theory of literary servitude
like Classicism, lent itself to political oppression an
depressed the vital and spiritual forces of the country
when a young and vigorous movement was makin;
literature free and stood for liberty all round, h
necessarily took his stand for the latter. Ther
could be no political or social regeneration for Italy
till she had a literature that made for freedom an
progress. "These literary disputes," he urged, "ar
bound up with all that is important in social an
civil life"; "the legislation and literature of a peopl
always advance on parallel lines," and "the progres
of intellectual culture stands in intimate relationshi
with the political life of the country." It was th
aim of the Romanticists "to give Italians an origina
national literature, not one that is as a sound c
passing music to tickle the ear and die, but one tha
will interpret to them their aspirations, their idea
their needs, their social movement." And thus, whil
generously recognising Manzoni's worth, he looke
rather to Alfieri and Foscolo, who had scourge
political wrong-doing and preached resistance t
tyranny; he praised the writers of the *Conciliator*
the short-lived Milanese journal of Silvio Pellic
and Confalonieri, which, like himself, had turne
Romanticism to political purposes. Here and ther
in his writings of this time a more or less dire
political allusion manages to escape the censor's ey
He speaks for the first time of "Young Italy," a nam
soon to ring through Europe; he pays his tribute

the political exiles; he slips in a remark that the spirit of a state cannot be changed without recasting its institutions. More than this he could not do in a censor-ridden press; perhaps literature was struggling still with politics to command his mind.

As it was, he had trouble enough with the censors. His first published articles appeared in the *Indicatore Genovese*, a commercial paper issuing at Genoa, whose editor was persuaded to admit short notices of recent books, which gradually swelled into literary essays. Among his later contributions were an article on the historical novel and reviews of Friedrich Schlegel's History of Literature and Guerrazzi's Battle of Benevento. They do not read very well. They are juvenile and exaggerated, and it is amusing to find the twenty-three years' old author telling his coeval Guerrazzi, the young Leghorn novelist, that he had not drunk enough of the cup of life to be a pessimist. The *Indicatore* gradually became a literary paper, and for a few months the censorship did not see what it was tending to. At the end of 1828, however, about a year after Mazzini began to write in it, it was suppressed. Mazzini easily transferred his energies. Guerrazzi had founded another paper at Leghorn much on the same lines, the *Indicatore Livornese*, and asked Mazzini to send contributions. Mazzini readily responded; he wrote, besides minor papers, an article on Faust, and attacked the defects of the Romanticist School in an essay on *Some Tendencies of European Literature*. His writing is still effusive, and generally dogmatic and sententious, but the style has improved. The censorship was comparatively lenient in Tuscany, and though the young writers were barred from direct reference to politics, they were able to make the political allusions sufficiently transparent. But the paper grew too daring even for the somnolent Tuscan censors, and, like its predecessor, it was snuffed out after a year of life. Mazzini and Guerrazzi parted, to go on very different ways, and meet again nineteen years later when both were famous.

In the meantime Mazzini had with some difficulty got a footing on the *Antologia*, the one Italian review of the time that ranked among the great European periodicals. It had been founded some ten years before, in the hope that it might become an Italian Edinburgh Review, by Gino Capponi, the blind Florentine noble who traced his race from the Capponi who bearded Charles VIII., and Vieusseux, a Swiss bookseller who had settled at Florence and opened the one circulating library of any note in Italy. Most of the leading Italian writers of the day contributed to it; and though its aim was avowedly nationalist, and in a sense Liberal, it had succeeded so far, thanks probably to its influential patrons, in eluding the censor's ban. Mazzini wrote for it three articles *On the Historical Drama* and another *On a European Literature*. His work had rapidly matured, and there is no trace now of the juvenilities of his earlier efforts. Every page has the mark of the strong, original thought, which made him one of the greatest critics of the century.

Meanwhile he was practising at the bar in a desultory fashion. Sometimes he pleaded in the lower courts as an " advocate of the poor," and was much in demand for his attention and skill. According to the etiquette of the profession, he read in the rooms of a barrister, who limited his interest to seeing that his pupils sat with a book in front of them. The vacations were generally spent in a little country villa at San Secondo, in the Bisagno valley, within sight of a house which the Ruffinis occupied ; and he shared in attentions to the Ruffinis' mother, who was now his spiritual guide and dearest friend, or went on botanical walks or shooting expeditions in the lovely hill country. He did not do much of the shooting himself, and when he was more than fifty, he remembered with remorse a thrush that he had mangled when sixteen.

His interests became more and more absorbed by politics. His Genoese home no doubt encouraged this, for the nobles and the working-classes were still unreconciled to Piedmontese rule, while the liberals of the middle classes looked on the annexation only as a step to some wider Italian state. But the local environment was only a minor influence, and Mazzini would doubtless have become a conspirator, had he lived in any other town of Italy. About the time that he began to write in the *Indicatore Genovese*, he was admitted into the Society of the Carbonari. The Carbonari were at this time suffering from the decadence, which sooner or later palsies every secret society. They had grown out of Neapolitan Freemasonry in the days of the French rule, and when, after Napoleon's fall, reaction came and the old dynasties returned, they swept into their ranks the mass of discontented men, who, with very varying political ideals, were at one in resenting the small tyrannies, the bigotry and obscurantism of the princes, who had come back from

exile to misgovern and sometimes to oppress. The
high level of their tenets, their appeals to religion
and morality, the esoteric symbolism of their rites, the
vague democratic sentiment that was often only skin-
deep, had made them a vast Liberal organisation.
Since they had made and wrecked the revolutions of
Naples and Piedmont seven years before, they had
kept the skeleton of their party together with considerable skill and persistency. But the conspiracy
had changed its character. It was no longer a purely
Italian society, for the exiles had carried it into France
and Spain, and the headquarters were now at Paris,
where Lafayette and the Orleanist conspirators were
using it to upset the Legitimist monarchy and dreamed
of a league of Latin countries to balance the Holy
Alliance. In Italy the democratic sentimentalism
had left it, it had lost touch with the masses, and
its leaders were mostly middle-aged men of the professional classes, who discouraged young recruits,
and had no wish to step outside their meaningless
small formalisms and barren talk of liberty.

Mazzini had little stomach for their ritualism and
lack of purpose, their love of royal and noble leaders ;
and probably the subordinate position, that as a young
man he necessarily took, sat uncomfortably on him.
But at all events they were the only revolutionary
organisation in the country, and he admired the
bravery of men, who risked prison or exile for however inadequate an end. Though fitfully in practice,
he had a theoretic belief in subordination, which
prepared him for the moment to act under orders.
But as soon as he joinèd the Carbonari and swore
the usual oath of initiation over a bared dagger,

he began to see the futility of it all. He found
that he was sworn only to obey his unknown
chiefs, and he was allowed to know the names of
two or three only of his fellow-conspirators. He
suspected that their political programme, if they had
any, was but a thin one. All the Italian in him
revolted against men, who talked lightly of their
country, and preached that salvation could only come
from France. The subscription to the Society's funds,
of which, needless to say, no account was rendered,
was sufficiently heavy to bear hardly on his slender
purse. He was so sickened by a melodramatic
announcement, perhaps in bluff, that a member was
to be assassinated for criticising the chiefs, that he
threatened to withdraw. His unknown superiors,
however, apparently thought well of him, and he
was commissioned to go on propagandist work to
Tuscany, where he made a few recruits. He seems
to have returned in better spirits as to the future of
the Society ; and if we may believe Giovanni Ruffini,
he began with a few young co-affiliates to organise
on his own account, nominally in the name of the
Carbonari, but really to substitute a more vigorous
association. His plan was apparently to bring the
Carbonari of Tuscany and Bologna into closer touch
with those of Genoa and Piedmont. He asked for
a passport for Bologna on the pretext that he wanted
to examine a Dante manuscript, but was told by the
police, that if he had no more important business, he
could wait. Baffled in this, he returned to his semi-
independent conspiracy at home. The July Revolution
in France had raised the hopes of liberals everywhere ;
and he and his friends enrolled affiliates, discarding

the Carbonaro lumber of oaths and secret signs, and simply pledging them to act, if an insurrection proved possible.   Bullets were cast, and other juvenile pre- parations made.   How far he succeeded in enlisting followers, we do not know, for he himself has left hardly any record of the plan.

At all events, it was abruptly nipped.   The government had its secret agents among the Car- bonari, and Mazzini was arrested on the charge of initiating one of them.   It is probable that the authorities had suspected him for some time.   He was, as the governor of Genoa told his father, " gifted with some talent, and too fond of walking by himself at night absorbed in thought.   What on earth," asked the offended officer, " has he at his age to think about ? We don't like young people thinking without our knowing the subject of their thoughts."   Mazzini was taken to the fortress of Savona, where he consoled himself by watching the sea and sky, which made all the prospect from his cell windows, and taming a serin finch, which would fly in through the gratings, and to which he " became exceedingly attached."   His case came before the Senate of Turin, the highest court in the country.   In the eyes of the law he was supremely guilty ; but, with an adroitness that he afterwards recalled with pride, he managed to destroy all compromising papers, and there was only one witness of the initiation, whereas the law required two.   Mazzini stoutly denied the fact.   The denial was more than a plea of not guilty in an English court ; perhaps he thought that a conspirator is bound to put his government outside the pale of moral obligation.   But whatever we may allow for his position, the plain man will count his action as one of the disingenuous lapses, that rarely, now and again, stain the clear honour of his life.

The court had to acquit him, but the authorities had too much evidence of his activity to leave him unmolested. They gave him the choice between internment in a small town or exile. Contemporary events decided him. The revolution had just broken out in Central Italy; the French government had encouraged the Carbonari to expect direct or indirect assistance, and Mazzini thought that he would serve the cause best at Paris, whence, he confidently hoped, he would soon return to a liberated Italy. In February 1831 he said his good-byes to his family, who had hastened to Savona, and crossed the Apennines and, for the first time, the Alps, afterwards so familiar and beloved. He watched the sunrise from Mont Cenis, and has left a memorable description of it, drawn with all the wealth of his artistic imagery. At Geneva he made the acquaintance of Sismondi and his Scotch wife. While there, he was advised to join the Italian exiles at Lyons, and, giving up the projected journey to Paris, he made his way to them.

Chapter II

Young Italy ·

Condition of Italy—The Revolution of 1831—Young Italy—Its principles
  belief in Italy; inspiration of duty; social reform—Its politica
  system : Republicanism ; Italian Unity ; war with Austria—Secre
  societies.

THE governor of the prison at Savona had allowe
him to read the Bible, Byron, and Tacitus, innocentl
thinking that they contained no revolutionary material
Out of these and Dante sprang Young Italy. Italy
was ripe for the teaching of the epoch-making society
The country was " a geographical expression." Con·
querors, whose appetites had been tempted by the
Southern land, had carved it into appanages foɪ
themselves. Austria held Lombardy and the lands
of the Venetian republic ; the King of Piedmon¹
ruled the North-West, and Sardinia, and Savoy acros:
the Alps ; the Bourbons of Naples had the South
the Pope, the grand-duke of Tuscany, the petty dukes
of Modena, Parma, and Lucca divided up the Centre
Nor had there been any serious demand for unity.
History and character sundered North and South
the great medieval cities still cherished their inde·
pendence too dearly to wish to sink it in a commor
country. Napoleon, while he ruled, had gone far tc

unite the land both in form and substance; and the aspirations he did so much to create survived him. Weak though they still were, practical grievances were ever enforcing the argument for unity; and Italians were chafing more and more against the artificial barriers, which stopped the circulation of the nation's life. The customs-lines, that met the trader on the confines of each state, strangled commerce. Literature circulated with difficulty, and the Genoese could hardly get access to books published at Florence or Leghorn, a hundred miles away. In the smaller states at all events, the area was too small to offer any field for enterprise, and every lawyer and engineer and civil servant was cribbed by the restrictions, that confined his activities to a handful of towns. Through all the peninsula there was a more or less intolerable misrule. Political disabilities allowed no voice in legislation, no control of taxation or the executive, no rights of public meeting or association, small liberty of speech or writing. There were more present grievances in the discouragement of education, in the clerical tyranny, in the obsolete and partial legal system. And the misgovernment had its yet more evil and intimate aspect in the power of the police, which threatened each man's home and honour and career. Governments, that breathed and moved in chronic dread of revolution, sought safety in a system of covert terrorism. The police had their spies everywhere,—in the streets, in men's households, in the churches, in the universities, —to scrape up any idle word or act, that seemed to mark a possible critic of government. There were mitigations of the misrule in Piedmont, Tuscany, and the Austrian territories. But in the Pope's states and

Naples there was little or nothing to relieve the crying corruption and incompetency ; and everywhere there was more or less a vexatious intolerance and oppression, that showed the blacker after the relative liberty and progress of Napoleon's rule.

The Carbonari had voiced somewhat fitfully the national protest. And just at this time they made their final attempt at revolution. Early in February 1831,—just before Mazzini was released from Savona, — the insurrection broke out in Modena, and spread at once to Parma and the Papal province of Romagna. In three weeks the greater part of the Pope's dominions were free, and the insurgent army was marching towards Rome. The leaders knew that, however easy it was to upset the rule of the Pope and Dukes, they could make no effective resistance to an Austrian attack ; but they counted on the promised backing of France to ward off invasion. " Non-intervention,"—the European equivalent of the Munroe Doctrine,—was one of the formulas of the July Monarchy, and by it Austria had no right to interfere in the domestic concerns of an Italian state. The French government had assured the Carbonari, that, if she violated the principle, it would declare war against her. But only a section of the ministry was sincere in the promise, and Louis Philippe saw that a war in the name of nationality might easily slide into a revolutionary movement, which would shake his own unsure throne. His government let Metternich know that non-intervention was a phrase that stopped at words. By the end of March, despite some fine fighting by the Italian levies, the Austrians had stamped out the ephemeral insurrection. Its feebleness courted failure. Not that the programme of the leaders wanted breadth and boldness. Mazzini's after criticism that it was neither nationalist nor democratic was exaggerated and unjust. During their few weeks of rule, the chiefs had showered projects of social reform. Some of them at all events wished to make Romagna the centre of a great national rising, and aimed at an independent federation of all Italy with Rome for its capital. But they made two irreparable mistakes. They did not face the facts; they failed to win the people. They were for the most part, like the rest of the Carbonaro leaders, middle-aged professional men, out of touch with the masses, possessed by the dread that popular imprudences might scare the diplomatists, on whom they built their hopes. Under an inspiring chief, the people would have fought perhaps, as they fought seventeen years later, when they drove the Austrians in confusion from Bologna. But the leaders were not the men to touch their enthusiasm. They had, in fact, miscalculated what the movement meant. These comfortable men of peace flinched from the fact that Austria must be fought and beaten. They had no stuff for a desperate guerilla fight, that meant the wasting of the country, privation and disease and death, for an uncertain hope that France might come eventually to the rescue. Still less were they prepared to launch on a forlorn enterprise, where friends were none and immediate disaster certain, that they might be precursors of their children's victories.

Their failure, so consonant with all the later Carbonaro policy, confirmed Mazzini in his belief that a new organisation was needed and new men to lead it. As usual, he saw only one set of facts. He exaggerated the mistakes of the revolutionary governments, and left out of his reckoning the unreadiness of the people. The insurrections had failed, he convinced himself, simply because they had been badly led. In the main, indeed, he was right. The revolution had been in the wrong hands. The Carbonaro chiefs kept at arm's-length younger men, whose energy might have made up for their own unforwardness. If the next revolution was to fare better, it must have these younger men to captain it, men of confidence and enthusiasm and fresh ideas, men with a message that would nerve "those artisans of insurrection, the people and the young." Mazzini had at this time a supreme faith in his generation; he had already written in the *Antologia* of "this young Italy of ours," so vigorous and cultured and warm-hearted, that no new movement, however bold and difficult, was beyond its powers. "Place," he said now, "the young at the head of the insurgent masses; you do not know what strength is latent in those young bands, what magic influence the voice of the young has on the crowd; you will find in them a host of apostles for the new religion. But youth lives on movement, grows great in enthusiasm and faith. Consecrate them with a lofty mission; inflame them with emulation and praise; spread through their ranks the word of fire, the word of inspiration; speak to them of country, of glory, of power, of great memories." They had been muzzled in the past; they must not be again. So rigidly did he insist on this, that the rules of Young Italy excluded from membership, except in special cases, all who were over forty years. Mazzini had no diffidence to curb the magnificent egotism of a design, in which he consciously destined for himself the leading part. As one of his closest friends of those days said, "his confidence in men was great and in himself unlimited." "All great national movements," he wrote in later years, "begin with unknown men of the people, without influence except for the faith and will, that counts not time or difficulties." It is worth noting that Camillo Cavour, five years younger still, was at this same time writing to a friend that "he would one fine morning wake up Prime Minister of Italy."

When we disentangle Mazzini's ideas from the superfluous verbiage that sometimes wraps them, two leading principles are found to differentiate them from those of earlier movements,—the principles, that, with his trick of making watchwords, he summed up in the phrase, "God and the People." The new movement must have the inspiration and power of a religion. Italy needed something that would shake her from the hopelessness of disillusion and defeat, something that would prove she "had a strength within her, that was arbiter of facts, mightier than destiny itself." Action must be roused by action, energy by energy, faith by faith,—the faith that made Rome great and inspired Christianity and sent forth the armies of the Convention, the faith that makes the weak strong in the knowledge they are carrying out God's will. Mazzini had two arguments to persuade his countrymen to this believing and conquering patriotism. He hoped to fire them with his own superb faith in Italy and her destinies. He

called up "that old name of Italy, hung round with
memories and glory and majestic griefs, that centuries
of mute servitude could not destroy." Twice had she
been queen of the world; many times had she, the
land of Dante and Vico, of the Papacy and the
Renaissance, inspired European thought. " Italy,"
he said, " has been called a graveyard ; but a graveyard peopled by our mighty dead is nearer life
than a land that teems with living weaklings and
braggarts." Her task was not yet done ; she had
still to speak to the nations "the gospel of the new
age, the gospel of humanity." He pointed Italians
to " the vision of their country, radiant, purified by
suffering, moving as an angel of light among the
nations that thought her dead." Rightly he judged
that men, who shared his faith, would never despair
of their country. But he had a more sounding note
to strike. He had the genius to see that he who
would have men rise to high endeavour, must appeal
to their unselfish motives, that only when some great
principle calls, will they lift themselves to heroism and
sacrifice of all that makes life dear. The effort to
make Italy meant the loss of thousands of lives,
meant exile and imprisonment and poverty, the
blighting of homes and the misery of dear ones ; and
men would only face it at the call of duty. The
Carbonari had no call ; they came of a school that
appealed to interested motives, and the appeal inevitably broke down in the day of disappointment
and defeat. Mazzini offered his countrymen " a
national religion "; Young Italy was no mere political
party, but " a creed and an apostolate "; it taught that
victory came "by reverence for principles reverence

for the just and true, by sacrifice and constancy in sacrifice." As individuals and as a nation, they had a mission given them by God. God's law of duty bade them follow it ; God's law of progress promised them accomplishment.

/The other principle of Young Italy was social reform. Earlier liberal movements had thought or attempted little for the masses, though at all events the recent rising in Romagna aimed higher than Mazzini gave it credit for, and had more of a democratic tendency than contemporary movements in France and England. Mazzini exaggerated the revolutionary impatience of the masses in 1821 and 1831 ; but it was true that such enthusiasm as they had, had been cooled by the disappointment of their hopes. Revolutions, as he said, had been Dead Sea apples to them. They would be slow to stir again, till they saw that the liberation of their country had tangible social results in store. / The gospel of duty would rouse the cultured middle classes, but at this time he seems to have thought that the uneducated, down-trodden, priest and official-ridden masses could not respond to the higher call, and must be won by some visible prospect of relief from present evils. Pope Julius' cry of " Out with the barbarian " would not touch men, who did not see how every social injustice leant in the last resort on Austria, how dear food, conscription, all the petty tyranny, were fruits of the foreign domination, that sheltered the princes who misgoverned them. Till the masses felt this, there was no hope of a successful war of liberation. " Revolutions," he said, " must be made for the people and by the people, and so long as revolutions are, as now, the inheritance and monopoly of a single class, and lead only to the substitution of one aristocracy for another, we shall never find salvation." The cry of the poor, unheard by most Italian statesmen from his time down to yesterday, was ever with him. "I see the people pass before my eyes in the livery of wretchedness and political subjection, ragged and hungry, painfully gathering the crumbs that wealth tosses insultingly to it, or lost and wandering in riot and the intoxication of a brutish, angry, savage joy; and I remember that those brutalised faces bear the finger-print of God, the mark of the same mission as our own. I lift myself to the vision of the future and behold the people rising in its majesty, brothers in one faith, one bond of equality and love, one ideal of citizen virtue that ever grows in beauty and might; the people of the future, unspoilt by luxury, ungoaded by wretchedness, awed by the consciousness of its rights and duties. And in the presence of that vision my heart beats with anguish for the present and glorying for the future." That they would rise in insurrection, he had no doubt. Once make them see whence sprang their wretchedness, where stood its remedies, once make them feel that "God is on the side of the down-trodden," the people of Italy would be again what they had been in the days of the Lombard League and the Sicilian Vespers.

Out of these principles, — social reform as the immediate end of revolution and duty as its inspiration,—Mazzini built up an elaborate political programme. He loved system-making and hardly apologised for it. You cannot have unity or harmony without it, he urged, and to a certain extent he had practical justification. It were better, as he said and as subsequent events proved, that the nationalists should argue out their differences before the time for action came, and not paralyse themselves by quarrels in front of the enemy. It was this want of a positive programme, that was, he thought, largely responsible for the failure of the Carbonari. Their policy had hardly gone beyond the overthrow of the existing governments ; and they had mustered under their flag royalists and republicans, conservatives and liberals, with the inevitable result that after their first successes they split their ranks and fell an easy prey. It were wiser, so Mazzini pleaded, to be few but united. "The strength of an association depends not on its numbers but on its homogeneity." But the principle was necessarily an intolerant one. It barred many a true patriot, who could not swear to the whole Mazzinian doctrine. For such he had no pity. In his view it was only fear, "the Almighty God of most politicians," that prevented the Moderates from accepting his position. "There can be no moderation," he said at a later date, "between good and evil, truth and error, progress and reaction." Unluckily truth to him too often meant adhesion to his own theories ; and he could never forgive men, who, starting from his premisses, could not follow his logic to the end, though, like most men who pride themselves on being logical, he was often singularly incapable of accurate reasoning. It was this intolerance that wrecked so much of his after life, that made him waste his splendid powers in fighting men, by whose side he ought to have been working.

However, for better or worse, Mazzini required

Young Italy

his fellow-workers implicit acceptance of his theories,—theories which embraced every sphere of national life, religion and politics, literature and art. His chief political doctrines were republicanism and Italian Unity. How he pieced republicanism on his general theory of things, is the subject of another chapter. It is sufficient here to note that he was a republican, chiefly because he thought that democratic legislation was impossible under any form of monarchy. The belief was natural enough at the time. Few had been the popular reforms under any European crown, while the one genuine series of democratic laws had been passed by the French Republic or while the French monarchy was tottering to its fall. Mazzini may be pardoned, if at that time he sharply sundered monarchies and republics, and failed to see how imperfect was the classification. In Italy, Mazzini saw special circumstances that made for a republic. Her great memories were republican, though even he must have recognised how little the republics of medieval Italy had in common with his ideal polity. At Venice and his own Genoa the republican tradition was still dear. Italian republicanism was free from any recent memory of outrage and proscription, such as tarnished the name in France. And above all, he urged, there was no possible king for a united Italy. Each prince was pledged to Austria, each had proved his sympathy with reaction. Monarchy in Italy had "no splendid annals, no venerable traditions," no powerful nobility to buttress it. Two princes only had an army, which could help in the war of liberation ; and neither the King of Piedmont nor the King of Naples would submit to the other without a bitter civil struggle.

And the antipathies of North and South, though they might bow to the principle of a common republic, would never allow the Neapolitan to take a king from Piedmont. History has proved how wrong was his diagnosis, and temporarily and reluctantly he had glimpses of his error. More than once in after life, as we shall see, he alternated his republicanism with fits of half-belief in the Piedmontese monarchy.

His advocacy of Italian Unity rests on a surer bottom. That the country was fated to stagnate till the foreigner had gone, was common ground with every school of patriots. But when the Austrians had been driven out, was Italy to be a federation of states or one united country? Mazzini pleaded that the point at issue between him and the federalists was mainly one of practicability. This hardly took sufficient account of the school, which looked to Switzerland and America for its types, and preferred a federation on its own merits. But on the whole his contention was right. Every argument that told for federation, told yet more forcibly for unity. /The strength of the federalist movement lay in the belief that unity was impossible. As yet, though Napoleon had foretold that unity must come, only a handful of Italians had dared to speak of it as a possible ideal. The great majority doubted whether Italy even wished to be united, whether, if she did, the facts of the European polity made it possible, whether unity could permanently stand the strain of the old provincial animosities. It was easy for them to adduce a host of facts,—the differences of race and temperament and tradition, the various habits formed by dissimilar

systems of law and land tenure and education, the
jealousies, still far from dead, that sundered province
from province and city from city.   Mazzini himself
had felt the force of their arguments, and there was
a moment, when even he had been shaken in his
faith.   He had little tangible reasoning to back his
confidence.   But he had the prophetic assurance of
a great possibility, and his contagious faith made it a
reality./ He saw, when hardly another of his con-
temporaries saw it, that Italian Unity was a practicable
ideal ; his teaching informed the national resolve, that
changed the seemingly impossible into a fact.   To
few men has it been given to create a great political
idea ; to fewer still to be not only the creator, but the
chief instrument in realising it.   Mazzini was both,
and it gives him title to rank among the makers of
modern Europe.

/ But there could be no unity, no republic, no
political advance of any kind, till the inevitable war
with Austria had been fought and won./ She would
not surrender her Italian provinces, unless by force
of arms.   She could not tolerate free institutions side
by side with her own despotic rule.   She had crushed
the Neapolitan and Piedmontese risings ten years
before ; she had done the same in Modena and
Romagna yesterday. / "She robs us," said Mazzini,
"of life and country, name, glory, culture, material
well-being."/ As Giusti said more pointedly a few
years later, the Italians "ate Austria in their bread."
Mazzini and many another patriot knew that any
peaceful solution was utopian. / "The destinies of
Italy," he preached, "have to be decided on the plains
of Lombardy, and peace must be signed beyond the

Alps." Mazzini rather welcomed war in a just cause. It would redeem the torpid, disillusioned Italian, who was brave enough, as Napoleon's campaigns had proved, but required much to nerve him to effort. It would give Italy again her national self-respect, her claim to the esteem of other peoples. "War," he said, "is the eternal law, that stands between the master and the slave who breaks his chains." But Mazzini in his saner moods saw the futility of any local or ill-prepared rising. In words, that condemn only too eloquently much of his after action, he declared that only victory could justify a rising against Austria. It was only when the great mass of the people had been won to the nationalist cause, that the patriots "might stretch their hand to Lombardy and say, 'There are the men who perpetuate your servitude,' towards the Alps and say, 'There stand your confines.'" Mazzini's plan of campaign was guerilla fighting. It was, as he said, the natural resource of an insurgent people, that had to win its freedom against disciplined armies,—the method chosen by the Dutch against Philip II., by the American colonists against England, by the Spaniards and Greeks in more recent times. Had he lived now, he might have added another illustrious example. Italy, with her long chain of mountains that no enemy could hold in force, had special fitness for the strategy. "Italians," he cried, "look to your mountains, there stand strength and infallible victory." In the meantime the work of Young Italy was to organise and educate ; and the only possible organisation was that of the secret society. Mazzini did not see its inherent weaknesses. Young Italy soon became as much the quarry of the spy and police agent

as the Carbonari had been ; and to the end of lif
Mazzini was the victim of informers, who won hi
easy confidence. The society developed an uncon
trolled and irresponsible leadership, and its chie
eager as he was and sincerely eager to disclaim an
desire to dictate, was too impatient, too self-confiden
to allow fair play to other men's convictions. As
means of preparing for war, it failed disastrously ; an
it proved an ill school for the parliamentary politic
of later days. But in a country, where any open ex
pression of liberal sentiment meant prison or exil
if not the scaffold, there was no alternative ; and a
an educating influence it came to be the greatest c
the forces that made Italy. / Its writings, smuggle
into every corner of the land, moved many a youn
thinker to a passionate resolve, that bore its fruit i
after times. At this stage, however, Mazzini wa
hardly looking to the slow results of political educa
tion. The hour of insurrection, he confidently believe
was near ; the European revolution was threatening, an
Italy must not be behind the sister nations. He wa
certain of success. / Whatever difficulties might com
to a nationalist movement without a backing from th
native governments, however much Italians might di
trust their own unaided strength, there was " no re
obstacle for twenty-six millions of men, who wishe
to rise and fight for their country." Austria, h
calculated, could at the best put two hundred thousan
men into the field ; he fondly counted on four millic
Italian volunteers. A people, that even under th
leading of the Carbonari had made three revolutior
in ten years, would rise again more readily and mo
victoriously at the inspiration of a nobler faith. /

Chapter III

Marseilles

At Marseilles—Spread of Young Italy—Letter to Charles Albert—
The Army Plot in Piedmont—At Geneva—The Savoy Raid.

WHEN Mazzini arrived at Lyons, he found an unhopeful
plan in preparation for raiding Savoy. Some 2000
Italian refugees, many of them Piedmontese who had
fled through Genoa ten years before and stirred his
boyish enthusiasm, were ready to march under the hardly
concealed protection of the French government. It
was still in the early days of the July monarchy, when
it had yet not quite forgotten its revolutionary origin.
But before the expedition could start, Louis Philippe's
swift lapse into conservatism, which had already made
him break his promises to the Romagnuols, abruptly
ended the patronage of the authorities. The would-be
raiders were scattered, and Mazzini joined a small
party of republicans, who were starting for Corsica,
on their way to join the insurgents in Romagna. The
Corsicans were still Italian in sentiment as well as
race, and the Carbonaro influence was strong in the
island. Two thousand men offered themselves for
service with the insurgents, but no funds were forth-
coming to pay their passage, and before arrangements

35

could be made the news arrived that the rising ha
collapsed.

Mazzini returned to Marseilles, and found himse
among the refugees who had escaped from Centra
Italy. He recruited a few young patriots among then
and with their help he began to give body to h:
schemes. In a small room at Marseilles the youn
Titans started, with nothing but their own sincerit
and daring, to revolutionise Italy. \ "We had no offic
no helpers," he wrote of them in after years. "All da·
and a great part of the night, we were buried in ou
work, writing articles and letters, getting informatio
from travellers, enlisting seamen, folding papers, faster
ing envelopes, dividing our time between literary an
manual work. La Cecilia was compositor ; Lamber
corrected the proofs ; another of us made himself literall
porter, to save the expense of distributing the paper
We lived as equals and brothers ; we had but or
thought, one hope, one ideal to reverence. The foreig
republicans loved and admired us for our tenacity an
unflagging industry ; we were often in real want, bi
we were light-hearted in a way, and smiling becaus
we believed in the future."

In later life Mazzini looked back longingly to th
freshness and enthusiasm of those days, before failui
had disillusioned him or misunderstanding estrange
him from his friends. When he was well and happ
all the charm of his nature—his radiant idealism, h
warm-hearted friendship, his contagious unselfishne
—made him the beloved inspirer of the little ban
that worked under his orders. "He was," said a
Italian of him at this time, "about 5 feet 8 inche
high and slightly made ; he was dressed in blac

ienoa velvet, with a large "republican" hat; his long,
urling black hair, which fell upon his shoulders, the
xtreme freshness of his clear olive complexion, the
hiselled delicacy of his regular and beautiful features,
ided by his very youthful look and sweetness and
penness of expression, would have made his appear-
nce almost too feminine, if it had not been for his
oble forehead, the power of firmness and decision
1at was mingled with their gaiety and sweetness in
1e bright flashes of his dark eyes and in the varying
xpression of his mouth, together with his small and
eautiful moustachios and beard. Altogether he was
: that time the most beautiful being, male or female,
1at I had ever seen, and I have not since seen his
1ual." [1] But sometimes even now overwork and
npatience told on him, and he felt ill and exhausted.
1 such moods he must have been a trying man to
2 much with—irritable, exacting, requiring absolute
1bmission from his fellow-workers, angry if they
1ought well of men whom he disliked.

For two years the little band worked on, sowing the
eds of revolution. It was a heroic enterprise. A
w young men, without birth or wealth to help them,
1d, except for their leader, of no great ability, were
anning to change the future of their country and pre-
1ring for war with a great military empire. To an
1tsider it must have seemed a madman's dream.
1t their masterful chief had taught them his own
ith; and they, and thousands of their countrymen
ter them, found in it the power, to which few things

[1] This description was given to, and published by Mr W. Shaen.
ere is reason for thinking it was written by Enrico Mayer, the Tuscan
1cationalist.

are impossible. They worked with remorseless energy, month after month, corresponding with sympathisers all over the peninsula, planting lodges of Young Italy wherever a chance opened, drawing together the threads of conspiracy. They found abundant backing in Italy. Mazzini appealed to his followers there to work among the people by every road that the despotism left open, to bring children to school and teach them, to hold classes for men in the country districts, to circulate pictures and pamphlets and almanacs, which would insinuate patriotic ideas without exciting the suspicions of the police, to carry the cross of fire from town to town and village to village. "Climb the hills," he asked of them, "sit at the farmer's table, visit the workshops and the artisans, whom you now neglect. Tell them of their rightful liberties, their ancient traditions and glories, the old commercial greatness which has gone ; talk to them of the thousand forms of oppression, which they ignore, because no one points them out." His appeal found a ready response. Hundreds of young Italians, fired by his own passion, gave themselves to the dangers and toils and the thousand small annoyances of a conspirator's life. It was no light call. " I know of no existence," said one of them in later life, " which requires such continual self-abnegation and endurance. A conspirator has to listen to all sorts of gossip, to soothe every variety of vanity, discuss nonsense seriously, feel sick and stifling under the pressure of empty talk, idle boasting, and vulgarity, and yet maintain an unmoved and complacent countenance. A conspirator ceases to belong to himself, and becomes the toy of anyone he may meet ; he must go out when he would rather

ay at home, and stay at home when he would rather
o out ; he has to talk when he would be silent, and
ᴐ hold vigils when he would rather be in bed." And
ᴇhind these petty vexations, which meant more to the
ːalians of that day than to a generation trained in
ːrenuousness, lay the knowledge that discovery meant
rison or exile, perhaps death. But they faced it with
ᴉe courage of men who believed that the "wear and
ːar was smoothing the way, inch by inch, towards a
ᴐble and holy end," who looked to the day when
trough their labours their country would be lifted
om the slough of misgovernment and low ideals.
ife and everything they were ready to give for that.
Here are we," said Jacopo Ruffini to his fellow-
ᴐnspirators at Genoa, "five young, very young men,
ith but limited means, and we are called on to do
ᴐthing less than overthrow an established govern-
ᴇent. I have a presentiment that few of us will live
ᴉ see the final results of our labours, but the seed we
ᴉve sown will shoot forth after us, and the bread we
ᴉve cast upon the waters will be found again."

Mazzini might well be sanguine, with men like
ᴉese behind him. He looked to his literature to
ᴐ the rest. The journal of Young Italy was, as he
ᴇscribed it, "a collection of political pamphlets," each
ː the infrequent and irregular numbers consisting of
hundred to two hundred pages, badly printed on
ᴉd paper. Later on, it was set up by French com-
ᴐsitors, who knew no Italian, and whose misprints
ᴉve him infinite concern. He himself did most of the
riting. It was terribly diffusive often and wanting in
recision, but his articles redeem their literary defects
y the glow of noble purpose, that made them thrill

their readers, and gave them a potency, that perhaps
no other political writings of the century attained to
Most of the remaining articles came from his fellow·
workers.   Mazzini tried to persuade Sismondi to con·
tribute, but the historian, though sympathetic, was too
opposed to some of his teaching to respond.   Louis
Napoleon, drawn by a fellow-feeling for conspiracy
and scenting a chance to preach Bonapartism, sent an
essay on Military Honour, with the thesis that soldiers
are not bound by their oath to act against a revolu·
tion.   Mazzini consented to insert it with many
emendations, which apparently left little of its Bona·
partist intention ; but for some reason that does not
appear, it was not published.   The journal had a small
circulation, and only reached a limited number of
young educated men ; it was indeed too literary for
popular consumption.   There seems to have been
larger demand for rules and instructions and popular
tracts written by Gustavo Modena, afterwards t
become one of the most famous Italian tragedians of
his day.   At all events there was a considerable con
traband of printed matter, smuggled to Genoa o
Leghorn or across the passes into Piedmont, inside
barrels of pitch and pumice stone or bales of draper
or packages of sausages.   So great became the deman
that secret presses were set up in Italy and the Ticin
to supplement the output from Marseilles.

The results surpassed even Mazzini's sanguine hopes
The first lodges of Young Italy were planted at Geno
and Leghorn, and they spread thence to a good man
towns of North and Central Italy.   The chief strengt
of the society lay at Genoa, where the nationalist an
anti-Piedmontese parties made common cause, and me

of every class came in—nobles and commoners, lawyers and civil servants and priests, seamen and artisans. Outside Genoa the working men seem to have kept aloof as a rule ; years had yet to pass before Mazzini's social teaching reached them. The recruits came chiefly from the young men of the middle classes, sons of the men who had had their importance under the French rule and had been cribbed and kept under since the restoration. Here and there a young noble joined ; in Piedmont and at Genoa at all events there was a sprinkling of older professional and business men ; a few priests welcomed a movement, which bore so strong a religious imprint. Everywhere the scattered remnants of the Carbonari enrolled themselves. Buonarrotti, *doyen* of the conspirators, descendant of Michelangelo, friend of Robespierre and Babœuf and Napoleon, attached his society of the *Veri Italiani*. Early in 1833 Mazzini, it is impossible to say with what accuracy, put the number of affiliates at fifty or sixty thousand. / Many a man, who came to the front in the later nationalist movement or in the first Italian parliaments, began his political life as a member of Young Italy. Garibaldi, a young sailor who wrote verses, just promoted to be captain in the Genoese mercantile marine, whose fearlessness and charm of manner made him the idol of the men under him, and who had already learnt from Foscolo a belief in the destinies of Italy as ardent as Mazzini's own, met the chief at Marseilles and joined the society. Gioberti, who was teaching a transcendental and literary patriotism to the novices in the Archbishop's seminary at Vercelli, sent warm words of encouragement to the cause of God and the People.

All Mazzini's preparations centred round Piedmon
and Genoa. He realised, with the bulk of patriots c
whatever school, that though the other provinces migh
play a secondary part, Piedmont must take the leac
It was the only state that possessed the militar
training and traditions, essential in a war; it was th
natural base for an invasion of Lombardy; Alessandri
and Genoa were two all-important strategic point:
and if the Italians were defeated in the plains, the
could fall back on the Alps and Apennines. Ther
were few republicans among the Piedmontese, bu
they were nationalists with all their race's tenacity c
purpose. The Genoese were zealots for the cause, a
the more if it were under a republican flag; in Savo
there was a strong strain of liberalism, and its positio
made it a connecting link with sympathisers in Franc
/ Mazzini's first public act—some three or four month
after he left Italy—was to write an open letter to th
king. / Charles Albert had just ascended the throne c
Piedmont; and expectation ran high, as it had ru
ten years before, that he would lead the nationalist
This time there was small bottom for the hop·
Charles Albert had had his phase of liberalism; i
his youth he had relations with the Carbonari, an
encouraged the Piedmontese conspirators of 1821 t
look to him to lead the army to a war for Lombar
independence. Had he had the courage, he woul
have stood by his word. But as he was then, so wε
he now, a moral coward, buffeted by irreconcilab
ambitions. / He was still a nationalist, but no libera
Liberalism had come to loom before him as a spectr
of Revolution, to be fought and crushed without pit
But priest-ridden absolutist as he was, he never quit

forgot his patriotic faith, he always had some vision, faint though it often was, of an Italy untrodden by the foreign soldier. It is probable that even now, in his worst years, he was waiting dubiously for the distant day, when he would measure himself with the enemy. But he knew that as yet this was impossible. He had a saner view than Mazzini of the possibilities of the time, when France—on the high road to the *juste-milieu*—would give no help, and a single-handed fight with Austria was foredoomed to defeat. He would have scorned an offer of Mazzini's guerilla bands ; but had he been as ready to welcome the volunteers, as his son was twenty-eight years later, they had little prospect of existence at this time outside Mazzini's visionary hopes./

Such was Charles Albert, when Mazzini appealed to him to lead the nationalist movement. What was the exact purpose of the letter, will probably never be known./ In after life Mazzini denied that there was any serious intention in it ; he pleaded that he expressed the hopes of others rather than his own, and wrote it in the certainty that its appeal would not be heard. At the time he disclaimed, though not so emphatically, any hope of a response, and suggested that its object was to disillusion the Piedmontese of any belief in their king. / There is some reason for thinking that the disclaimers must not be taken quite literally. When he wrote twenty years and more afterwards, he was anxious to prove that he had never lapsed from his republican faith. His earlier commentary was in a letter to a man, whom he did not know, and to whom he was not likely to express himself unreservedly. There are indications

that he had not quite escaped the glamour that Charle
Albert threw over the liberals, had not entirely abar
doned all hope of winning him.   The secret instruc
tions of Young Italy, written a few months late
accepted the possibility of a monarchy as a "syster
of transition"; and in the subsequent army plc
Mazzini intended to offer the King the leadership c
the revolution.   One would fain believe that his ow
interpretations do him injustice, that he did not writ
his glowing prose in utter insincerity.   Were it othei
wise, we must bow the head and sadly own a stai
upon that noble life.

The letter, it must be confessed, was hardly calcu
lated to make a convert.   Threats alternate with ovei
done praise; the assumption of political omniscience
the claim of the young exile to speak for Italy, th
magniloquent parade of the obvious, must have, lik
much else of his earlier writings, offended Italia
common-sense and been extremely irritating.   Muc
of it reads like a declamatory school essay on th
duties of a constitutional king.   But the lesson wa
true enough on its negative side.   Charles Albei
could find no safe foothold outside popular govern
ment; coercion, administrative reform, the support c
Austria or France—none would permanently conten
or overawe his people.   And if Charles Albert ha
retorted that to grant a constitution meant war wit
Austria, Mazzini would have welcomed the corollary
The King was right and Mazzini was wrong as to th
inopportuneness of a national rising at the momen
But for the policy of another day, the letter ha
passages that speak like a trumpet call.   "Sire, ther
is another road, leading to true power and a glorio

...mortality; another ally, safer and more strong than
...ustria or France. There is a crown more brilliant
...d sublime than that of Piedmont, a crown that
...aits the man, who dares to think of it, who
...edicates his life to winning it, and scorns to dull its
...lendour with thoughts of petty tyranny. Sire, have
...ou never cast an eagle glance upon this Italy, so fair
...ith nature's smile, crowned by twenty centuries of
...oble memory, the land of genius, strong in the infinite
...sources that only want a common purpose, girt round
...ith barriers so impregnable, that it needs but a firm
...ill and a few brave breasts to shelter it from foreign
...sult? /Place yourself at the head of the nation,
...rite on your flag, 'Union, Liberty, Independence.'
...ree Italy from the barbarian, build up the future,
...e the Napoleon of Italian freedom. Do this and we
...ill gather round you, we will give our lives for you,
...e will bring the little states of Italy under your flag.
...our safety lies on the sword's point; draw it and
...row away the scabbard. But remember, if you do
...not, others will do it without you and against you."/
The letter was published in May or June 1831, and
few copies found their way into Italy. Mazzini
...ought he had evidence that the King read it. At
...l events his police did, and ordered the writer whose
...onymity did not conceal him, to be seized, if he
...ossed the frontier. Whatever Mazzini's hopes may
...ve been, this proved that the letter had failed in its
...tensible object, and he threw himself feverishly into
...s preparations for a revolt in Piedmont. His detailed
...heme shows that he had not yet planned or had
...andoned for the time the strategy of guerilla fighting,
...d intended to rely on the Piedmontese army. Charles

Albert was, if possible, to be persuaded to lead the revolution, and the army was to be mobilised for an immediate advance on Lombardy. Should the King decline the offer, a provisional directorate at Genoa would assume the government. Mazzini had better ground for his hopes than often afterwards. The army had not forgotten that it had led the constitutional and nationalist movement ten years before. Many a soldier, who had served in the *Grande Armée*, cherished the democratic sentiment that clung to it all through, and was eager to avenge himself on the enemy, whom he had routed in old days. These feelings were especially strong among the non-commissioned officers. Many of them were men of the middle classes of good standing and education, for in many, if not all, the regiments commissions could be held only by those of noble birth, and no bourgeois, whatever his capacities, could rise above the ranks. A few officers joined the society, and a general or two promised to throw in his lot, if the movement proved successful. At Alessandria and Genoa, the two chief garrison towns, the society had a considerable strength. The government, though quietly tracking the civilian conspirators seems to have had no suspicion of the army plot; and had the revolt broken out early in 1833, it would have had its chance of success at home, though the inevitable disaster must have come, when the little army faced the Austrians.

But the conspirators waited too long, and late in the spring an accident led to the discovery of the plot. The government cautiously followed up the clue, till it possessed itself of every detail of the conspiracy. Then it threw itself on its prey with a savage ve geance, that outside the Austrian provinces has had no parallel in Italy since the days of Fra Diavolo. Charles Albert, pitiless with fright, surrendered himself to the reactionary court party and fed their thirst for blood. Moral, sometimes physical, torture was inflicted on the victims to extort confession of their own or their confederates' guilt. Jacopo Ruffini, given the choice between execution and the betrayal of his friends, committed suicide in prison. Ten soldiers and two civilians were shot; fourteen more only escaped by flight; numbers were sent to longer or shorter imprisonment. Italy still execrates those courts-martial. Not all Charles Albert's later patriotism has purged his memory from their indelible shame; and while yet he reigned, the Genoese erased from their city every record of the brutal general who was his worst instrument. The humble lawyers and sergeants whom he shot, have a deathless homage from their country. " Ideas ripen quickly," said Mazzini, " when nourished by the blood of martyrs." It was the memory of these and other victims of tyranny, that helped to nerve Italian arms and send Italians to die in the battles that won their country's liberty.

Meanwhile, since the previous August, Mazzini had been driven into hiding at Marseilles. The French government decreed his banishment and broke up his press. Mazzini eluded both blows. He started a secret press and got French compositors to work it. He himself found refuge in the house of a French sympathiser, Démosthène Ollivier, father of Louis Napoleon's last premier, under whose roof he remained " a voluntary prisoner." Twice only in the year he passed its threshold, and then only at night, disguised as a woman or a *garde national.* It was at this time that the French government, whether maliciously or itself deceived, brought against him a false charge of encouraging assassination, for repeating which in after years Sir James Graham wore sackcloth.[1] Mazzini was still at Marseilles, when the news of the Genoese executions came ; and so terrible was his anguish, for in Jacopo Ruffini he had lost his dearest friend, that his health and mind nearly broke down. The devotion of a noble woman, whom he loved,[2] saved him from insanity or death.

About the beginning of July 1833 he moved to Geneva. He came there to be on the spot for a new plan of insurrection. The failure of the army plot only impelled him more feverishly into his fixed idea of a rising in Piedmont. He wished no doubt to punish Charles Albert, and well may he have been maddened by the savagery, which had sickened Europe. He wanted to "moralise" his party by proving that the terrorism had no fears for him and striking back at the victorious and brutal enemy. He thought that, if he was to keep his following together, he must make his cast now or never. Once allow the fire to slack down, and it would be beyond his power to rekindle it. He believed that half Europe was on the brink of revolution, that a republican movement in Italy would be the signal for republican risings in France and Spain and Germany. It was probably a fantastic dream ; but he had surer ground for thinking that a revolt would fire the tinder

---

[1] See below, p. 104
[2] See below, p. 68

throughout Italy. Exaggerated as his hopes were even here, the revolutionary spirit, that Young Italy created, had sunk deep. In the Genovesate and Savoy, in the Papal States and parts of Naples there was a good deal of material ready for an insurrection ; and Mazzini had assured himself that on the appointed day guerilla bands would take to the mountains in several districts. / The chances of success, indeed, were not bright at the best ; but the raid was not quite the unpardonable playing with brave lives, that it seems at first sight. Mazzini, taking up a plan of the Carbonari at Paris, chose Savoy for the starting-point of the insurrection. He expected that the troops there would join the insurgents, and the revolutionary army would cross the Alps into Piedmont, 'while another band would land in the Riviera and rouse the Genoese country.[1] /

By the autumn of 1833 several hundred exiles had been enrolled in Switzerland. Many of them were Poles and Germans, a few were French ; and Mazzini welcomed assistance, which he hoped might cement an international alliance of democrats, and develop into a " Young Europe," which would do elsewhere what Young Italy was doing for his own country. He had the help of several officers, Bianco di San Jorioz, author of a clever book on guerilla warfare, which had much influenced him, and Manfredo Fanti, the future organiser of the Italian army. They saw the importance of giving the command to an experienced officer, and the Savoyard conspirators insisted that the choice should fall on a certain General Ramorino, a cosmopolitan adventurer of

[1] For Gallenga's plot to assassinate the King, see below, c. ix.

Savoyard birth, who had fought under Napoleon, and had an undistinguished command in the Polish rising of 1831. Mazzini's slender preparations were completed by October, and about eight hundred men were armed and ready to march. There were plans of simultaneous risings at Genoa and Naples, in the Marches and the Abruzzi; and Garibaldi enlisted in the Piedmontese navy in the quixotic hope of bringing it over to the revolution. / But what chance there was of success was spoilt by Ramorino. He had no real interest in the expedition; perhaps he was paid by the French government to wreck it. / At all events he lingered at Paris, squandering much of the war-fund, that Mazzini had collected with infinite labour. Every week added to the difficulties. The foreign governments put pressure on the Swiss to break up the volunteers. Buonarrotti, suspicious of the whole design, did his best to discredit Mazzini among his own men. When Mazzini at last insisted that the volunteers must wait no longer, the conspirators in Savoy refused to cooperate unless Ramorino came. Mazzini worked desperately to undo the mischief, and at last, in January, Ramorino arrived. It was too late. The Swiss authorities harassed the volunteers, and on February 1 only a small body of the raiders could gather on the frontier near St Julien. Ramorino marched them aimlessly about. Probably he saw from the first how desperate were the chances, and wished to spare a useless loss of life. On the 4th, before hardly a shot had been exchanged, he disbanded his men, and the insurrection was still-born.

Chapter IV

Switzerland

Life in exile — Mental crisis — Principles of the revolution — Young
Switzerland — Young Europe—Literary work—Women friends :
Giuditta Sidoli—Madeleine de Mandrot.

During the raid Mazzini's health collapsed. The
strain of work and anxiety might have broken down
a stronger man ; he had not touched his bed for a
week, and fatigue and cold and the crushing responsibility brought on fever. There was a false alarm one
night, and a patrol fired ; and Mazzini, hurrying up
excitedly with his musket, lost consciousness and did
not regain it till the volunteers had recrossed the
frontier. The collapse unstrung him for the time,
and perhaps it was only the letters of the woman he
loved, that kept him from a worse fate. " I have
moral convulsions," he writes to her ; " there are
moments when I could roll on the ground and bite
myself. I have fits of rage at every human face and
voice." When he recovered, he found his residence
in Switzerland threatened. The foreign governments
rained threats on the Federal Diet to make it expel
the refugees. The Diet was easily frightened, but
even had it been braver, it could not tolerate acts

contrary to international law, or allow Switzerland to be a recruiting ground for raids upon a neighbouring power. The Swiss could not be expected to risk foreign complications for the sake of men who, from any ordinary standpoint, had abused their hospitality. After what had happened, it was difficult for the raiders to plead at once even the traditional right of asylum for political refugees ; and though after a lapse of time a stronger government would have reverted to the more generous policy, and though some of the cantons were restive at its continued deference to foreign pressure, it is not easy to blame the Diet, even at a later date, for its unwillingness to shelter the raiders.

Many of them were sent at once across the frontier ; others succeeded in hiding themselves. Mazzini was determined not to leave Switzerland. It was essential to his plans that he should be near Italy, and he dreaded moving further from the beloved land. He grew fond of Switzerland, and came to " love the Alps almost as one loves a mother." England and America were the only other countries open to him, and he feared that if a Tory government came into power in England, he would find no shelter even there. " Besides," he said, in words to be recanted later, " there is no sympathy there, no help, no anything." For nearly three years he led a more or less hunted life—at Lausanne, at Berne, at Soleure and Bienne and Grenchen, in the house of a Protestant pastor at Langnau ; sometimes hotly sought by the police, sometimes with the connivance of the government, but generally a virtual prisoner in the houses where he found a refuge. For seven months, at one time, he fled from place to place, living in apparently untenanted houses, with mats at the windows, never setting foot outside, except in his fugitive removes by night across the mountains. Exhausted in body and soul, he had to taste an exile's life in all its bitterness ; " the existence mournful and dull as a stormy sky or the ashes of a dead fire ; the suffering that has no name, that finds no vent in tears or words, that has no poetry save for the distant sentimentalist ; the suffering that makes a man wan and hollow-cheeked but kills not, that bows but does not break ; while the weary eyes follow the driven clouds, that the wind wafts away to the skies of fatherland, beyond the everlasting Alps, those icy cherubim that guard the gate of the heart's Eden."

There was little interruption to his desolate solitude. Save for occasional glimpses, he was parted from his old comrades, except the Ruffinis ; and though he found a few sympathetic friends in Switzerland and caught greedily at their affections, it could not make up for the loss. He had few books ; " I could well live all my life shut up in one room," he wrote wearily, " if I had all my books at hand, but without books, or guitar, or view, it is too much." The sedentary life told on his health, and he obstinately declined the medicines his mother sent him. Toothache wore him down, though sometimes he welcomed it as a diversion from his sickness of heart. Money difficulties came, with their sordid complications. His mother sent what she could spare ; friends helped him with loans. But he could never refuse an exile in need, and they importuned him, till even he rebelled against their exigencies. The organisation of Young Italy—such of it as still was left——and expenses of publishing and postage absorbed most of the rest, for there were few subscribers to the party funds. He denied himself all but bare necessities and cigars, even the two small luxuries he valued——scent and good writing paper. He borrowed what few books he had. He went short of clothes, and sends his mother lean inventories of his wardrobe, which she and his old nurse did their best to replenish. Sometimes he found himself in absolute want, and writes " with a blush on his face " to the mother who never refused him. Aching fits of home-sickness came on him, " a physical craving for home, for Italian clouds and winds and sea." " The other day," he writes to a little girl friend, " I was looking at the Alps in the distance——beyond them is my country, my poor country that I love so much, where my father and mother are, and my two sisters, and another sister who has been dead many years, and the tomb of the best friend of my youth, who died for liberty, and meadows and hills and beautiful lakes like your own, and flowers and oranges and a beautiful sky——all that one needs to make one die happy, and I thought sadly on it all."

He had more pungent thoughts to trouble him. The disastrous raid demoralised his party. From Italy came news of discouragement and desertion. The exiles loaded him with the responsibility of the fiasco ; he found himself the centre of a miserable cross-fire of recrimination, and he repaid the criticism with scorn and suspicion. The want of response in Italy made him at times very bitter against his countrymen. " Oh, how cold those Italians are, and how they hunt for excuses for their apathy. They will not see that they are slaves, without a name, accursed by God, and mocked among the nations."╱ The human sweetness in him was half dried up, and a misanthropy, so new and alien to him, made him querulous and captious. Friends were cold, or at all events seemed so to his sick mind. He wrote peevishly to the best of them; probably he talked more peevishly still. The society, even of those who were dearest, worried and distressed him, and he preferred to be left alone with a favourite cat. "I am inclined to love men at a distance," he writes; "contact makes me hate them." The sorest pain, one that obsessed him and dragged him to the abyss, was the thought of his suffering friends, suffering because of him, though for a cause for which he too had given all. It was the Gethsemane of every true-hearted man, who calls his fellows forth to sacrifice and battle. The friends of his youth were in exile. Men who had loved him and whom he had loved, were laying their misery to his charge. The Ruffinis' home was desolate—one son the victim of his own hand, two more in exile, the mother, whom of all women he reverenced most, sitting in loneliness and mourning. Another woman, to whom he had given his love, but to whom a fugitive exile could not give a home, was hunted by the Italian police, worn and desperate. "What gives me pain and very sad moments," he writes to his mother, "is the past and present and future of the few beings who love me and whom I really love, you, and the Ruffinis, their mother, my sisters, and Her. If I could see you all and my few other friends, I will not say happy, for that we can never be again, but tranquil, quiet, smiling, and united, I would die that day with rapture." "I wanted to do good," he writes to a friend, " but I have always done harm to everybody, and the thought grows and grows till I think I shall go mad. Sometimes I fancy I am hated by those I love most." Once, at all events, it made him doubt of all that he had done. " I think over it from morning to night, and ask pardon of my God for having been a conspirator ; not that I in the least repent the reasons for it, or recant a single one of my beliefs, which were, and are, and will be a religion to me, but because I ought to have seen that there are times, when a believer should only sacrifice himself to his belief. I have sacrificed everybody."

The black misery settled on him. " I felt alone in the world, except for my poor mother, and she too was away and unhappy for my sake, and I stopped in terror at the void. In that wilderness I met Doubt." The men whom he had sent to a patriot's death, had they died in vain? Was it all a frightful error, an empty dream born of ambition and pride of intellect? Was it for some grandiose, impossible chimera, that he had taken men from quiet useful lives and the simple round of kindliness? What authority had he still to preach a creed, which meant the sacrifice of thousands more, the unhappiness of many another mother? In his nightly terrors, in his little lonely room, while the wind howled round, he heard Jacopo Ruffini's voice calling to him. He was of course verging on insanity, and thoughts of suicide passed through his mind. His strong moral nature and the influence of two women—Madame Ruffini and one unknown—saved him. Characteristically, mental health returned in the shape of a philosophy of life. It was his theory of Duty, expanded till it penetrated every cranny of the individual soul. His old enemy, the utilitarian theory, had taken subtle root in his affections. " I should have thought of them, as of a blessing from God, to be accepted with thankfulness, not as of something to be expected and exacted as a right and a reward. Instead of this, I had made them a condition of fulfilling my duties. I had not reached the ideal of love, love that has no hope in this life. I had worshipped not love but the joys of love." And so he put away that last infirmity of the true man, took to himself not only toil and danger and opprobrium, but unloved solitude of soul, the desert life of him who has no friend but God. He, who ached for sympathy and love, took duty for his hard task-master—duty, " an arid, bare religion, which does not save my heart a single atom of unhappiness, but still the only one that can save me from suicide." " There are four lines of Juvenal," he said, " that sum up all we ought to ask of God, all that made Rome the mistress and the benefactress of the world :——

> ' Pray for the soul, that has no fear of death,
>   That holds life's end among kind nature's gifts,
>   Brave to endure each pain and labour ; nought
>   Vexes it, nought it covets.' "

" When a man," he writes to a friend, " has once said to himself in all seriousness of thought and feeling, I believe in liberty and country and humanity, he is bound to fight for liberty and country and humanity, fight long as life lasts, fight always, fight with every weapon, face all from death to ridicule, face hatred and contempt, work on because it is his duty and for no other reason."

Long indeed before his mental crisis, the light and joy had gone out of his work. There were times when he felt he had neither strength nor time nor capacity for it, when his theories became cold, emotionless abstractions, far other than the passionate beliefs of other days. God was " a geometrical solution," his own task " a fated mission." All life seemed drab and purposeless. " There is so much agony in life," he writes, " that when I see a baby quiet, smiling, at peace, I can only wish for death for it." Perhaps though such moods were the exception. " He is almost always good-tempered and sometimes gay," wrote Giovanni Ruffini. Certainly during these three years he wrote some of his warmest and humanest pages. At times he was even hopeful of his immediate political schemes. / He was strong in the sense of his mission. " I know," he said, " there is the future in this life of mine, little matter if I see it." " We have made," he writes, " the cause of the people our own, we have voluntarily taken on ourselves the sorrows of all a generation. We have snatched a spark from the Eternal God, and placed ourselves between Him and the people ; we have taken on ourselves the part of the emancipator, and God has accepted us."

Alike in hours of insight and of gloom he remained ever constant to his work. His friends advised him to retire. His father threatened, his mother entreated. To the latter he " would have yielded, if he could." He would gladly have withdrawn, at least he thought so, if anyone else had come forward to take up the work ; but this of course was impossible. He would have liked to fall back on the Manzonian policy, and devote himself to quiet moral and literary education.

But this seemed an impossible solution in a country, where there was no freedom of speech or writing. The only way, he thought, to rouse his countrymen was to give them the example of a life, that no adversity could turn back, no want of response dishearten, ever labouring and suffering for their sake and the ideal's. There must be no folding of the hands, because others were slow to follow.

He set himself to think why the revolutions of the last five years had failed, why the people, whether in Italy or France or elsewhere, had been so deaf to the call to liberty. He was always asking himself why it was that Christianity had succeeded, and why a movement, that had so much in common with it, the movement for the social and political redemption of the people, had failed. He found his answer in the fact that the Revolution had missed the spiritual power, that made Christianity triumphant. It was the substance of his Marseilles teaching, but informed with a more mystical, transcendental spirit, due no doubt to the apocalyptic results of his depression, and partly too to the influence that Lamennais had over him at this time. The French Revolution had appealed to men's selfish and personal interests, their rights, their desire for happiness. It had been a rebellion against evil, not a mission in search of good. It had had its use, but now it had done its work. The principle of liberty and human dignity was accepted everywhere in theory, however much realisation lagged. The nineteenth century was plagiarising the eighteenth, and following precedents whose day was past. A new principle was needed to carry progress one step further, and that principle must be a spiritual one. "We fell as a political party, we must rise again as a religious party." The new revolution must find its strength in "the enthusiasm, which alone begets great things"; it must appeal to men's sense of duty, it must bid them work not for themselves but for humanity./ Then and not till then, the pettiness and party feeling and want of earnestness, which had wrecked the movements of 1831 and his own Italian schemes, would vanish in the light of a great faith, and that same light would be a beacon, which would draw the masses after.

/He was still, in spite of disappointment and the scepticism of his friends, convinced that Europe was ripe for revolution, if only one country showed the way. He was equally convinced that Italy would be that country./ France, he thought, had disqualified herself by her adherence to the traditions of her Revolution. The strong dislike of France, which marked him all through life, was now especially prominent, and he declared that popular progress throughout Europe depended on emancipation from her political and literary influence. / Why he appropriated for Italy the revolutionary hegemony, he would have found it difficult to give a convincing reason. At bottom, probably, with the sublime prophetic confidence that went hand in hand with all his searchings of heart and absence of personal ambition, he claimed the primacy for his country, because he hoped to inform her with his own principles./

/His Italian programme remained almost unaltered. He was indeed prepared, though regretfully, to support a royalist movement, if it declared for Italian Unity. But he would not countenance a royalist programme with any lesser goal. He still believed in the Republic, both for Italy's own sake and for the example it would give to other democracies. And he still believed in insurrection as the only possible road to reformation in a country, where there were no constitutional liberties to make constitutional progress possible. Gioberti urged to him in vain that unsuccessful insurrections only discouraged the patriots and intensified the oppression. Mazzini, though he promised that he would not again encourage an insurrectionary movement, unless it started inside the country and independently of the exiles, argued that insurrection was the only means to rouse the masses. It mattered little if the first risings failed ; they would keep alive the spirit, that one day would lead to victory. His hopes of the early triumph of the revolution grew slowly fainter ; he began to see that time, perhaps a generation, was needed to quicken the inertia, that ages of despotism had instilled. But every effort brought them nearer to the goal ; every slackening made it more remote. He would not believe that sacrifice and struggle could go unrewarded, or quiet waiting spring from ought but cowardice. He still, though fitfully—for want of money and the need of secrecy and his own deepening gloom hampered him at every turn—went on with his preparations. The sixth number of *Young Italy* appeared in July 1834 ; this was its last issue, but he persevered in the thankless work of organisation, carrying on a voluminous correspondence, raking in sympathisers from every quarter, sending agents to Italy, who brought back the same monotonous tale of discouragement and unreadiness.

He found time meanwhile to interest himself in Swiss politics, and tried to organise a party to do for Switzerland, what Young Italy had been doing for his own country. Many of the Swiss naturally resented the intrusion of a stranger. Mazzini brushed away the objection, though he would perhaps have been the first to criticise a foreigner, who had preached to the Italians, as he preached to the Swiss. Switzerland, he urged, played so important a part in the European polity, that no one could be indifferent to its destiny. At this time, certainly, Swiss politics offered abundant scope for a reformer. The Federal Pact of 1815 had undone Napoleon's comparatively liberal constitution. The cantons were connected by the loosest of ties ; many of them were governed by small oligarchies ; class privileges depressed the artisans and peasants. The return of the Jesuits stirred a bitter religious struggle, which from time to time threatened to blaze into civil war. A vigorous reform movement had indeed recently swept away the worst abuses inside some of the cantons ; but, nothing had been done to strengthen the bonds between them, and the narrow cantonal life threatened to smother the country in a " mud-death." It was impossible for Switzerland to assert her independence or maintain her traditions, when she had no central authority worthy of the name. To Mazzini it meant too the absence of any real national life, the adhesion to a policy of neutrality, which prevented the one republican state of Europe from throwing its weight into the European balance. Mazzini's ideal for Switzerland was to include it with the Tyrol and Savoy in a federation of republics, and substitute for the settlement of 1815 a true federal authority, representing and responsible to the whole people and not to the separate cantons. He founded a "Young Switzerland" society, and published a paper, *La Jeune Suisse*, which appeared twice a week in French and German, till after a year's existence (the usual life of Mazzini's journalistic ventures) the Diet suppressed it and decreed Mazzini's perpetual banishment. In some of its articles Mazzini appears at his best,— more tolerant, less dogmatic and theoretical. The movement does not seem to have found any great measure of success, though it attracted a certain number of the finer spirits among the younger men and Protestant clergy. But, whatever may have been the immediate fruits of Mazzini's work, at all events his ideas triumphed. The Swiss constitution of 1848 embodied their essentials, and it is worth noting that Druey, one of its two draughtsmen, was his personal friend.

Italy and Switzerland together were not enough to occupy his energies. Two months after the collapse of the Savoy raid, seventeen of the exiles, Italians, Germans, Poles, signed a "pact of Young Europe," which was intended to be an alliance on Mazzinian principles of the republicans of the three countries. When one remembers that its vast scheme of transformation was the work of a few young exiles, it reads like pure rhodomontade. Mazzini himself recognised afterwards that the plan was too embracing to lead to practical results. But at the time he seems to have expected a good deal from it. It was to be a kind of "college of intellects," which would watch and give information on the popular and nationalist movements of the Continent, and at the same time be an organised propagandism with its machinery of agents "and countless other means." One thing in particular he hoped from it, that it would assist towards "the emancipation from France," and encourage another country, Italy of course by preference, to initiate the new age of religion and the republic. As a matter of fact, nothing seems to have been done beyond the despatch of a few agents to France and Spain, and an attempt to organise meetings in England. But it loomed large in the public eye, and did something to teach democracy that its interests are international.

Meanwhile, in addition to his political correspondence and journalism, he found time for literary writing. It was partly in the vain hope of earning a little money for himself and his political work. " I think over schemes day and night, as every man in want does." It was partly too to encourage "a religious and poetic sentiment" in Italy, and combat the dominant scepticism and materialism. For literary fame he cared nothing. Friends, who wished him to retire from political work, advised him to "honour Italy with his pen." " Excuse me," he answered, " but this has no meaning for me. I don't know what or where Italy is. We must try to regenerate and create her, and honour her afterwards." His articles on *Byron and Goethe* and *The Philosophy of Music* date from this period. He collected materials for the edition of Foscolo's works, which was so near his heart now as at a later time. He wished to edit a collection of translated dramas, and wrote introductions to Werner's *Der vierund-*

zwanzigste Februar and De Vigny's *Chatterton*. "No other critic," says a recent Italian writer, "has written at such length or so profoundly on Werner as did Mazzini." The essay was published later at Brussels with Agostino Ruffini's translation,—the only instalment of the projected series. He planned a *Foreign Review*, to be published at Genoa, but an indiscreet friend betrayed his editorship, and the censorship promptly withdrew its sanction. Another scheme for a *Review of European Literature*, to be issued in the freer air of Lugano, broke down, apparently for want of funds. Another venture, which had a brief life, was the *Italiano*, a literary and scientific magazine, which appeared at Paris for a few months in 1836, to which he and Tommaseo and some of the best Italian writers of the day contributed, and where Guerrazzi published the first chapters of his *Siege of Florence*. Mazzini, who drafted the prospectus, seems to have been especially anxious to include novels and poetry. "It must be remembered," he writes, "that fancy and the affections make up at least four-fifths of man. Poetry is not the gift and privilege of a few, the masses are full of a living and speaking poetry." He urged too that women's questions should have adequate attention.

It is to this period chiefly that belong the only love-episodes of Mazzini's life. He had a lofty conception of womanhood. "Love and respect woman," he once wrote. "Look to her not only for comfort, but for strength and inspiration and the doubling of your intellectual and moral powers. Blot out from your mind any idea of superiority;

you have none.   There is no inequality between man
and woman; but as often is the case between two
men, only different tendencies and special vocations.
Woman and man are the two notes, without which
the human chord cannot be struck." "Marriage," he
wrote to a young wife many years afterwards, "is
sacred, because it is one of the most potent means of
accomplishing life's mission.   It gives the almost
superhuman strength that comes of love, the supreme
comfort that makes sacrifice a joy, the dew that
tempers the scorching heat upon the flower." But
"now, as a rule," he says, "we do not love.   Love,
the most holy thing that God has given to man, has
become a febrile need, a brutish instinct; the family
is perverted into a denial of all vocation and social
duty; male and female have cancelled man and
woman." He himself was a man, not likely to be
easily in love.   His work absorbed his vital force, and
he had no pity for men who forgot public work in
domestic happiness.   And though his unsoiled·purity
and gentleness, together with the sympathy that
allowed him to understand women as few men can
do, won him the devotion and affection of many
women, especially Englishwomen, the sentiment, on
his side at least, was, save in two cases, one of
"intense friendship" only.

He had two or three boyish passions, one for an
English girl who lived near his home at Genoa, another
for a Genoese, Adele Zoagli, who afterwards became
the mother of the patriot-poet Mameli.   When he
went into exile, the only women who had a place in
his heart were his own mother and Madame Ruffini.
His affection for his mother was very serious and

deep, more masculine and less sentimental than in
the common course of Italian filial love. Perhaps
after his boyhood she did not influence him in details,
and intellectually there was some lack of sympathy
between them. But her strong pride in him, that
made her " thank God day and night for having given
her that son," her faith in his political, though not in
his religious beliefs, the love that watched year after
year over the son she saw not, the courage that made
her bear long years of parting rather than ask him to
deny his call, made the most lasting human inspiration
of his life. In time of deep trouble a man will turn
to his mother and his God, and he looked to her, as to
one whose love would never change, to whom he could
pour out, not indeed his spiritual misery, but all the
little material worries which a man tells only to his
mother and his wife, certain that her sympathy would
never fail. His love for Madame Ruffini was of
another kind. She was a very noble woman, with
intense and unconcealed sympathies, wise with the
experience of age and motherhood and sorrow ; and
Mazzini was not the only one in the circle of friends
at Genoa, who loved her with the reverential affection,
that an elderly woman of saintly life and understanding will call forth from young men. It was she, whose
own deep religious faith had saved him in youth from
his short episode of scepticism. Another woman would
have reproached him with Jacopo's death ; to her the
common memory of one so dear only fed the affection,
that many memories and the same intense religious,
almost mystical, beliefs had already made so strong.
He calls her " mother, friend, and all that is more
sacred," " the purest, whitest, holiest soul he had ever

met on earth." As far as we can tell, it was from no fault of his that their friendship closed afterwards in misunderstanding and silence.

His devotion to these two women had a deeper and more lasting influence on him than any lover's passion There was, however, at least one other, whom he loved in another way, one to whom he gave his troth and whom he would have married, had an exile's life allowed it. Giuditta Sidoli was the daughter of a noble Lombard family, where she had been brought up in a school of patriotism. Her brother, Carlo Bellerio was a follower of Young Italy, and was banished for his faith. She had been married, when a mere girl, to Giovanni Sidoli, a wealthy Reggian, a patriot and an exile too ; and he swore her on his death-bed to be true to the cause to which he had given his life. She was one year older than Mazzini, a quiet-moving, gracious woman, almost beautiful, with a gentle, blonde Venetian face, warm, golden hair, and dark, thoughtful eyes ; sober and unemotional in her manner, but with deep springs of enthusiasm and devotion. Mazzini first met her, a five years' widow, at Marseilles and afterwards in Switzerland ; their liking and common interests soon deepened into love, and he was engaged to her before he left France. A few months before the Savoy Expedition, her yearning for her children, who were left at Reggio, drove her to Florence in the hope that with or without the Government's consent she might see them. Thanks to the Tuscan police who opened and copied Mazzini's letters to her we have some fragments of their correspondence " There are words in your letter," he writes, " which make me still thrill with joy. In these last days

I have learnt the strength of my love. I have covered your lock with kisses. Oh, that I could sleep for once with my head resting on your knees." To a common friend he writes, probably a little later, "I love her more than she thinks, much more than she loves me. I dream of her day and night, and it becomes more and more a fixed idea with me; and yet I know with absolute certainty I shall never live with her, not even if Italy were free."

Up to a point they doubtless loved; but, especially when one remembers Mazzini's emotional epistolary style of this time, one is tempted to question whether their love had very much passion in it. It was the tender, strong affection of two absolutely good and kindred souls, and with neighbourhood it might have ripened into more. But long separation cooled it, and neither was inconsolable. To Giuditta probably at bottom her children were dearer than her lover, and Mazzini felt this. She seems to have made no effort to join him afterwards in England; she went to Parma to be near her children and importune the ducal brute, who forbade her access to them, at last going to Reggio in his despite and apparently seeing them for a moment. Mazzini for his part was wrapped up in his work and the struggle with exacting poverty. In England he hardly corresponds with her, partly because his letters might have brought fresh persecution on her, but partly, one is forced to conclude, because there was no lover's ardour to find out a way. But he still considered himself as in honour bound to her, and in a sense no doubt he loved her still. He writes in the summer of 1838, "Giuditta loves me, I love her, and have promised to love her," but he speaks as if he feared a rupture rather for its effects on her than on himself.   Two years later he writes as if his love were dead.   But, if love was dead, friendship, and a very strong and true one, remained to the end.   It is probable that they never ceased entirely to correspond. In the fifties, when she was living in the Valle dei Salici, near Turin, a grey-haired woman, with all the gracious gentleness and culture of her earlier days, Mazzini would come to see her in his secret visits to Piedmont, and she was still the tolerant but ardent believer in his policy.   When she was on her death-bed, a year before he died himself, he wrote "as an old friend" to "one of the best spirits he had ever met."

In a sense Giuditta had a rival.   During his Swiss wanderings, the daughter of de Mandrot, a friendly *avocat* at Lausanne, whom he had met casually,[1] became strongly attracted to him.   And what was at first a woman's pity and a disciple's adoration, changed to passionate love.   She was a girl of some sixteen years, of rich, emotional nature and spiritual yearnings, that echoed to his own.   When he went to London, and she saw no more of him and heard of his uncared-for loneliness, her hopeless love and pity worked on her, till she pined into melancholy and illness, and her friends begged him to return and save her by his presence.   What response he made to her love, it is not easy to say.   If one may judge from the meagre references in his letters, he felt at first no more than affectionate gratitude for the rich gift

---

[1] Her niece, Mademoiselle Dora Melegari, tells me that her aunt's real name was not Madeleine, as given in the *Lettres Intimes*; what it was, Mademoiselle Melegari does not at present feel justified in disclosing.

he could not take. But later, as he learnt more
of her constancy and unhappiness, and his love for
Giuditta wore away, and he ached for a woman's
loving hand, his affection ripened into something that
was probably nearer passionate love than anything he
felt before or after. Not that his permanent, reasoning self was disloyal to Giuditta. " Am I free ? " he
writes to a friend, who would gladly have seen him
and the girl united ; " before society and men, who
recognise only actual bonds, I am ; but before my
own heart and God, who watches over promises, I am
not." Sometimes indeed he balanced the results to
the two women, and was tempted for the moment
to think that " the imperious duty " of saving the one
from death or life-long misery might justify the breaking of his promise to Giuditta. But he knew that it
would be a cruel blow to the woman to whom he had
pledged himself; he felt he would gladly escape from
an attachment, which stained his loyalty to her ; and
his common sense told him that his gloomy companionship and the privations of an exile's life would
never make a young girl permanently happy. And
so he never seriously faltered in crushing down the
rising love within him or trying to crush it out in
her. He steadily declines to admit more than a
brother-and-sisterly relationship ; he prays she may
forget him and begs his friends to do their best to
kill her love by painting him in his defects ; he
refuses to correspond with her, and though at last
at the earnest prayer of her friends he promises to
come, if he can find the money, it was only to save
her from the pining that was bringing her to her
grave. But though he put her aside as a beautiful

and impossible dream, he could not stop the yearning. "Do you think," he writes, "that I easily give
up having near me one like her, a creature of God,
young, pure, religious, enthusiastic, into whose heart I
could pour all the world of feelings and dreams and
beliefs and love that is in me?" He finds his comfort in the thought that theirs is "a mystical, spiritual
union," that she will meet and make him happy in
another world. In this world he never saw her again,
and it seems that her passion soon fretted her frail
life away. Love of wife and love of family were not
for him, and bitterly he felt it. "He, who through
fatality of circumstances," he wrote long after, "cannot
live the serene life of family, has a void in his heart,
that nothing fills; and I who write these pages, well
I know it."

Chapter V

London

1837-1843.   AETAT 31-38

Life in London—Spiritual condition—English friends—The Carlyles—
Lamennais and George Sand—Literary work—Decay of Young Italy
—The Italian School at Hatton Garden—Appeal to working men.

EARLY in 1837 Mazzini and the Ruffinis came to
London.   The determining cause was the inability of
the latter to bear the privations of a life of hiding.
They travelled by slow diligence stages through
France, the French government, which was only glad
to get them out of Switzerland, giving them every
facility for the journey.   In London at all events they
were free men, able to live under their own names
and move where they liked, untroubled by the police.
But the change from the snows and sunsets and
silences of Switzerland to the squalor and noise of a
back street in London added to Mazzini's desolation.
In this "sunless and musicless island," with the
dreary stretches of houses and the wearing din, he
pined for the peace of the Alps, where nature had
brought him an occasional respite from his heart-ache.
" We have lost," he writes, "even the sky, which the
veriest wretch on the Continent can look at"; and in
time the desolate walls across the street worried him,

73

till he would not go to the window. The one thing in London that appealed to him was the fog. "When you look up, the eye loses itself in a reddish, bell-shaped vault, which always gives me, I don't know why, an idea of the phosphorescent light of the Inferno.[1] The whole city seems under a kind of spell, and reminds me of the Witches' Scene in Macbeth or the Brocksberg or the Witch of Endor. The passers-by look like ghosts,—one feels almost a ghost oneself." The half-glimpses of the buildings, harmonising with their sombre colouring, gave him a sense of mystery and indefiniteness, that redeemed London of "the positive and finite" of a Southern town, and responded to his growing faith in the poetic and unseen.

For a few weeks he lived at 24 Goodge Street, Tottenham Court Road, with the Ruffinis and two other exiles, who had helped him in the Marseilles days. In March the quintet moved to 9 George Street, near the Euston Road, where they suffered many things from the maid-of-all-work, who no doubt did much as she liked with the five inexperienced males, only two of whom could speak English at all well. Here they lived for three years, on the whole a very miserable household. Mazzini himself was "an angel of kindness and good-temper and enthusiasm," ever ready to sacrifice himself to others' whims and comforts. But the unhappy mystic was no cheerful companion, he was unpractical and dogmatic, probably sometimes peevish, half-lost in the empyrean

---

[1] For once his knowledge of Dante seems to have failed him. Many years after he quotes the expression to " Daniel Stern," but owns that he cannot refer to the verse.

of his ideals, beyond the ken or sympathy of the others. Agostino Ruffini's petty selfishness and ungovernable tongue were the source of frequent scenes, which one day brought Mazzini to tears, " tears which nothing else could have drawn from him," as he writes plaintively to Agostino's mother. At bottom young Ruffini recognized Mazzini's worth and devotedness, and swore himself on paper to keep his temper, with other salutary resolutions, to be read over three times a week ; but he was quite incapable of reaching to Mazzini's mind, and he longed to enjoy himself in a freer life, where the gospel of duty was never heard. Giovanni was more equable, and knew Mazzini better, but he too had small belief in the gospel, and there was little except old associations and the common love of his mother to bind him to his transcendental friend. The general irresponsiveness at home bitterly hurt and saddened Mazzini. " I love no one and want to love no one," he writes of his English surroundings ; and in his letters to his friends in Italy and Switzerland, he returns again and again to the lack of sympathy around him, as the heaviest trial of those unhappy days.

There was nothing to distract him from the sordidness of the bickering household in George Street. He seldom went out of doors, except to the British Museum. He had no money to buy books and complains that nobody would lend them. He saw few besides a few exiles, as poor and perhaps as unhappy as himself. He was " lost in a vast crowd of strangers, in a country where want, especially in a foreigner, is a reason for a distrust, which is often unjust and sometimes cruel." In common with his companions, he was miserably poor, often living on potatoes or rice. His father advanced him money to speculate in olive oil; naturally he lost it, and after an angry letter from the hard old man, refused for several years to accept help from home. He tried to find employment as a proof-reader, but in vain. He had an offer of work at Edinburgh, but the Ruffinis would not leave London, and he felt himself tied to them. Literary work came in very slowly, and for a year or two his articles in the English reviews brought in little profit, when the translator had been paid. The income of the rest of the household was not much larger, and the bad house-keepers found that in England "francs were little better than sous." Mazzini, as ever, could not shut his purse to the needy exiles, who importuned him and, as Agostino grumbled, "in the name of this chimera of human brotherhood thought they had a right to make themselves at home in his house." His few possessions soon found their way to the pawn-shop. He pledged his mother's ring, his watch and books and maps; his cloak went to buy cigars, "the one thing I don't think I can do without." On one black Saturday he pawned a pair of boots and an old waistcoat to find food for the Sunday. One winter he risked his health by giving away his only overcoat. His mother, finding that good clothes got sold at once to buy suits for his friends, thought it better to send several suits of cheaper garments, so that he could keep one at least for himself. Sometimes his wardrobe was so depleted, that he had to stay at home, and could not go to the British Museum to carry on his literary work. His generosity was well-known to his better-off friends, and it is not surprising that their patience in lending him money was exhausted. He tried a few years later to negotiate a loan on the security of yet un-written manuscripts; but the ingenuous scheme met with no better success. Once some friends at Paris lent him £120; another by a ruse persuaded him to accept what was practically a gift;[1] but when towards the end of his first residence in England a proposal was made at Turin to raise a subscription for him, he obstinately declined it, partly because, if it reached his mother's ears, she "would have died of shame." There were thus only two roads open to him, suicide or the money-lenders. The thought of suicide came to him again and again, but he put it away as a coward's act and for his mother's sake. So more and more he fell into the money-lenders' hands, borrowing at thirty or forty or sometimes nearly one hundred per cent. from loan societies, that "rob the poor man of his last drop of blood and sometimes his last rags of self-respect." Year after year he plunged desperately in the morass, and though £320 seems to have been the limit of his indebtedness, it was a crushing sum for one so utterly destitute. It was the common lot of the exiles, and some of them fared worse. In the midst of wealthy London, with men of means all round them, who shared their political views and made speeches for their cause, Karl Stolzmann, the Polish leader, one of Mazzini's nearest friends, went sometimes literally without food, and Stanislaus Worcell, born a rich Polish noble, was saved from a pauper's burial by an English acquaintance.

[1] He subsequently discovered that it was a loan, and insisted on repaying it shortly before his death.

Apart, however, from money troubles, Mazzini's external life gradually brightened. In 1840, after a short stay at 26 Clarendon Square, not far from their George Street house, where happily Agostino left them for work in Edinburgh, he and Giovanni moved to 4 York Buildings, which then stood in the angle between King's Road, Chelsea, and Riley Street. He came there to be near the Carlyles, and escape from London gloom and noise and importunate visitors. An Italian artisan, an exile from Perugia, kept house with his English wife, who proved an excellent house-keeper and saved them from servant-girl worries. In those days there was a hay-field on one side of the house and market-gardens on another, some trees in view " of a very sombre green, but still trees," and not far off the Thames, " equally sombre with its muddy dirty-yellow water, but beautiful at night, when its colour is lost in the dark, and the water shines silver in the moonlight, and the barges go down, black, silent, mysterious as ghosts." After a year Giovanni left him after a violent quarrel, and went to Paris. They were never really reconciled again, and Giovanni repaid his friend's devotion with a coldness and con-tempt almost as unworthy as his brother's, though he did something to atone for it by the sympathetic picture of his old comrade as the Fantasio of his *Lorenzo Benoni*.

Uncomfortable as his relations with them had been, Mazzini felt the loss of the Ruffinis. With them or without them, the early years of his English life were, if anything, more utterly forlorn and miserable than his worst days in Switzerland. His intellect, indeed, was safe now, though there are indications still of a mental weariness and strain, that bordered on hallucination. There was no longer any fear of a spiritual collapse, like that which had threatened a year or two ago to wreck his moral faith. But he was more wedded to his misery, more desolate, alone in "the solitude of a damned soul." "A man cannot live alone," he writes, "and I have nobody who cares to know what I am thinking of and what I want." His heart sank, when he came home from the British Museum to his bare, dark room, where there was no friend or woman to welcome him, and Agostino's querulous temper to add to the loneliness of it all. More and more the want of response around him made him seal up his thoughts and aspirations. His friends' ingratitude, the desertion of his followers added to the "terrors" of his spiritual solitude. It seemed to him "an age of moral dissolution and unbelief, an age like that in which Christ died." The sense of failure still lay heavy on him, a brooding, unhealthy feeling that his work had been in vain, that it was his doom to bring ill-fortune to his friends that he had sacrificed himself and made no one happier by it. He felt like "one irrevocably condemned, though without fault." "Pray for me,' he writes to one of his best friends, "that, before I die, I may be good for something."

Two things saved him from despair, perhaps from suicide. In the crisis in Switzerland he had put away, once for all, any thought of personal happiness. Sometimes still the natural man rebelled. "Do you think," he writes of Madeleine, "that in my hours of desolation I would not, if I could, seek a breast on which to lay my brow, a loving hand to place upon my head." But he knew that to look for happiness led imperceptibly but certainly to selfishness, that " sacrifice was the one real virtue," that duty " to God, and humanity, and country, and all men " was the only law of life for the true man. And what he had worked out once in cold philosophy, now mellowed into religion, mystical sometimes, but beautiful and saving. Jacopo Ruffini and his own dead sister were praying for him, watching over him, inspiring him with strength and love. Life was an expiation, to purify the soul for another stage, where friends would meet again, and misunderstandings pass, and love reign over all. And even in this world, though sorrow might be the portion of the individual man, Humanity, the great collective being, would go ever forward to new knowledge, and new hopes, and nobler rules of life.

Perhaps, even more than by his faith, he was saved by his intense affections. True that they centred on ever fewer persons. He had hardly a real friend left among his old political associates. For the men and women, whom he was coming to know in England, he felt as yet gratitude but little more. His love for Giuditta Sidoli was fading into a sincere but un-passionate esteem. Madeleine was an impossible dream, that he resolutely shook away. But the dear ones of his boyhood, — Madame Ruffini, his mother, his unmarried sister, even his dour father, — were loved with an affection that was pitifully, almost morbidly sad, but ever more intense. It was the only sunshine in his clouded life. " I feel God's power and law more every day," he wrote to Madame Ruffini, " but He cannot weep with me or fill my soul's void

for I am a man still and tied to earth. I worship
Him more than I love Him, but you I love." And
he pours out, in words that read extravagant but came
in truth from his inmost being, all that reverential
love, which he felt for her, who had been more than
mother, but whose affection for her devotee was
cooling all too quickly. Agostino did his best to
damage his friend in her eyes ; there seems to have
been friction between her and Madame Mazzini ; and
no doubt she sided with her own sons, when the
estrangement with them came. At the beginning of
1841 Mazzini's correspondence with her appears to
have abruptly ceased.

To his parents he turned yearningly in a new
sorrow, that was bowing them down. His one surviving unmarried sister died. She had been his favourite,
the one of the family who had sympathized most with
his political schemes, and encouraged him in his work,
and pleaded for him with his father. Her death
obsessed him with an unhealthy depression ; but he
felt most for his parents, left in the solitude of old
age, bereft of the one who had been a needed link
between them, for the father had grown morose, and
there was evidently some want of harmony between
the old people. Then the father himself fell very ill
and recovered with difficulty. His son brooded over
the thought that he had not been enough to his
parents while he was with them, that the life he had
chosen for himself had been the cause of all their
trouble. Plans for their comfort worked in his mind
"like a never-resting wheel." He would have risked
the death-sentence that still hung over him, and gone to
live with them in hiding, but he knew that the dread

of discovery would only have added to their cares. It seems indeed that in 1844 he paid a visit to them in disguise.[1]

The gloom lifted somewhat, as he began to make friends in England. He was not yet, it is true, in sympathy with English life. He found little liking here for his transcendentalisms, his big indeterminate generalizations ; and English love of facts and suspicion of theories seemed to him "materialism incarnate, pure critical analysis," fatal to spiritual or philosophic thought. "Here," he writes, "everybody is a sectarian or a materialist" ; and now, as always, he never understood or valued Protestantism. He had a poor opinion of English statesmen, especially of the Whigs, who irritated him by the folly of their attempts to put down Chartism. Nor did he think much better of the Chartist leaders, who were "Englishmen, which means materialists, utilitarians, Benthamists *par excellence*, with no principle except that of the greatest possible happiness." The severance between the middle and working classes portended, he thought, an imminent and terrible revolution. But he came by degrees to recognize the better side of English life. He admired its tolerance, its insistency and tenacity, the "unity of thought and action, which never rests till it has

[1] The only evidence for this is contained in Cagnacci, *Giuseppe Mazzini e i fratelli Ruffini*, pp. 287, 290, from which it seems probable that Mazzini saw Madame Ruffini between June and November, 1844, and therefore, almost certainly, was at Genoa. Signor Donaver thinks it doubtful whether *la Cugina* of the Ruffinis' letters refers to Mazzini, but the internal evidence seems to me to favour the identification. Signor Cagnacci's note on p. 290 seems to imply that he has seen a memorandum by Elia Benza to the effect that Benza saw him at Porto Maurizio about this time disguised as a Capucin.

carried each new social idea into practice, and when it has taken a step, never retraces it." He watched the Chartist movement sympathetically, and contrasted its great following with the scanty disciples of the French socialists. Though he cared little for its doctrines, he saw in it something that rose above "the narrow egotism, which characterizes English politics," and he especially approved, when the Chartists put aside national prejudices and sent their good wishes to the Canadian rebels.

Gradually he came to feel more at home in England. "There," he says, "friendships develop slowly and with difficulty, but nowhere are they so sincere and lasting." "Never," he wrote in after days, "shall I forget, never without a throb of gratitude shall I mention the land, which became a kind of second country to me, where I found friendships that brought an enduring balm to my weary and unhappy life." After a year or two his circle widened almost too rapidly, for clothes and bus fares and the drain upon his time made society an expensive matter to him. One of the first English persons who took an interest in him, was Mrs Archibald Fletcher of Edinburgh. A few months after he came to England, she met him, "a young, slim, dark man of very prepossessing appearance," who could not speak English and wanted admission to a public library. So profoundly unhappy he seemed, that the kind old lady feared suicide and wrote to gently warn him. Mazzini replied that no one but "a man, who wished only to enjoy and has made that his chief thought, will destroy his life as a child does its plaything."

His first close English friendship was with the Carlyles. "They love me as a brother," he wrote in 1840, "and would like to do me more good than it is in their power to do." For Carlyle he had for several years a very sincere liking. "He is good, good, good ; and still, I think, in spite of his great reputation, unhappy." He respected Carlyle's sincerity, his freedom from insular narrowness, his outspokenness. "He may preach the merit of ' holding one's tongue ' ; —to those, in truth, who do not agree with him, are such words addressed,—but 'the talent of silence' is not his." He welcomed him as one "who served the same God" as himself, "though with a different worship"; his ally in the attack on utilitarianism, in the exaltation of the spiritual. "His motive is the love of his fellow-men, a deep and active feeling of duty, for he believes this to be the mission o man on earth." Their common love of Dante, n doubt, too, helped to draw them together. But in hi criticisms of his books he condemned, however gentl and respectfully, his individualism, his hero-worship his depreciation of the great common march of th race, his ineffectiveness and timidity, when he cam to practical political applications. And the antagonis grew on him, till in time they seemed to be "diametri cally opposed." "Why," he said long afterwards to girl, who had been reading and admiring Carlyle, " yo are fast drifting down the road to materialism. Yo are lost. Carlyle worships force, I combat it with al my might. Carlyle is the sceptic of sceptics. He i grand, when he pulls down, but incapable of recon structing something [anything] fresh. If instead o loving and admiring nations and humanity, you onl love, admire, and reverence individuals, you must end by being an advocate of despots." Carlyle on his side had little sympathy with Mazzini's opinions, which to him were "incredible and (at once tragically and comically) impossible in this world." He was impatient with his "Republicanisms, his 'Progress' and other Rousseau fanaticisms."[1] He valued him none the less for "a most valiant, faithful, considerably gifted and noble soul." Once the Piedmontese minister spoke lightly of Mazzini in his presence. "Sir, you do not know Mazzini at all, not at all, not at all," Carlyle angrily replied and left the house. At the time of the Bandiera episode, though they had recently been quarrelling, he wrote to the *Times*, "Whatever I may think of his practical insight and skill in worldly affairs, I can with great freedom testify to all men, that he, if I have ever seen such, is a man of genius and virtue, a man of sterling veracity, humanity, and nobleness of mind, one of those rare men, numerable unfortunately but as units in this world, who are worthy to be called martyr souls; who in silence, piously in their daily life, understand and practise what is meant by that." Mazzini, mindful of their late coolness, was much touched by the defence. "That I call noble," he said of it to a friend.

For Mrs Carlyle Mazzini had a warmer feeling; and she reciprocated it not only with an intense personal confidence, but for a time at all events by sharing his political beliefs. Gradually she came more to her husband's view of these; and Mazzini and she had

---

[1] Carlyle's statement (*Reminiscences*, ii. 182) that he "once or twice" talked with Mazzini is rather startlingly inaccurate. See Carlyle's *Life in London*, i. 488.

"warm dialogues," when he unfolded some wild design of throwing away his life in Italy. "Are there not things more important than my head?" he asked her. "Certainly," she replied, "but the man, who has not sense enough to keep his head on his shoulders till something is to be gained by parting from it, has not sense enough to manage any important matter." But "to the last," says Carlyle, "she had always an affection for him"; in 1846 she came to him for advice on her troubled married life, and he appeals to her to "send her ghosts and phantoms back to nothingness" and make it bearable by communion with her dead parents and work and love. "Get up and work. When the Evil One wanted to tempt Jesus, he led Him into a solitude."

Mazzini was a frequent caller at their house; coming in all weathers, "his doe-skin boots oozing out water in a manner frightful to behold" upon her carpets. Sometimes he would come with any story that he could think of to amuse her; sometimes he would discuss Dante with John Carlyle, who was then writing his translation of the *Divina Commedia*, till Carlyle grew weary of the talk and reminded both that the last bus was starting. Margaret Fuller has left a description of an evening spent with the trio; how Mazzini turned the conversation "to progress and ideal subjects, and Carlyle was fluent in invectives on all our 'rose-water imbecilities,'" how his flippancy saddened Mazzini, and Mrs Carlyle said to Margaret, "these are but opinions to Carlyle, but to Mazzini, who has given his all and helped bring his friends to the scaffold in pursuit of such subjects, it is a matter of life and death." On another occasion

Carlyle, after monopolizing the talk while he passed
in long review the silent great ones of earth, turned
to Mazzini, saying, "You have not succeeded yet,
because you have talked too much." The contests
between them became more frequent and painful.
They would argue, so the tradition has been handed
down, the one courteous, deeply moved, pleading
with his whole heart, eloquent in his rather broken
English ; the other exaggerative, splenetic, scornful in
the wild flow of his language. All the time Mazzini
would sit pale and quiet in his chair, sometimes excited
almost to tears, nervously smoking his small cigar ;
while Carlyle with his long clay pipe shifted restlessly,
as he stormed out his sentences.[1] None the less
Mazzini's intimacy with them went on unbroken, at
all events as far as Mrs Carlyle was concerned, through
all his first stay in England. When he left for Milan
in 1848, he told her with a kiss to be "strong and
good until he returned"; and when he came back
aged and worn, she sadly stroked his grey beard.
She found lodgings for him ; she went to comfort him,
when prostrated by his mother's death. But the
severance between him and her husband gradually
widened, till two or three years later they completely
parted, to respect each other's character and detest
each other's opinions to the end. Once more they
met, years afterwards, and "talked in a cordial and
sincere way with real emotion on both sides."
"Mazzini," Carlyle noted at the time, "is the most
pious living man I now know." / Even for his politics
he had at last some tolerance. /"The idealist has

---

[1] There are some interesting descriptions of the Carlyles in Giovanni
Ruffini's letters to his mother. See Cagnacci, *op. cit.*

conquered," he confessed, "and transformed his utopia into a patent and potent reality."⁄

· With the Carlyles, however, even in the days of his closest acquaintanceship, he was never at home as he came to be in other English households. His best friends in the forties were the Ashursts of Muswell Hill. They were, he says, "a dear, good, holy family, who surrounded me with such loving care as sometimes to make me forget I was an exile." W. H. Ashurst was a solicitor, who had been a friend of Robert Owen, and who made Mazzini's acquaintance at the time of the letter-opening episode. To Mrs Ashurst Mazzini, forgetful of Madame Ruffini's expired title, gave the name of "second mother." One daughter married James Stansfeld; the other, at this time "the favourite of his English sisters," afterwards became Madame Venturi, and has left the best English memoir of him. Both they and their brother for long years after gave him much quiet help in his work. Through the Ashursts he came to know the Stansfelds and Peter Taylors, but his intimate friendship with them belongs rather to the time of his second residence in England. Among his other friends· were William Shaen, whom the Italian refugees knew as their *angelo salvatore*, Joseph Toynbee, the father of Arnold Toynbee, Joseph Cowen, afterwards member for Newcastle, and George Jacob Holyoake. J. S. Mill wrote of him as "one of the men he most respected." Margaret Fuller, who had come to England prepossessed against him, lost her prejudices when she visited his school for organ-boys, and began the friendship which was to be renewed in the days of the Roman Republic. "She is," he writes of her to a friend, "one of the rarest of women in her love and active sympathy with everything that is great, beautiful, and holy." IIe had some intercourse with the two, next to himself, most notable Italian exiles in London at that time, Gabriel Rossetti and Antonio Panizzi. Mazzini interested Rossetti in his school, and they had common acquaintances among the exiles; but they never came into close touch, and Mazzini tried in vain to persuade him to help in his patriotic work. At a later date political differences completely sundered them. Panizzi was already Keeper of Printed Books at the British Museum. He had been a Carbonaro in his Italian days, and he and Mazzini had common ground in their cult of Dante and Foscolo. He backed Mazzini warmly in the incident of the letter-opening a few years later; but they disagreed on Italian politics, and they saw little of one another, though they seem to have been never entirely estranged. Among other foreigners that he met were Prince Napoleon (" Plon-Plon "), then busily conspiring against the Orleanists, and Conneau, afterwards Louis Napoleon's doctor and a general go-between for the Emperor and the Italian patriots. But he hated anything that tasted of fashionable society. The mistress of a famous London salon once persuaded him to come to her house, but when he found that she wanted him to adorn her society and not from any interest in his cause, he refused to go again.

He came at this time much under the influence of Lamennais. They began to correspond soon after the *Words of a Believer* were published, and once at least they met. Mazzini saw a kindred soul in this

" priest of the Church Universal," who " preached God,
the people, love, and liberty " ; this man " whom I saw
but lately," so he writes in 1839, " so full of sweetness
and love, who weeps like a child at a symphony of
Beethoven, who will give his last franc to the poor,
who tends flowers like a woman, and steps out of his
path rather than crush an ant." ⁄He recognised how
much Lamennais' teaching had in common with his
own in its reaction against the sceptical, destructive
school of the Revolution, in its belief in tradition and
humanity, in its appeal to duty as the principle of life.
In some degree, perhaps, Lamennais' *Words of a
Believer* inspired his own *Duties of Man.*⁄ He had his
own plans for him.　He saw in him " a Luther of the
nineteenth century " ;　he hoped, though not very
confidently, that he would come frankly forward as a
teacher of the religion of humanity, and he urged him
to " do something better than write books," and become the missionary of the new faith.　Lamennais
replied, that though Christ could preach in the high-
ways, four persons could not meet now in a field to
speak of God and humanity without being taken up by
a policeman.　Mazzini was grievously disappointed
at the refusal, and he felt that Lamennais regarded
him with some diffidence, as indeed was natural
enough.　He " loved him as a friend and revered him
as a saint " ; but he felt that Lamennais returned hi
love " as it were in spite of himself."　" This goo<
Mazzini, one cannot help loving him," Lamennai
once said in his hearing ; and the phrase left an unhappy sense in Mazzini's mind.

　　Lamennais and " George Sand " were in his judgment " the two first living writers of France " at this

time, and he looked to the latter too as one of his
own faith. At the time of his mental crisis in
Switzerland he read her *Lettres d'un Voyageur* (he
always thought it her best production), and the book
was "sweet to him as is the cradle song to a weeping child." He corresponded with her, and in 1847
visited her in the Vallée Noire. She impressed him
above all, as she did Matthew Arnold the year before, by her simplicity. "Madame Sand," he wrote
back to England, "is just as we wanted her to be;
good, noble, candid, simple, calmly suffering, even
more than can be seen in her books." He warmly
defended her in England; not that he thought that
all her books were to be lightly put into everybody's
hand; but "the evil she has portrayed is not *her*
evil, it is ours," and her realism was informed by
a passionate moral purpose. Genius, he said, can
in the long-run do nothing but good, and it is
bound to make itself heard. "You may sound
your alarm against her in your old *Quarterly*, and
forbid your youth to read her: you will find some
day, without well knowing how, the best places in
your library usurped by her volumes." He saw in
her "an apostle of religious democracy"; he responded to her sense of the Divine, her belief that
the decay of the old creeds restored allegiance to
the true Godhead, her faith in a future which should
be built on love. He delighted to repeat her words,
"there is but one virtue, the eternal sacrifice of self."
And he saw in her, too, the voice of down-trodden
womanhood; "thank God," he says, "she is a
woman," and her books were a revelation of the
"inward life of woman," a woman's pleading for

justice and equality. At this time few writers appealed to him more; but her later works and her acceptance of the Empire alienated him, and afterwards he "sadly and unwillingly" convinced himself that what he had hailed as the sincere and conscious "utterance of a high priestess," was but the artist's passive echo of a faith that was not hers.

Slowly, besides making friends, Mazzini began to find work. The difficulties were great. He was at first too worn-out and unhappy to care to write. He could not yet write in English, and the expenses of translation absorbed a large part of the remuneration. It was a painful effort to trim his pen to the likings of the English public. "My ideas and style frighten them," he says. "What is old to us is new to them. One cannot talk to them of mission or humanity or progress or socialism." One editor refused an article in praise of Byron, "because Byron was an immoral poet." Kemble, the editor of the *British and Foreign Review*, politely declined his articles, after some experience of them, on the ground that the English public were "conceited asses," who could only gradually be broken in to listen to generalizations. Mazzini sometimes promised to do his best, but the effort came unwillingly, and it was only the pressing need o money and his resolve to ask no more from home, that made him write in an alien style on subjects that often had little interest for him. To an English reader, however, the discipline appears a salutary one; and his English articles have a precision of thought that his earlier writings lacked. His literary out-put was considerable. Some of his articles were more or less pot-boiling; thus he wrote on Fra Paolo Sarpi in the *Westminster Review*, on Victor Hugo and Lamartine—brilliant and suggestive essays—in the *British and Foreign Review*, on contemporary French literature in the *Monthly Chronicle*. He put more heart into those on English subjects,—his masterly criticisms of Carlyle in the *British and Foreign Review* and the *Monthly Chronicle*, and his papers on Chartism in *Tait's Edinburgh Journal*. But what he cared for most was to bring Italy or his own religious faith before English readers. He wrote for the love of it, when he discoursed on Dante's Minor Works in the *Foreign Quarterly* and on Lamennais in the *Monthly Chronicle*, or when he wrote on Italian politics for the same magazine, and on recent Italian literature, and probably on Italian art, for the *Westminster Review*. In the *People's Journal* under John Saunders' editorship he began the *Thoughts on Democracy in Europe*, which were afterwards expanded into *I sistemi e la democrazia*,—a very able criticism of the utilitarian and earlier socialist schools; in his own *Apostolato Popolare* he wrote the first six chapters of the noblest of all his writings, *The Duties of Man*. He seems to have written a novel, which never saw the light.

He found one literary task very near his heart. From the days of his early studies at Genoa, he had had a supreme admiration for Ugo Foscolo, as the one modern Italian writer, besides Alfieri, who had a virile political teaching for his countrymen. While in Switzerland, he had planned to write his life, and made researches for his manuscripts and rare and scattered publications. His interest strengthened, now that he was living close to where Foscolo's bones lay in Chiswick churchyard. He knew that Pickering, one of Foscolo's English publishers, possessed the manuscript of his unfinished notes on the *Divina Commedia*, already published, but with many inaccuracies, in 1825; and in a dusty corner of Pickering's shop he found the proof of part of Foscolo's *Lettera apologetica*, a kind of political testament, which apparently had not been published. Mazzini undertook the task of getting both re-published with more zeal than candour. Pickering would not sell the *Lettera* apart from the Dante manuscript, and asked £420 for the two. Mazzini " cursed his bookseller soul, and would have stolen them without scruple, if he could." A Tuscan lady, Foscolo's *donna gentile*, lent the money for the proofs; and Rolandi, the Italian publisher in Berners Street, was disposed to buy the Dante notes. Mazzini found that the notes were very incomplete, and feared that Rolandi would not buy, if aware of the deficiencies. He concealed the fact, and with immense labour completed the notes and the revision of the text. Rolandi, who, it seems, did not discover the pious fraud, bought the manuscript, and in 1842 published the edition in four volumes with an anonymous introduction by Mazzini, who took no pay for his known and unknown labours. The edition had its value at the time, though its interest now is historical only. Meanwhile he discovered the remaining manuscript of the *Lettera apologetica* in an old trunkful of Foscolo's papers; and thanks mainly to his friend, Enrico Mayer, the educationalist, this and others of Foscolo's political writings were published at Lugano in 1844. Mazzini gave much assistance to

Le Monnier, the Florentine publisher, in the complete edition of Foscolo, which he brought out a few years later. But the life remained undone. For years with the true student's fever he hunted up every letter and record of Foscolo, to which he could find a clue. But as time went on, politics and social work commanded him again, and the biography, on which so many cares had been spent, was never written.

Gradually he returned to political work. At first the moral prostration produced intense lassitude ; and he found it as difficult to settle down to politics as to literature. There were moments indeed of nervous reaction, when his brain teemed with " daring projects, titanic presentiments, limitless conceptions." But generally the struggle with depression used up his strength, and he felt too weary and discouraged to revive Young Italy. He seems, a few months before he left Switzerland, to have taken some sort of formal step to abdicate leadership. But where no actual organization survived, and there was no one to step into his place, the retirement meant nothing. / Young Italy was so completely himself, that the society was non-existent, till he took up the reins again./ There had been something of a stampede among its members. /In Italy many had made their peace with the governments ; others were nourishing their faith in silence ; few carried on the work, at least in the old spirit. Conspiracy, it is true, was not quite dead ; but the few secret societies, that still lived on, mostly harked back to Carbonaro traditions, or turned to an agrarian and free-thinking agitation, which was as hateful to Mazzini as apostacy itself./ It was no better among the exiles. " There are not two of us," he complained, "who think the same on any single subject." " You cannot find one Young Italian among us." Many took advantage of the Lombard and Piedmontese amnesties to return home. Gioberti was attacking the society. ⁄ Even those nearest to Mazzini had little faith in its methods or hopes, and Mazzini would compromise on no tittle of his creed to win them. ⁄In his high singleness of purpose⸱ he could not understand or tolerate the faintness of men, who had sworn to fight for an idea, but deserted at the first defeat⁄ If his countrymen had not responded, that was only an argument for renewed and yet more strenuous effort. It was all so pitiful to him,—this want of faithfulness unto death. " When I write in favour of Italy," he says, " I feel myself blush, as if I were lying." For a time, though, he himself felt powerless to act. He was tempted to go to Italy, and throw away his life in some desperate act of protest. But he had too fine a nature to be long content with inaction or despair. " If you only knew," he writes early in 1839, " how this absolute uselessness of existence weighs on me." He dreaded dying with his work undone. Jacopo Ruffini's memory was ever present with him, and he felt that he was dedicated to the cause for which his protomartyr had died. ⁄ He had taken on himself a task " in the face of God and Italy and himself" ; he thought of himself as blasphemer and hypocrite, if he slackened in it ; and though he knew that his enthusiasm had gone, sometimes too his confidence in Italy and himself, yet duty still remained, and he could trust in God and the righteousness of his cause. " I know," he wrote, " that Jacopo is not dead, that he and we are forerunners, not of a new policy, but of a new faith, which we perhaps shall see not, but whose advent no human force can stop."/

It was not however till the summer or autumn of 1839,[1] that he decided to return to active political work "with an almost fierce resolve.' At first he had no definite plan, except to accentuate the popular side of his programme and appeal more than he had yet done to the working classes. He had at present little means of reaching those at home, but he could do something among the Italian population in London, the shopkeepers and organ-grinders and hawkers of terra-cotta casts. Hitherto he had been little in contact with his working-class compatriots; now in the whirl of a foreign city he came to know them. It began with his intense feeling for suffering, that for the remainder of his life made him happiest when relieving individual cases of misery. About this time, going out one winter morning, he found a young girl on the doorstep worn out with cold and hunger. With the sympathy for forlorn womanhood, which he had in common with the greatest of English states-men, he took her in and put her in his landlady's charge. When the girl afterwards married, and was deserted by her husband, he undertook the education of her children, and for many years devoted to it a large share of his scanty income. The same charity now drew him to the waifs of his own land. Talking to the Italian organ-boys, who went about the streets of London with a barrel-organ and its squirrel or white

---

[1] Madame Mario says in her *Della vita di Mazzini*, in the middle of 1838; but I think it is quite clear from *Lettres intimes*, 197 and 205; Giurati, *op. cit.*, 11-12; Cagnacci, *op. cit.*, 447 that 1839 is the true date.

rat, speaking a patois half Comasque half English, he learnt the details of the "white-slave traffic," how a few Italians living in London brought over poor peasant-boys under contracts, which promised high pay and good living, but which had no validity in England ; how when the boys got there, they were beaten and half-starved and cowed. He brought the worst offenders to justice, and did something to frighten the masters into better treatment of their victims. But he cared more to influence the boys themselves. In 1841 he opened a school at 5 Hatton Garden (afterwards removed to 5 Greville Street, Leather Lane), where the boys came in the late evenings to learn the three Rs and some elementary science, and on Sundays had lessons in drawing and Italian history. The school was very dear to Mazzini, and the boys, says an English observer, " revered him as a god and loved him as a father." One of them, returning to Italy, travelled to Genoa expressly to tell Madame Mazzini what her son had done for him. Italian and English friends (Joseph Toynbee among them) taught gratuitously, and the annual supper was a great event for him and his circle. Mario and Grisi sang at concerts to help the school's finances. The school flourished in spite of the noisy opposition of a neighbouring Italian priest, —an opposition, which Mazzini repaid by his first angry attack on the Papacy.

Already, before the school was opened, he had started a political society for the Italian workmen in London, and was publishing a paper, the *Apostolato Popolare*, which came out at intervals till 1843. In it he makes his appeal to the working-men of Italy.

He felt more strongly even than in his Marseilles days that a revolutionary movement must depend for its main support on the working classes and have their good for its ultimate goal. / English life had brought him into touch with the social thought of the time, and he felt that political movements were dwarfing beside the question of the condition of the masses. / He began to speak of the Italy to-be as the " Italy of the People." It was the people, he wrote, who suffered most from her dismemberment and misrule. While other classes had their compensations, there were no distractions for the unknown poor, no true home life, no intellectual interest. He tried to rouse them from their provincialism, their self-absorbed indifference to politics. He appealed to them to be patriots and republicans, proud of their country's glorious past, working for its future and their children, and remember that God would judge them not by what wages they earned but by what they had done for their fellows. But however much he laid stress on the democratic side of his agitation, on working-class organization and social reform, he was careful to safeguard Young Italy from becoming a class movement. / It was at this time and in his papers for working men, that he first began the crusade against socialism, which he continued, sometimes with less discernment, to the end of life.

Chapter VI

The Revolution

1843-1848.   Aetat 37-43

Politics in Italy—The Bandieras—The Post-Office scandal—The People's
International League—Life in 1845-47—Letter to Pio Nono—
Attitude towards the royalists—The Revolution of 1848—At Milan.

WHILE Mazzini was watching from England in discouragement, and the waves seemed to gain no
painful inch, in Italy the main came flooding in.
How far exactly the sudden tide of national impulse
owed itself to his teaching, is perhaps an insoluble
problem. But when one remembers how wide had
been the influence of Young Italy, how many of the
men who were now coming to the front had been its
members, it seems unlikely that the impetus could
have come without him. Young University men
who treasured secretly at home his pamphlets or
numbers of the *Apostolato Popolare*, artisans who had
fingermarked his or Gustavo Modena's tracts, were
pondering his teaching and waiting for the times to
ripen. But Mazzini's influence, even if the most
powerful, was not the only one. Traditions still lived
on, handed down from the Carbonaro revolutions;
the old belief in Charles Albert was flickering into
life again; the mild Catholic nationalism, that came

from Manzoni and his school, flowed strong; and all
the time the daily witness of oppression and misrule,
was there to preach against the Austrians and the
native tyrants. And though there were many currents
in the swelling crowd of nationalists, at two points all
moved together. Austria must go, and there must be
some guarantee for good government. /

In spite of censors and police, the rising spirit
showed itself in literature. " The shade of Dante, the
poet of the regenerated nation, began to brood above
the speech and silence of the land." Students, in the
footsteps of Foscolo and Gabriel Rossetti, drew all the
reading world of Italy to the great national seer, who
more than five centuries before had pleaded for unity.
Dramatists and historians and novel-writers spoke of
the ancient glories of their country. Social reformers
came in to swell the liberal movement, founders of
schools and savings banks, agricultural pioneers,
builders of railways that would " stitch the boot."
Their interest in politics was a secondary one, and
such political sympathies as they had, were generally
with the Moderate politicians, just rising to a prominence, which was soon to eclipse Mazzini's waning
light. Gioberti had already published his *Moral and
Civil Primacy of the Italians*, which, while it echoed
Mazzini's faith in Italy and Rome, banned democracy
and unity, preached federalism and half-hearted
liberalism, and looked for salvation to Charles Albert
and a reforming Pope. Cesare Balbo in Piedmont
was pleading for the same mild policy, without its
faith in the Papacy. Theirs was an easy creed
beside Mazzini's. They had little of his religious
faith, none of his passionate democracy, his demand

for sacrifice and martyrdom.   It was a creed for the doubting and half-hearted, for the royalist and Catholic, for the courtier and the rich man and the priest ; and also for the level-headed man of the world, who turned from Mazzini's fancies and idealism, who laughed at Italy's mission to humanity but cherished a more modest hope for her own regenera- tion.   But at all events the teaching had two notes in common with his own.   It strove to lift the nation to healthy ambition and strenuous effort ; it cried as earnestly as he did for the expulsion of the Austrian. And so it made the complement of his work.   Less noble in its spirit, more halting in its patriotism and uninspiring of great deeds, yet it marshalled for the cause a host, that would never have swelled the thin ranks of Young Italy. It supplied the common movement with qualities that Mazzini conspicuously lacked,—a political sense of the possible, and, among its better exponents, a patience and tolerance, a comprehensiveness that prejudged no class and welcomed all, who, gladly or reluctantly, offered them- selves for the great task.

One of the sources of the Moderate movement was the impatience at the little insurrections, that only led to useless loss of life and an embittering of the tyranny.   One of its postulates laid down that there should be no revolt against the better native princes, and that the fight with Austria should be waged by regular armies.   But the traditions of revolt could not die out at once, indeed were all the stronger for the new spirit of hope that was abroad.   All Central Italy was alive with plots. Mazzini, though he was coming partially to recognize the futility of these petty risings, still had a standard of preparation that was pitifully inadequate. / He was elaborating a scheme for a rising in the Papal States, to be followed by movements in the North and South and supported by the exiles. ⁄ He was still persuaded that a few small guerilla bands would draw the people after them, that daring and a clear programme were the only necessary conditions of victory. ⁄ He found few men and less money for his plot. Among the handful, who put themselves at his disposal, were two young Venetian nobles, Attilio and Emilio Bandiera, officers in the Austrian navy, which was chiefly manned by Italians and Dalmatians. They were high-minded lads, and, one is bound to add, sentimentalists and prigs, naively self-conscious and immature; but with the supreme virtue that they were ready to take their lives in their hands. Mazzini wished to use them for his designs in Central Italy; but there were police agents of the governments around them, who had their ear and sent·them with a handful of followers, including a man in the pay of the police, to help an imaginary rising in Calabria. ⁄ The English government, too, had opened their correspondence with Mazzini, and put the government at Naples on its guard. Thus they went, as they foreboded, to their death. The trap was ready for them; and when they landed near Cosenza, they were captured easily and shot.

⁄ The ignoble action of the English government brought Mazzini into English political life. ⁄ He suspected that his correspondence had been tampered with in the post, and careful experiments proved to him that his letters had been opened, sealed with

new wafers, and the postmark altered. He put the
matter into the hands of Thomas Duncombe, the
member for Finsbury ; and the storm of indignation,
that followed Duncombe's disclosures in the House
of Commons, showed how angrily the better English
opinion felt it, that the government had violated
elementary ethics and "played the spy" in the
interests of continental tyranny. Shiel and Macaulay
denounced it in parliament. Carlyle wrote to the
Times that "it is a question vital to us that sealed
letters in an English post-office be, as we all fancied
they were, respected as things sacred ; that opening
of men's letters, a practice near of kin to picking
men's pockets, and to other still viler and far fataler
forms of scoundrelism, be not resorted to except in
cases of very last extremity." The government tried
to ride out the storm with quibbles and constructive
falsehoods, which proved, as Mazzini said, that they
adopted different standards of honour for their public
and their private lives. Sir James Graham repeated
the stale charge that Mazzini had promoted assassination in France, and honourably withdrew it, when he
knew the facts. But public feeling was too heated
to let the matter rest there ; and secret Committees of
enquiry were appointed by both Houses. They reported that letters had been constantly opened at the
Post-Office, at all events since 1806 ; that even letters
of members of parliament had been tampered with ;
that in this case the government had issued a warrant
to open Mazzini's letters (his letters had in fact been
opened several months before the date of the warrant),
and had sent information extracted from them to "a
Foreign Power." It is true that this information

seems to have been of a general character, but that did not affect the ignominy of the whole business or the fact that an English government had sent a warning to the Bourbons, that helped them to entrap the hapless patriots.

The incident gave Mazzini a welcome opportunity to appeal more directly to English opinion on behalf of Italy. He had a supreme contempt for English foreign policy, which "opposes everything that introduces a new fact in the European polity, and is the first to recognize it when it shows its strength." It was an unfair criticism, at least of Canning and Palmerston, tied though the latter's hands were by court and colleagues. England was still on the whole the champion of the cause of men. But it was true that the Foreign Office gave small attention to the great nationalist movements that were maturing in Europe. The wise policy for England, as he urged, was to encourage these movements, and win the gratitude of the rising nationalities, not necessarily by armed intervention (he expressly disclaimed asking for that), but by her moral backing. Perhaps it was partly owing to the seeds he sowed at this time, that Palmerston afterwards did for Italy so much of what he asked for. We may regret that he never gave a generous recognition to the great Foreign Secretary's policy.

On individual Englishmen and Americans he knew that he could count for practical sympathy. He exploited well both the anti-Papal feeling in the country and the old love of Italian liberty, which had descended from the days of Byron and Hobhouse. English and American travellers carried his secret letters and literature into Italy. He had plans for utilizing the Christian Alliance, an American society for Protestant propagandism. A year or two later he induced his English women-friends to organize an Italian bazaar, which was held at Mrs Milner-Gibson's, nominally for the expenses of his Italian school, but with the secret intention of devoting any surplus from the Italian contributions to a National Fund, which he was trying to raise for political work. In the same year, 1847, he founded a People's International League to resume the interrupted work of Young Europe, but mainly with the object of enlisting sympathy for Italy. Stansfeld, the Ashursts, Peter Taylor, W. Shaen, Thomas Cooper, Henry Vincent the Chartist, W. J. Fox (the Unitarian orator, afterwards M.P. for Oldham), served on the Committee. They used to meet once a week at Mr W. J. Linton's house in Hatton Garden, and Mazzini "with those wondrous eyes of his lit up with a power that was almost overwhelming," infected them with his own enthusiasm and faith. Men among them, like Thomas Cooper and Peter Taylor, who had denounced physical force remedies in England, demurred at his gospel of revolution. "You are right about your own country," he passionately answered. "You have had your grand decisive struggle against tyrannous power. You need no physical force. But what are my countrymen to do, who are trodden down under the iron heel of a foreign tyranny? They have no representation, they have no charters, they have no written rights. They must fight."

The business of the League brought one of the very few occasions, on which, so far as is known, he expressed his views on Ireland. Some Repealers complained to the League that it had omitted Ireland in its report from the list of the nationalities of the future ; and Mazzini was asked to draft an answer to them. His argument was addressed to Separatists, but it would apply almost equally to Home Rulers ; it proves how radically he misunderstood the Irish movement, and he seems to have felt himself on unsafe ground. He regarded the Irish demand as at bottom one for better government only ; and he had every sympathy with their "just consciousness of human dignity, claiming its long violated rights," their "wish to have rulers, educators, not masters,' their protests against "legislation grounded on distrust and hostility." But he believed that the nationalist movement was not likely to be permanent, and he refused to see any elements of true nationality in it, on the grounds that the Irish did not "plead for any distinct principle of life or system of legislation, derived from native peculiarities, and contrasting radically with English wants and wishes," nor claimed for their country any "high special function" to discharge in the interests of humanity. On which it may be noted that the first objection shows Mazzini's ill-acquaintance with Irish life and feeling, and that the second involves a condition, which, save in his own theories, has not been asked of any nation.

In place of the enforced idleness of a few years before, he was now only too busy. Political corre- spondence, literary work, the school, the bazaar, visiting and being visited crowded on his time. He hardly left London, except for two visits to France and one

perhaps to Italy, and once for a pilgrimage to New-
stead Abbey and other places of Byronic memory.   He
had left Chelsea, and moved first to Devonshire Street,
near the British -Museum, and afterwards to Cropley
Street, near the New North Road.   He was somewhat happier and more hopeful.   His active life left
little time for the old broodings.   The Post-Office
scandal had brought him new friends, and the desolation of his solitude had gone.   He joined the Whit-
tington Club, largely for the sake of playing chess,
at which he was an adept and did not like being
beaten.   He was much perturbed by a proposal to
allow no chess on Sundays, and jokingly threatens a
rider that smoking too shall be forbidden, except to
those who undertake to sit silent for an hour in
religious contemplation, and that, as further penance
for the members, one of them shall "read twelve
minutes every hour *alta voce e con declamazione* a
parliamentary speech from Mr Plumpton or Sir Robert
Inglis or a chapter from the second volume of Tancred
by D'Israeli."   But when back in his lodgings, he was
often depressed and miserable again.   He was "giddy"
with writing, worn down with work and want of proper
food and clothes ; and for the first time he writes in
bad spirits about his physical condition.   The burden
of poverty and debt still "dominated his life."   He
was now in receipt of a small allowance from his
mother, to find which she stinted herself of every
luxury and more.   But he was generous as ever, and
probably as bad a housekeeper ; and he found himself
powerless to reduce the mountain of debt.   His literary
earnings were again very small.   The life of Foscolo was
still waiting to be begun, for he thought it better now

"to supply new materials for Italian history than make an inventory of the old." The better-paying reviews no longer took his articles, and he was "writing on Switzerland and heaven knows what for a petty Edinburgh magazine." He fretted because the need of hack-work and his multifarious occupations left little time for writings that would help the cause, as they had helped it fifteen years ago. "For the wretched sum of some 8000 francs," he writes, "I am a slave ; I am growing old in body, in soul, in power, and I am not allowed to help my country and fulfil my mission." And from causes that we can only guess at,—perhaps the worry and publicity, perhaps the partial lifting of his unhappiness, perhaps the loss of physical health,— there is a perceptible, though slight decline from the moral height of a few years before. He is less the apostle, more the politician, too fond of coming forward as the practical man—a part that ill became him,—not always straightforward in his utterances and methods, more reasonable, it is true, and tolerant, but at the same time sliding into occasional reticences and equivocation.

The result of the Bandiera episode was to leave Young Italy yet more friendless than before. Its miserable mismanagement was set down to Mazzini, unfairly on the whole ; and cruel slanders charged him with egging others to a desperate task, while he stayed safe behind. In reality, he was more impatient than ever to lead a fight in Italy "before he grew quite old." But he seems again to have recognized that any fruitful action was impossible. All his efforts for the National Fund brought in a poor £100. And he knew that he was losing his hold on the middle classes, and must wait till he had formed a party among the working men of the towns. The Rimini revolt of 1845, with its poor programme of local reform and silence on the bigger issues, proved what influence the Moderate movement in its worst and weakest form had even in those parts of Italy, from which he had hoped most. / A year later the Moderates leaped into overwhelming prominence with the accession of Pio Nono to the Papacy. / Here was a Pope, the Italians fondly thought, eager to bless Liberals and Nationalists, while Charles Albert in the North was threatening to bare his sword for war. The mass of Italian Liberalism caught at their protection, and was ready to pay the price. Some no doubt hoped to push on the King, till he was " moral," if not actual " lord of Italy "; others dreamed that circumstances might make Pius president of an Italian Republic. But the majority willingly accepted the limitations of the policy, were ready to safeguard the Temporal Power, to make Italian union no better than a loose federation, to stop short at administrative reform or at the most at middle-class constitutions.

/ Mazzini was very suspicious of the new development ; jealous that the nationalist movement had passed into other hands, that the credit of it went to men like Gioberti, who had halted in their faith, while he alone had held the banner high ; sceptical of Charles Albert's and the Pope's intentions ; angry at the tentative, compromising ambitions of the Moderates, at their repudiation of democracy, their trust in diplomacy and its pretences and deceptions. / He knew Charles Albert's " rabbit-nature "; he judged Pio Nono much at his own estimate. " They want," said the Pope, "to make a Napoleon of me, who am only a poor country parson." "An honest parson but a bad prince," was Mazzini's verdict. ⁄The triumph of the Moderates meant that Unity would be put indefinitely back, and federalism inflict "perpetual impotence" on Italy.⁄ But he saw the impossibility of standing out against the new spirit. And he was prepared, as he had been in 1833 and again in 1844, to waive his republican agitation, if the Moderates for their part would abandon federalism and declare for unity. "If I thought," he said, "that Charles Albert would rise to rare ambition and unite Italy for his own behoof, I would say Amen."⁄ "Let the Moderates," he wrote, "give us, if they like, a Pope, a single king, a dictator ; we can compromise on everything but federalism." And on these lines he was working through 1847 to bring the exiles at Paris together on a common programme of Unity, to which both monarchists and republicans could rally⁄

It was in this spirit that in September of the same year he wrote his famous letter to the Pope. As with the parallel letter to Charles Albert, he was anxious afterwards to explain away in part its implied belief in the Pope's patriotism and its anxiety to see him leader of the Italian movement. But his private letters of the time would seem to show that this was an afterthought, and that he was sincerer than he gave himself credit for. In one of them, written apparently just before the letter to Pius, he says in somewhat Carlylean style, "I consider this as the last agony of popedom authority. And in my own way of feeling I would not be sorry to see a great institution dying, for once, in a noble manner ; transmitting the watchword of the future before vanishing, rather than sinking into the Crockford or Tuileries mud of the English aristocracy and French monarchy. A moral power, like a great man, ought always to die so ; uttering the words of dying Goethe, ' let more light in.' " In another letter, written in the same month, he says that he wrote to the Pope " in a moment of expansiveness and juvenile illusion," as he would have written to his friend himself. He was excited and sanguine at the great European drama, that was developing so fast. He still probably had moments, when the old faith in men broke through his later suspicion and exclusiveness. /He was ever looking for a new religion to issue forth from Rome,[1] and for the moment dreamed that a nationalist Pope might be its herald. His appeal, however, was ludicrous in its miscalculation of the facts. " Be a believer," he said to Pius, "and unite Italy." He told him that he, the foremost man of the moment in Europe, had duties of corresponding magnitude. He could guide Italy to her appointed future, make of her one great state, based on the people and justice and religion, with " a government unique in Europe, which would end the absurd divorce between the spiritual and temporal powers." If Catholicism were capable of revival, he under God might be the instrument ; if it were destined to give place to a new creed, based on the same Christian principles, he could be the leader, who would guide the Church securely through its passage/ One can imagine the horror with which Pius read the part so tactlessly suggested to him ; and we know that the only result of the letter was to thoroughly alarm him.

[1] See below, p. 127.

In fact Mazzini's fits of belief in Pope or King were very transitory. Only five months before he had written in an open letter, that he "did not believe that from prince or king or pope Italy would now or ever find salvation." His mind was in a state of flux, wavering between his old simple, but for the time impracticable, creed and some compromise with the new order. It would read him wrongly, if we charged him with downright insincerity ; but his whole conduct through this period is a disingenuous one, too subordinate to unavowed intentions, too much akin to that "substitution of Macchiavelli for Dante," which he condemned so unsparingly in the Moderates. While professedly ready to work with the monarchical nationalists, while abstaining from any active republican agitation, he was encouraging republican beliefs, anxious even to keep something together of a republican organization, that when "the Moderate farce was hissed off the stage," the republicans would be again in a position to captain the nationalist cause and lead it to their own goal. He wants to spread the literature of Young Italy broadcast. He urges that his followers, while nominally joining the Moderate ranks and "shouting for Pio Nono louder than the rest," should quietly prepare to seize the movement for themselves. At the same time, outside Italy they were to depreciate the Pope with equal vehemency, that when the inevitable disillusioning in Pius came, they could put in a claim to foresight. Apart from this underhand diplomacy, his hesitation was largely justified. He had no security that the Moderates would accept the offered compromise or declare for Unity. And he feared that the enthusiasm of the masses might evaporate in noisy demonstrations, that reform would prove an opiate to lull the nationalist impulses to sleep again. / Towards the end of 1847 his chief anxiety, as Cavour's was for different reasons twelve years later, was to irritate Austria into taking the offensive, and force the Italians to fight for independence. He was confident that she would intervene. Sometimes he hoped that the popular pressure behind would force Charles Albert to head the national defence ; at other moments he welcomed the thought that the native governments would decline the challenge, and Young Italy be left alone to lead the war. /

/ For once he underrated the strength of the nationalist feeling. / The new year opened with revolutions in dramatic sequence. Its first day saw the Tobacco Riots at Milan,—the overture to the maturing Lombard rising. Two days later the social revolution mildly reared its head at Leghorn, and Mazzini's old collaborator, Guerrazzi, was master for a few days of the insurgent city. In another fortnight Sicily, with one great effort, threw off the Bourbon yoke ; and before the month was out, the Neapolitans had forced a constitution on King Ferdinand. In the first half of February Tuscany and Piedmont had their constitutions too ; in a few days more the Second Republic was proclaimed in France, and the face of European politics was changed. Pio Nono, ever more fearful of liberalism, but carried helplessly along, gave the Romans a constitution ; and, save in the Austrian provinces and dependant Duchies, all Italy had won its liberties. War with Austria was now only a question of weeks, and the nation waited breathlessly till the signal came from Milan or Turin. Charles Albert was still the " Wobbling King," drifting towards war, thirsting for national applause and revenge on Austria, but timorous of the democratic forces that pushed on behind, dreading republican France as much as the real enemy across the Ticino.

/ While he paused, the great uprising came. / The news of revolution at Vienna passed the signal through the North. The heroic Milanese after five days of memorable struggle drove the great garrison out in flight. Venice, Bergamo, Brescia, Como, well-nigh every city in the Lombard and Venetian lands, fought for and won their liberty. The Austrian power crumbled in a week, and save at Ferrara and the fortresses of the Quadrilateral,—themselves too all but lost,—no foot of Italian ground remained to Austria. From all Italy the forces of the nation were hurrying to complete the work. Piedmont and Tuscany declared war. The Pope and King of Naples let perforce their troops march to the front. From town and village, from plain and mountain valley the volunteers poured up. Princes and statesmen, clergy and nobles, students and artisans,—all were swept along by the great flood of patriotism, some lightly or with purpose to betray, but the mass with the enthusiasm of crusaders, glad, for the day at all events, to give up comfort and home and life./ It seemed as if Mazzini's vision were fulfilled, and Italy, transfigured by a holy call, had risen in unconquerable might. ◢

Mazzini hurried to Italy at the glad tidings. He

was already in Paris, where he had gone again directly after the Revolution, and had just founded a National Association to carry out his policy of bringing royalist and republican exiles together in the cause of independence and unity. He crossed the St Gotthard with some danger. "The scene," he wrote back to England, "was sublime, Godlike. No one knows what poetry is, who has not found himself there, at the highest point of the route, on the plateau, surrounded by the peaks of the Alps in the everlasting silence that speaks of God. There is no atheism possible on the Alps." He stopped to pick the first pansy he saw, when he left the snows, to send it to an English friend. He reached Milan on April 7. He could not go to Piedmont or Genoa, for the sentence of 1833 still hung over him, and, besides, Milan was the centre of everything at the moment. But the scene of the Five Days did not bring the sense of exultation he had expected. "As for Italy," he writes, "I have grown old, and seem only too much to bear the chains of exile with me." But he "cried like a child" with enthusiasm, when he saw two thousand Italians, who had deserted from an Austrian regiment, march through the shouting crowd ; and the reception he found must soon have cheered him. The very customs-officers on the frontier had known him from his portraits, and repeated his phrases to him. A procession met him at the gates of Milan, and took him in triumph to his hotel. His position was in fact a very strong one. He stood before his countrymen as the prophet once cast out and stoned, who had preached in the wilderness, what was now a commonplace on every tongue. His beliefs of yesterday—utopias to other men—were potent facts to-day. Italy was free or nearly so. Throughout the land democracy seemed on the eve of·triumph. Even the republicans and unitarians had shown an unexpected strength. / And he, who through long years had preached and suffered, while others fell away or doubted, had the grateful homage of his country-men. At this time, probably, his word was law at Milan.

It remained to be seen if he had the talent for actual political life, whether he could put away accumulated prejudices, see clear to the supreme and indispensable end, and waive all secondary things for that. His professed position was a sound one. / While the war lasted, so he laid down, there must— apart from the postulate of Unity—be a truce to party struggles. Monarchy or republic must await the decision of the liberated and united nation ; and meanwhile the whole strength of the country must be given to the war. His earlier actions were true to this programme. / He supported the Provisional Government, and discouraged the extremer republicans. Probably, as he hinted later, he was half inclined at first to believe that Charles Albert was the fittest instrument for the deliver-ance of Italy. And though he soon abandoned any hope in the King, he repeated to the end that, while the war lasted, there should be no republican agitation.

So far as the war itself was concerned, he did his best in the one way open to him, the encouragement of the volunteers. He exaggerated their military value, just as he had always exaggerated the possi-

bilities of guerilla fighting in Italy.   But his advice
that every available man should be thrown on the
enemy's communications in Venetia was better
strategy and patriotism than the poor jealousies, that
made the regular army and the politicians depreciate
the volunteers from fear lest their influence should be
cast for a republic.   In a fight, where the Italians had
no single commander of genius, the Moderates had
the folly to reject the services of men, like Garibaldi
and Fanti, who twelve years later were the first
generals in Italy.   But, sincerely as Mazzini tried to
help the war, he was not equally loyal to his professions of political neutrality.   His refusal to let
unity remain an open question deprived them at once
of any seriousness.   Even his ostensible attitude
towards the monarchy was no doubt in part a matter
more of necessity than principle.   He seems to have
gone to Milan undecided what exact policy to adopt ;
and as soon as he arrived there, he wrote that he was
occupied in organizing the republicans, and that,
should Charles Albert fail to gain a speedy and
brilliant victory, he had hopes of success for them.
But he soon realized that a republican agitation meant,
if not civil war, at all events a fierce dissension in the
face of the enemy, a dissension on no point of vital
principle or honour,—which would have shamed its
author.   And, though the republicans were strong at
Milan, they were perhaps a minority even there, and
in the rest of Lombardy a handful, while Piedmont
and its army stood solid in their loyalty to the King.
And so, whether from choice or from necessity, he
stood in the letter by his promise to abstain from
republican agitation. / But the policy of neutrality sat

uneasily on him, and he soon broke from the spirit of his undertaking by loud professions of republican faith and suggestions quite inconsistent with the silence he was pledged to./

To some extent the policy of the Provisional Government excused his change of attitude. At the beginning of the war everybody had accepted the position, that there should be a truce to politics till the fighting was over. But as the war dragged on, the position became a hardly possible one. The government of Lombardy was hopelessly incapable, and everybody wished to see it superseded. The conservatives both at Milan and Turin feared to leave an opening for a possible Lombard republic after the war. Many of the democrats wished for annexation as a step to Unity. The agitation for "fusion" with Piedmont grew so strong, that the government, not unwillingly, capitulated, and ordered a plebiscite to be taken on the question whether fusion should take place at once. When the voting came, there was no doubt abundance of intimidation by the fusionists ; but the overwhelming majority that declared for them proved that the desire for a North Italian Kingdom was predominant in the politics of the moment.

/Almost irresistible as the forces were that made for fusion, Mazzini was strictly accurate in branding it as a breach of faith. The fusionists had tried to win him over. The King had sent a message, that, if he would use his influence with the republicans in favour of fusion, he should have an interview with himself, and exercise as much influence as he wished in drafting the constitution on

democratic lines.[1]   The offer was a generous and
patriotic one, but Mazzini consented only on condition that the King would publicly declare for Unity,
and sign a bombastic promise to be "the priest-king
of the new age."/ Naturally no answer came to this,
and Mazzini broke into polemics, that the bad faith
of the other side did something to excuse, but which
were none the less opposed to the spirit of his
pledge. /Italy, he said, would never be united, till
the flag of the republic flew at Rome. / He pleaded
that France should adopt a frankly "republican and
revolutionary" diplomacy. Royalty was "a hereditary
lie," and the republic the only government which
would put the best citizens in power. Now and
again he shot stinging phrases at his opponents,
that only added to the bitterness of faction ; for, as
often, even when Mazzini tried to be tolerant, his
pen ran away with him. He attacked the Turin
nobles, forgetting that they and their sons were at
the .war, giving their lives for the cause he loved.
No doubt he had provocation, and the baser Moderates
were even more intolerant, but none the less he was
playing a hurtful and ungenerous part.
/ He made, in fact, a grave blunder in staying at
Milan. His presence there did little to help the
war ; it was, whether he wished it or not, a standing
encouragement to the factiousness, that was not a
little responsible for the ill-fortune of the army/ His
place was at Rome. At bottom the Italians were
defeated through the feebleness of Charles Albert's

[1] According to Madame Venturi (English Edition of Mazzini, V. 96)
the King offered him the premiership ; but neither Mazzini himself, nor,
so far as I know, any of the memoirs of the time mention it. For other
overtures from the government see Donaver in *Rassegna Nazionale*,
Dec. 1, 1898.

generalship and policy and the defection of the Pope and King of Naples. Mazzini could do nothing to make a capable commander of the King; but he might have influenced his policy. Charles Albert, timid and conventional as he was, had had his hand forced already and was prepared to have it forced again, as his son's was a few years later. Mazzini judged the King accurately and not unkindly; but his attitude towards him was lacking in all tact. Bad-tempered attacks on the monarchy, melodramatic appeals for a "priest-king," suggestions that the united nation would proclaim the republic from the Capitol, could only alarm. But had the popular pressure been sufficient and well-directed, Charles Albert would, half fearfully but half gladly, have felt his way to the crown of Italy. He had a deep belief in nationality; he dearly loved popular applause. Romagna was only waiting for his signal to come over to him. Piedmontese agents were at work in Tuscany, and it is hard to believe that he had not approved their mission. He hesitated long before he declined for his son the crown that Sicily laid at his feet. Had Mazzini gone to Rome, he would have given a great impulse to the radicals and unitarians there. It would almost certainly have decided the Romagnuols; it would not impossibly have created such a force of opinion in all Central Italy, as would have overborne the autonomist parties and the King's own hesitations, and put all the Papal States and Tuscany under his suzerainty. Nay more, though the counter-revolution had triumphed at Naples, the nationalist elements were strong throughout the South; and had Mazzini organized them from Rome, and Garibaldi marched

South in the name of Unity and Charles Albert, the work of 1860 might have been done twelve years earlier. Even had the bigger consummation failed, Mazzini could have forced the Pope to choose between a nationalist policy and deposition from his temporal throne; he would have thrown all the energies of the Roman government into the war, and given Charles Albert another ten or twenty thousand men, enough to shift the scales of victory.

Chapter VII

The Roman Republic

1848-1849.   AETAT 43-44

The collapse of the war—The People's War—At Florence—The mission
of Rome—The Roman Republic—The Triumvirate—Attitude to the
Church—The French attack.

HAD he done this, he might have averted the
catastrophe, which quenched the nation's hopes in
swift disaster.   In one pitched fight after another the
Italians had won.   But courage could not repair bad
generalship and growing inferiority of numbers, and
Mazzini foretold disaster only too accurately.   At
the end of July the collapse came, and the army,
still fighting doggedly, but starved and outmanœuvred,
retreated on Milan.   For some weeks past Mazzini
had urged that a small committee of defence should
be appointed ; and when disaster threatened, he was
allowed to nominate his men.   He chose Fanti and
two others, who did their best in the short time to
organize the defence of the city.   The Milanese rose
again to something of the spirit of the Five Days ;
but it was too late to turn the tide of victory.   The
army made a gallant fight outside the city walls, but
were driven back within the gates.   The unhappy
king would fain have fought on still, but he knew

there was no hope of victory, and after long hesitation he surrendered the city. The people, maddened by the desertion, attacked the palace where he lodged, and it was with difficulty that his life was saved. Sullenly he and his army withdrew, followed by thousands of the citizens, intolerant of Austrian rule.

Mazzini left Milan, as soon as the army arrived, shouldering a rifle that Mrs Ashurst had given him when he left England. He had persuaded himself that a popular rising might have saved the city, but that the army could not. He started to join Garibaldi, who was in command of the volunteers at Bergamo, and met a detachment of them at Monza. Their flag had "God and the People" for its legend, and the volunteers chose Mazzini to carry it. Garibaldi's small force of three thousand men made a difficult retreat, in terrible weather and ever harassed by the Austrian cavalry. Mazzini, frail and exhausted, won their admiration by his endurance and intrepidity. He was happy doubtless to have a simple task, which only asked for physical courage, after the tangled politics of the last four months.

The volunteers disbanded when they had passed the frontier, for the national cause seemed desperate. The army had retreated into Piedmont, and the King had signed an armistice. The Roman and Tuscan forces hardly existed; Naples was at the mercy of King Ferdinand. The Austrians had triumphed swiftly and conclusively. They dared not indeed cross the Ticino for fear of French intervention, they were not strong enough as yet to advance into Central Italy, and Venice defied them in her lagunes; but

Lombardy and the Venetian mainland seemed lost past hope. Mazzini refused to own defeat. But he based his hopes more on partisan illusions than on cool possibilities. The royal war had ended ; the people's war would begin. The Italians, betrayed by their princes, would rise in their own strength, and crush the Austrians by force of numbers and enthusiasm. He was working feverishly at Lugano to create a national organization to this end, and prepare for a popular rising in Lombardy. Again he wavered whether or not to raise the republican flag. Providence, he thought, had by the recent disasters pointed the Italians to a republic. But, at all events after the fiasco of a mad rising near Como, he recognized the hopelessness of an un-supported insurrection in the Austrian provinces. He saw, as cooler heads saw all along, that the Piedmontese army was indispensable ; and, while urging the Romans to declare for a republic there, he was willing to postpone the political question elsewhere, and work with any, who would relegate it to the decision of a Constituent Assembly after the war and throw their strength into a new fight. He recognized at last that his own best field was in Central Italy. Various motives drew him there. He could use his influence at Florence and Rome to push on the military preparations ; he could perhaps secure a union of the two states, which would be a step towards unity ; he might, if circumstances favoured, help to plant the republican flag. Both in Tuscany and at Rome democracy was triumphant. The Pope had fled to Ferdinand's fortress at Gaeta, and the Romans, finding every overture for compromise rejected, and left without a stable government, were heading irresistibly for a republic.   At Florence the Grand Duke was at the mercy of the democrats, with no alternative before him but flight or unconditional surrender.   Mazzini left Lugano, and sailing from Marseilles, arrived at Leghorn on February 8, just when the news had come that the Grand Duke had fled from Florence.   He used his influence to prevent any attack on the ducalists and dissuade the Livornese from secession.   A week later he was at Florence.   Here he saw Giuditta Sidoli, at whose house he met Gino Capponi, and paid a visit to Giusti.   But he had little time for the society of friends.   Guerrazzi was now virtually dictator of Tuscany.   More practical in small things than Mazzini, but with none of his inspiring confidence or simple loyalty to an idea, he was trying to steer a middle course and keep clear of a republic.   He and Mazzini had hot words, and Mazzini, backed by a great republican meeting by Orcagna's Loggia, forced him to a nominal and insincere acceptance of its programme.   After fruitless efforts to promote union with the Roman states, and make the slow Tuscans prepare for war, Mazzini left for Rome.

Ever since the Pope's flight in November, he had been appealing to his friends there to agitate for a republic.   The road, he urged, was plain.   The Pope had virtually abdicated, and, without a blow, the republic was in their grasp,—a republic, which might grow into a republican Italy.   "You have," he wrote, "in your hands the destinies of Italy, and the destinies of Italy are the destinies of the world."   It was one of the master-ideas of his life, cherished through years of meditation from the first

days of Young Italy. The thought was a fantastic
one; a student's conceit, fed on his early classical
studies, on his later readings in medieval history,
above all on Dante's faith in Rome, the destined
seat of Empire; a strange historical survival, born
of what Cesare Balbo called "the importunate memory
of Rome's past greatness," which translated into
modern terms the theories of the Holy Roman
Empire./ Many an Italian in those days shared that
faith,—a faith that fed their inextinguishable resolve
that Rome should be the capital of Italy. Mazzini
and Gioberti went beyond, and looked to Rome for
some new word of truth for all humanity. / But
while Gioberti's destined instrument was a reformed
Papacy, Mazzini watched for a Pope-less, republican,
Italian Rome to bring the dawn of that "religious
transformation," Christian in spirit and in origin
but with another dogma, which would again unite
mankind in a living, universal faith. Indefinite as
his conception was, the thought of an all-embracing
unity, the "word of universal brotherhood"—the
necessary mark of any great religion—runs through it
all. As Imperial Rome had united Europe by force
of arms and majesty of law, as Papal Rome had
united it by thought and spiritual authority, so
"Rome of the People" would unite it once again
in some new gospel of social duty and progress,
would harmonize the temporal and the spiritual, the
Roman law of justice and the Christian law of sacrifice.
When nationality had remodelled Europe, then would
eternal Rome, destined alone of cities to rise more
mighty from each fall, be hailed its moral centre,
seat of a diet of the nations, to teach to them their

common duties to humanity.[1]   Who will say that this last more modest vision may not some day and in some sense be fulfilled? /

Partly in consequence of Mazzini's incentives, more from force of circumstances, the republic was proclaimed at Rome on the day after he landed at Leghorn.   The Assembly, a fairly level-headed body, elected on manhood suffrage and drawing its members from the larger landed proprietors and upper middle classes, had voted for it by a great majority; and the republican Triumvirs had discoursed in true Mazzinian phrases, and headed their acts with the rubric "God and the People."   On the fourth day of the republic the Assembly unanimously made Mazzini citizen of Rome, and invited him to come. He started as soon as he could leave Tuscany, and arrived on the evening of March 5, slipping into the city unobserved, "awed and like a worshipper," feeling, as he passed under the Porta del Popolo, "a spurt of new life," that for the moment swept away doubtings and disappointments.   His first thought was to organize for the impending war.   Piedmont, unreconciled to defeat and stung by Austrian brutalities in Lombardy, was about to denounce the armistice; there were formidable preparations for insurrection in the Lombard cities; Venice was undaunted and threatening from her lagunes.   Republican Rome must not be behindhand.   Mazzini made her anticipate the belated appeal from Piedmont by offering ten thousand men, and they had started for the North when the news of Novara came.

Piedmont lay crushed by one staggering blow,

---

[1] See below, c. xvii.

and the hope of freeing Lombardy had gone. The moment's task was to save Central Italy, and in the imminent danger the Romans turned to the man, who had won their reverence and lifted them to something of his own moral greatness. Mazzini was made a Triumvir, and henceforth became little less than dictator. He had probably at heart small hope of saving the Republic, and to foreigners like Clough and Margaret Fuller did not conceal his fears. But the cause was not yet desperate. He knew he could contemptuously disregard the Neapolitans, who were hovering on the Southern frontier; and at this time he could not foresee how base a part France was soon to play. The Austrians were the only serious enemy in sight; and with Hungary still untamed, with the chance that Piedmont might brace itself to a third effort, a desperate defence might yet keep them at bay. He intended to treble the Roman forces, and concentrating them at Terni, swoop down on the long line of Austrian communications, as they advanced along the Eastern coast.

Meanwhile, among the cares of war, he began to build a government that should be worthy of his ideal. "Here in Rome," he told the bickering politicians in the Assembly, "we may not be moral mediocrities." / He hoped to inspire government and people with one great purpose, that would leave no place for party-spirit or suspicion. He would have no exclusiveness, no intolerance, no war of classes or attacks on property or person. " Stiffness in principles, tolerance to individuals " was the motto of his rule, and to this, through all the troubled times that followed, he was nobly true. At a time when national danger

E

might have excused severe precautions, the press was hardly interfered with; there were few arrests, fewer penalties, for political offences; conspirators, with barely an exception, were left in contemptuous tolerance, or merely warned not to let the people know of their intrigues./ It was this very leniency to the men who were plotting the Republic's downfall, that led to the few outrages that stained its name. The civil service and police, left full of enemies and lukewarm friends, lacked vigour to repress the disorderly elements; and here and there a fanatic or criminal took advantage of the murmurings at Mazzini's tolerance to assassinate a Papalist. But save in a few provincial towns, where political murder was endemic, and for a few isolated outrages at Rome, there was absolute security alike for friend and foe. Mazzini's mild authority stands out in luminous contrast with the Papal terrorism, that scourged the unhappy land before and after.

The Triumvir's attitude to the Catholic Church is a strange commentary on the myth, that writes him down an anti-clerical fanatic. The man, who believed Catholicism a spent force, whose whole soul yearned for a new religion to issue forth from Rome, was yet superlatively careful not to shake the people's one religious creed. It would have been easy to do otherwise. There was fierce exasperation at the Pope's obduracy, at the ferocious fanaticism of men, who would see Rome bombarded rather than yield one tittle of their temporal power. Churches were half empty, and, but for the government's precautions, many another priest would have died the victim of the people's anger. But Mazzini made it one of his first cares to protect the clergy in their spiritual work. His deep religious instinct, old memories and friendships, his respect for men who in their way were witnesses to the spiritual, made him always tolerant towards them. " In Italy," he once said, "the priest is powerless for harm but powerful to do good"; and before this time and after he made impassioned appeals to them to take their part in the national work. He tried to win them now. It was from no ill-will towards the Church that he did something to repair the ecclesiastical misrule. Such reforms as he effected were bound to go to the strengthening of a church, made hateful by clerical domination ; and many were the priests and monks who defied the threatening cardinals at Gaeta, and gladly rallied to the republic. The nationalization of church lands, which Mazzini took over from his predecessors, aimed at improving the stipends of the poorer clergy. Religious services and processions went on uninterrupted, and his one act of severity towards the priests was to fine the canons of St Peter's for refusing to celebrate the usual Easter services. "It is the duty of the government," the Triumvirs said, "to preserve religion uncontaminated." "Do not be afraid," he wrote to a nun, who feared the suppression of her convent; " pray God for our country and for men of good intentions." Once in the fear of imminent attack upon the city, the crowd fetched a few confessional boxes from the churches to make barricades. Mazzini reminded them that from those confessionals had come at all events words of comfort to their mothers. It is perhaps the most convincing proof of his grip on the people's hearts, that the confessionals were taken back. With the Pope himself he was ever ready to compromise. True, he had postulated his expulsion and the downfall of his

authority as the condition of the new faith, for which
he yearned. But whether it was that the statesman
saw that the idealist must wait, or from his deep
respect for the institution round which hung so much
of Christian history, or that he wished to remove the
last pretext for the intervention of foreign Catholics,
his attitude went to the extreme of conciliatoriness.
At its first outset the Republic, while decreeing the
fall of the Temporal Power, had promised all necessary
guarantees for the Pope's spiritual authority; and
Mazzini, anticipating Cavour, tried to persuade the
Assembly to define the guarantees, and offer to consider any suggestions for them that the Catholic
Powers chose to make. We must distinguish, he said,
the Pope from the Prince, and claim our rights
without doing violence to religious faith.

Thus noble and thus gentle was the Triumvir's rule,
and finely the people responded to it. At first there
had been small enthusiasm for the Republic. The
Romans had accepted it calmly, as the one alternative
to the intolerable rule of priests. But Mazzini touched
them with his own great faith. He appealed to no
selfish interests. He promised social legislation, but
it went into the background behind the national question; and except for a land scheme to create a peasant
proprietary on the church lands, there was no time to
project much for their material well-being. His was
a pure spiritual ascendancy, that made a populace,
demoralized by bad government and charity, rise to
something of his own moral height and dare to bear
and die. There were some at all events, to whom
Rome, hallowed by a great ideal and noble rule, had
become as the city of God. Greatly their leader

merited their love. The equivocations of the past few months had gone, and in a clear position of command, untrammelled by the need to compromise with alien forces, he stood in all the majesty of his translucent soul. It shone in his face; worn and emaciated, he seemed to Margaret Fuller "more divine than ever." His personal life, of which we have grievously few records, was one of democratic simplicity. Lodged in the Quirinal, he hunted for a room "small enough to feel at home in." Here he sat unguarded and serene, " sadly ἀδορύφορος for a τύραννος," wrote Clough (for it was a country where political assassination was a tradition on both sides), as accessible to working men and women as to his own officials, with the same smile and warm hand-shake for all ; dining for two francs at a cheap restaurant, afterwards, during the siege, living on bread and raisins, his only luxury the flowers that an unknown hand sent every day, his one relaxation to sing to his guitar when left alone at night. The Triumvir's slender stipend of £32 a month he spent entirely on others. As an administrator, he was too gentle to be sufficiently prompt and stern. He even refused to sign the death-warrant of a soldier condemned by court-martial. But he made amends by his unbending energy and the quick and fertile intellect, that helped in every military detail of the defence and made his diplomatic notes, so Palmerston is said to have called them, "models of reasoning and argument." Through all the tangled cares of government he kept his calmness and serenity, the statesman's right to lift his people to new visions and new powers.

His hope was to leave a great republican example. Probably he dared expect no more. Sanguine no doubt he was, but in his cooler moments he seems to have realized from the first that the powers of evil were too strong for the noble little republic. The blow came from an unexpected quarter. This is not the place to dissect the causes, that led France to the meanest of modern political crimes, that impelled a state, pledged by its own constitution "never to employ its forces against the liberties of another people," to destroy an unoffending sister-republic. France paid at Sedan for the carelessness of honour, that allowed the Catholics and Louis Napoleon to do a great crime in her name. When Oudinot's expedition started, and, in spite of falsity on falsity, it was plain that the French government intended to crush the Romans, Mazzini's policy was clear. /He would not yield to brute, unrighteous force; Rome, he told the Assembly, must "do its duty and give a high example to every people and every part of Italy." But to him the enemy was not France but the French government. The true republicans at Paris were striving courageously to save the Romans and their own national honour; and on their efforts depended the one hope of safety. He would do nothing that would weaken their hands or unnecessarily hurt French pride./ When the Assembly resolved without a dissentient voice to resist at all cost, and Oudinot's troops were ingloriously driven back, defeated by the raw Italian levies, he refused to let Garibaldi make the rout complete. The French prisoners were released after generous and diplomatic hospitality. A monster gift of cigars was sent to the enemy's quarters, wrapped in handbills that appealed to republican fraternity.

Perhaps someone remembered that eighty years before
the American Congress had sent the same ingenuous
present to the Hessian mercenaries.

Fraud and force alike had failed to open the gates
of Rome, and the long chapter of deceit went on,
—deceit hard to parallel even in the diplomacy of
great nations. Ferdinand de Lesseps, then a bud-
ding attaché, was sent to parley with the Romans,
till Oudinot's reinforcements arrived, and the new
elections in France gave a Catholic majority in the
Chamber. ⁄It was a mere ruse, but de Lesseps was
Napoleon's dupe and negotiated in all good faith,
giving ample credit to Mazzini's " moderation and
loyalty and courage." Had they been left alone,
they would have concluded peace on terms honour-
able to both sides, and Mazzini seems to have hoped
that the danger from France was passing. ⁄Garibaldi
was sent to meet the Neapolitans, who had advanced
as far as Albano, and drove them back in rout across
the frontier. King Ferdinand brevetted Ignatius
Loyola field-marshal of his army, but the very
posthumous honour could not exorcise the superstitious terror, with which the great guerilla-chieftain's
name inspired his men. Had the Triumvirs been
free to let Garibaldi advance, the Bourbon power
would perhaps have crumbled, as it crumbled eleven
years later.

But at the moment when Mazzini and de Lesseps
had agreed on terms, the French government threw
off the mask, and Oudinot made a treacherous attack.
Then came the memorable siege, when for nearly a
month the badly-armed and badly-generalled Romans
kept at bay an army twice their number and a powerful

siege artillery.   Heroically they struggled on against the overwhelming odds.   The great majority of the soldiers were natives of the state; but some had gathered from all Italy, drawn by the spell of Rome to fight once more for country.   It was a band of heroes, such as never came again together in the Italian struggle; generals of the future like Medici and Bixio; Manara, the Lombard leader in the Five Days; Mameli, the war-poet of Italy, son of the woman who had been Mazzini's boyish love; Ugo Bassi, the priest-patriot, greatest Italian preacher of his day, nearest of spiritual kin to Mazzini's self; Bertani, the future organizer of the Sicilian Thousand and Pisacane their precursor; and the great protagonists themselves, Mazzini and Garibaldi;—a diverse band, patricians and plebeians, saints and sinners, royalists and republicans, all moved by one supreme redeeming love of Italy and Rome.   Within, the city showed a passive heroism as fine.   Calmly and patiently the people bore the destruction of their homes, the growing scarcity, the hopelessness of victory as the toils drew ever closer round the fated city.   Six thousand women came forward to offer their service in the hospitals.   When the women of the poor Trastevere were driven from their homes by the French shells, the government lodged them in the palaces of the fugitive nobles, on their simple promise that there should be neither theft nor injury, and the promise given in the name of "God and the People" was scrupulously kept.

To their leader those weeks must have been a time of fearful strain.   Garibaldi's bad generalship and bad temper shortened a resistance, that was hopeless from the first. The losses were heavy, and Mameli and Manara fell with many another of Mazzini's friends. After the ill-fated revolt of the Mountain on June 13, there was no hope of diversion from the republicans at Paris. ⁄At home, though the Assembly loyally supported him, he had to meet the petulant criticism of Garibaldi and the intriguers who made him their tool. To him it was a matter of clear duty that the Republic should fight on to the end. " Monarchies may capitulate, republics die and bear their testimony even to martyrdom." When the last defences broke down, he wished to make a desperate fight from street to street, or retire with the Assembly and the army to the Apennines, throw themselves on the Austrian lines, and keep the republican flag flying in Romagna. The army was prepared for either course; but the Assembly had no stomach for the sacrifice, and Mazzini, bitterly reproaching them, resigned his office on the eve of the city's fall. ⁄Sullenly Rome surrendered, and the victors, as they entered the city, hung back before the threatening populace. Garibaldi, with three thousand who disdained surrender, began his great retreat. "Hunger and thirst and vigil," he promised them, "but never terms with the enemy." Mazzini would have been more consistent, had he gone out with them. Perhaps he had no liking for a desperate fragment of his rejected scheme; perhaps the personal tension with Garibaldi was too great. For some days he stayed on in Rome. He was worn out and overstrung; he had not slept on a bed since the siege began, he had fed on coarse and insufficient food. In two short months he had grown old; his beard was grey, his face cadaverous, his manner, so Margaret

Fuller noted, "sweet and calm, but full of a more fiery purpose than ever." He wandered defiantly about the streets. It was partly that he wanted, by offering himself to any assassin's knife, to kill the lie of the Catholic press that he had forced a hated tyranny upon the Romans. Besides, he had a desperate hope that he might rouse the people and the remaining troops to one more struggle. His whole soul was possessed by the passion to protest on to the end against the triumph of brute force. It is strange that the French did not arrest him ; perhaps they knew too well the temper of the people. At last Gustavo Modena's wife and Margaret Fuller persuaded him to withdraw. He had no passport, but he found the means of sailing to Marseilles ; there he succeeded in eluding the French police and travelled on to Geneva.

Chapter VIII

London Again

1849-1859.   AETAT 44-54

In Switzerland—Life in London—English friends—English politics and
literature—The Friends of Italy.

MAZZINI stayed for a few weeks in a quiet hotel near
his old quarters at Geneva, then moved to Lausanne,
where he and a few more refugees, Saffi, his co-
Triumvir, and Pisacane among them, took a small house
(the Villa Montallegro) near the town on the hills that
overlook the lake.   Here he and his friends plunged
at once into the old eager work of correspondence
and journalism, as if the struggle at Rome had been a
holiday.   Another ephemeral paper, *L'Italia del Popolo*,
was launched on its short career.   His head was full
of literary schemes,—an Italian translation of the
Gospels with an introduction, a new Encyclopædia,
which should do for religious democracy what the old
Encyclopædia had done for the thought of the
eighteenth century.   It was a quiet, not unhappy
time, that must have recalled something of the old days
at Marseilles.   At times indeed he was miserable and
pessimistic as of old, brooding over lost friendships,
chafing at the triumph of brute force in Italy.   But
except in these hours of taciturn gloom, when he

avoided all companionship, he was serene and genial, sometimes brightening into anecdote and humour, when the party settled down to the evening's talk and chess.

In the spring of 1850 the agitation in France at the proposed revision of the constitution excited vague hopes of a revolution there; and with some fatuous idea that he could help to stop Louis Napoleon's progress to empire, Mazzini went to Paris, only to discover how empty was the expectation. On the journey he lost a note-book, in which for many years he had entered his thoughts on religion. The world would gain more from its discovery than from that of any lost Greek tragedy. He crossed to England for a few months, then returned to Switzerland. But the persecution of 1834 repeated itself. The governments put pressure on the Swiss to expel the refugees, and Mazzini after a month or two of hiding found it necessary to leave. One night in November he and two friends left Geneva, walking along the lake to Nyon, while they discussed Byron and Mickiewicz, and were taken on in a friend's carriage to Lausanne, whence he found the means to escape to England.

Here he made his home with few interruptions till the last years of his life, taking no small part in English society and politics, finding his best friends in English men and women. "Italy is my country, but England is my real home, if I have any," he said. He had come to love England and English ways, and in his brief political journeys to Italy his home thoughts went to England, and he was glad to be back again. His old horror of London changed to a real liking; and its conveniences for his work made it difficult to get him out of town, save for a rare visit to his friends, or for a day or two to recruit his health at St Leonard's or Eastbourne, which he liked, or at Brighton, which he hated. He longed sometimes, indeed, for "some secret nook in the country, to breathe fresh air and gaze on the sky or at the sea "; but when he was urged to take rest in the country, he railed affectionately at his "misled and dreamy friends" for supposing he could attend to his work anywhere out of London. The fogs still had their fascination for him ; he wrote once from Italy, "I think very often under these radiant skies of the London fogs and always regretfully. Individually speaking, I was evidently intended for an Englishman."

At first he lived at Cromwell Lodge, Old Brompton, a little house in the middle of orchards and gardens at what was then the extreme western end of London. Building operations drove him thence, and Mrs Carlyle found him lodgings over a post-office at 15 Radnor Street, near his old rooms in York Buildings. Here, at first with Saffi and three other exiles, afterwards alone, he lived the frugallest of lives. His income indeed was somewhat larger than it had been. At his mother's death he came into an annuity of £160 a year, which she, knowing how readily his money flowed to public work and charity, had wisely invested with obdurate trustees. His friends would gladly have helped him, but though he frankly asked money of them for his cause (always scrupulously repaying it, if borrowed on his personal responsibility), he never, so far as I know, would take from this time forward money for strictly personal needs. Once only he accepted some to pay

for a private secretary, and once again for cabs, when
his friends suspected that there were plots to assassinate
him, and feared for his walking in London streets,
unprotected save by a sword-cane.   Thus, even with
casual literary earnings, his income seldom reached
£200, and of this for some years £80 went to the
education of the Tencioni children, and often every
other available penny to finance his plots of insurrection.   While his enemies in Italy painted him living
in patrician luxury, he denied himself every comfort
(cigars always excepted), save the modest ones that
his friends forced on him.   Money he only wanted for
his political schemes.   " I have never felt so bitterly
the curse of not being rich," he wrote once, when
wanting rifles for one of his revolutionary plots.   For
himself, he was content with his humble fare and modest
lodgings.   Here in his small room, every piece of
furniture littered with books and papers, the air thick
with smoke of cheap Swiss cigars (except when friends
sent Havannahs), brightened only by his tame canaries
and carefully-tended plants, he was generally writing
at his desk till evening, always with more work in
hand than he could cope with, carrying on the usual
mass of correspondence, writing articles for his Italian
papers, raising public funds with infinite labour, stirring
his English friends to help the cause, finding money
and work for the poor refugees, or organizing concerts
in their interest.   The school in Greville Street went on
for three years longer, when, except for the Sunday
lectures, it was closed.   And amid all the exacting
cares of public work he spared himself no trouble for
his English friends, advising in their family affairs
writing long letters of tenderness and spiritual wisdom

to comfort a bereaved son or lead a young girl from a life of selfishness to higher things.

He had aged greatly since he left London less than three years ago. He was worn and thin, his beard was white, and the once dark features wore " a sort of grey, ashy halo." But it was the same high " cliff-like" forehead, the regular features, the strong, straight nose, " the exquisite curve of lips like a woman's in their expression of spotless purity," the piercing black eyes, whose like none ever knew who saw them, " of luminous depth, full of sadness, tenderness, and courage, of purity and fire, readily flashing into indignation or humour, always with the latent expression of exhaustless resolution "; " the only eyes," says another observer, " I ever saw that looked like flames." " His face in repose was grave, even sad, but it lit up with a smile of wonderful sweetness, as he greeted a friend with a pressure, rather than a shake, from the thin hand." [1] He carried his head a little forward, and he had a habit of sitting on the edge of a chair, perhaps, it has been suggested, because in his own room his books left but narrow margin for sedentary uses. He dressed, as ever, with perfect neatness, in a worn black frock-coat, a double-breasted velvet waistcoat buttoned high, despising collars and substituting a silk handkerchief wound round his neck, wearing a long thin gold watch chain, which had probably been his father's, and two rings, one at least no doubt his mother's, now rescued from the pawn-shop.

His personal life was centred almost wholly in his English friends. It is true, he felt his exile bitterly.

[1] I owe these particulars to one who knew him well, and to a contemporary description in a private letter.

" Wish for me," he writes to friends one Christmas,
" that I may die in the country and for the country,
in which I have been forbidden to live." But he had
no home ties in Italy now. His father had died in the
winter of 1848, leaving him to brood over the thought
that he had been but a source of pain to the grim
old man, who under all his moroseness and want of
sympathy had never lost his pride and affection for
his son. His mother, whom he had seen once again
when at Milan, with whom he had never relaxed the
close, affectionate correspondence, died in the summer
of 1852. It was a very heavy blow. There was no
one to replace her ; he had lost " the dream of his
individual life,—to see her in the joy of triumph," when
Italy was free. But he nerved himself, and took her
loss as an incentive to fresh effort. " My mother," he
writes, " seems to me to be present, perhaps nearer than
she was in her terrestrial life. I feel more and more
the sacredness of duties, which she recognized, and of
a mission which she approved. / I have now no mother
on earth except my country, and I shall be true to her,
as my mother has been to me." / So intensely actual
was she still to him, that once afterwards, when in
hiding and deep dejection, he thought she came to
him in veritable presence to strengthen and console
him. His lonely heart, athirst as ever for affection,
went out to his English friends, the men and still
more the women, who believed in him and in his
politics, and tried to bring some warmth and brightness
into his sad life. After a year or two he saw little
more of the Carlyles, but their place was more than
taken by the Ashursts, the Stansfelds, the Peter Taylors,
the Shaens, the Mallesons, the Nathans, the Milner-

Gibsons. When the day's work was over, he would generally spend the evening at one or other of their houses, most often with the Stansfelds, whose home at Bellevue Lodge was within an easy walk from his lodgings. Gradually he came to have a large outside circle of acquaintances. He corresponded with Grote and Mrs Gaskell; the Brownings, J. S. Mill, Jowett, Swinburne, Cairnes, Miss Martineau, probably Dickens were among the people he met.[1]

With these friendships a new light and happiness came to his life. Probably, too, the consciousness of having played a great part nobly added a new touch of dignity and gentleness. " The indescribable look of suffering for others," noted one who met him now after a ten years' interval, " has disappeared, and he is now a man full of experience, patience, and hope." / " The Roman revolution," wrote Carlyle to Emerson, " has made a man of him,—quite brightened up ever since." / All the human sweetness in him blossomed out. His friends provided the home care, which he had lost, since he left his mother and sisters at Genoa twenty years ago; and he loved to repay them by many little marks of affection, never forgetting birthdays, buying presents of books and jewelry out of his slender purse, taking them to the Opera, where his acquaintance with the great Italian singers sometimes put boxes at his disposal. In his evenings at the Stansfelds he was often full

---

[1] It has often been supposed that Browning had Mazzini in mind, when he wrote *The Italian in England*. I know of no evidence for or against this; but the poem was written in 1845, when the letter-opening affair had made Mazzini prominently public. Mazzini is said to have made a translation of it.

of merry fun; he could tell a story well, all the more piquantly for his Italicisms. One favourite anecdote (he had told it to Mrs Carlyle) was how he baffled an undertaker, who brought a coffin by mistake to his landlady's, and refused to take it away. " My dear," he said, no doubt with his sweet gravity, " we have not here a dead." Or he would, when quite alone with the family, sing to his guitar, or finger out on it the score of some favourite opera. His native gentleness came out in his kindness to children and animals. He does not seem to have been naturally very fond of children, but, when among them, he made himself easily at home. Some French children at a house which he visited, who got into disgrace when Louis Blanc came to see them, were always good with Mazzini, " because he was so kind and never failed to enquire after the dolls." They loved to sit and listen to his talk, not that they understood him, but because the beautiful voice fascinated them. With dogs and cats and birds he was always happy. He would make one of his hostesses angry, because he insisted on feeding her dog at dinner. " But, my dear," he would say, " I make Bruno happy." Ledru Rollin and he, once talking, probably, of the European revolution, put out their cigars, because the smoke made a dog uncomfortable. His most constant companions were his tame linnets and canaries. He had netting over the windows, so that they could fly about his room at liberty; and visitors would generally find a bird or two perched on his head or shoulders, or hopping among his papers, inured to the thick tobacco smoke, in which they and he lived.

He was a brilliant talker, because he was in earnest and his thoughts were clear, at all events to himself. There was no trace of effort or affectation ; he was always just himself and never played a part. / He would speak with a prophet's simplicity and conviction of his religious faith and the destinies of man, talking vivaciously, tenaciously, passionately sometimes, with the authority of one who had no thought of self and had lived and suffered for his creed. / Some of his hosts were the champions of every struggling cause, and the conversation turned naturally to American slavery or women's rights or nationality or cooperation. Music and poetry were favourite subjects with him, and he would contend pugnaciously in mock-earnestness for the superiority of Meyerbeer over Rossini, or inveigh to his heart's content against the abominated doctrine of "art for the sake of art." He once, when dining with Mr and Mrs William Shaen, forgot his dinner in his eagerness to convert his hostess from the heresy ; and when pressed to eat, pleaded that he had something else to do, for "here is Mrs Shaen travelling to perdition as fast as she can, and I must save her soul." He spoke English now well and fluently, but,—unlike his English writing, which was rarely unidiomatic,—with many little Italicisms. Among those he seldom met, he was sometimes nervous and silent ; at other times, perhaps from the same nervousness, he would monopolize the conversation, and was remorseful afterwards. Once, many years after this time, he met Jowett, and talked uninterruptedly for two hours, Jowett listening silently. When Jowett went, he observed, "he made me talk all the time, and I have no notion what he thought of it." Jowett, made careful notes of what he said, and years afterwards remarked, in allusion to their meeting, " Mazzini was a man of genius, but too much under the influence of two abstract ideas, God and the principle of nationality." He thought, though, very highly of him. " He was an enthusiast, a visionary," he said, " but he was a very noble character, and had a genius far beyond that of ordinary statesmen. Though not a statesman, I think that his reputation will increase as time goes on, when that of most statesmen disappears."

With those, who knew him well, constraining was the influence of this man, who spoke with authority of life and God and duty. Young people at all events, who came under the spell of those eyes, and heard the vibrating voice speak with passionate earnestness of the deep things of God, felt for him an awe and veneration, such as few, if any, of his generation inspired. Here was one who had given all for his ideal, who had taken poverty for his bride, yet without self-righteousness, too sad at the world's sin and struggle to be aught but humble ; one too, who had lived on a great stage, who was helping to remodel Europe, a great thinker, a great moral teacher, yet with infinite concern for the trials and temptations of some puzzled soul. " Thou noble Mazzini," said Clough after brief knowledge of his life at Rome. Much deeper was the feeling of those, who had the privilege of close companionship. And, though, perhaps, it would be difficult to prove it, it is probable that he has left no inconsiderable impress on English thought. Here and there one finds strong traces of his influence on men, who have helped to mould the best thought among us in the last forty years. "Mazzini is the true teacher of our age," said Arnold Toynbee. Never, certainly, did age more need his high idealism to teach a nobler rule in national and private life.

His literary work at this time was not remarkable. He was "still praying God to grant him, when Italy had become a nation, two years of hermit life," when he could write his long-cherished book on religion and a popular history of Italian nationality. But the hope of ever writing them was gradually fading. He was too absorbed through all this period by political propagandism, and in his controversial writings of these years he is generally far from being at his best. The latter chapters of his *Duties of Man*, however, date from this decade. He seems, despite his busy life, to have found a good deal of time for reading. His writings on the Slav question are evidently the result of careful study. Apart from political reading, English literature seems to have claimed his interests. Byron was still to him the greatest of English poets, and he read Byroniana with the zest of a devotee. He could not forgive England for her neglect of her "only poet who will live in times to come." "I wish," he once wrote, "I had time to write before dying a book on Byron, and abuse all England, a few women excepted, for the way she treats one of her greatest souls and minds." He was keenly interested in the controversy on Byron's treatment of his wife, refusing to believe that the husband was the more in fault, but owning himself too in-discriminating an admirer to be a fair judge.[1] He

[1] See below, pp. 359-360.

would contrast him with Wordsworth and Coleridge, criticizing the latter as contemplative poets, living remote from action among their lakes and mountains, —which proves that he had not read Wordsworth's patriotic sonnets. He liked Chatterton in a way, drawn doubtless to him by his sad end and de Vigny's drama ; " I have always," he writes, " had a sort of fondness for him, as I have for crushed flowers." Among contemporary poets Mrs Browning was probably his favourite. He reads *Aurora Leigh*, " admiring it very much, only wishing from time to time that she had written it in beautiful prose than—passages ex-cepted—in neglected poetry." Browning himself he is said to have read and admired. But perhaps he alludes to him when he writes, " the form in England begins to be systematically wrong, I think."

Meanwhile he had resumed his strong interest in English life and politics, stimulated no doubt by the keen thinkers he moved among, but always preserving his own original outlook. On the whole, his was not a very appreciative criticism. Sincerely and increas-ingly as he admired the freedom and seriousness of English ways, he keenly felt the decay of our religious life, and, what he regarded as its consequence, the selfishness and want of principle in our foreign policy. His knowledge of Protestantism was never very deep or sympathetic ; but he knew enough of it to apply his own tests of religious vitality. He condemned it for its soul-killing formalism ; he showed how it sinned against itself, when it ceased to be concerned with men as citizens ; he poured scorn on the Bible

Societies, that tried to proselytize his countrymen, and made no sign, when he and other Italians had fought at Rome for liberty of conscience. It was to this want of true religion, that he charged our insular selfishness. He detested the Cobdenites. "The 'peacemen' have no principle." /"Your Peace Societies," he wrote in an open letter to "the people of England," "allowing God's law and Godlike human life to be systematically crushed on the two-thirds of Europe,— your *believers* in liberty as the only pledge for man's responsibility, allying themselves with despots,—your Christians fighting for the maintenance of Mahommedan law on European populations,—seem to me to be the reverse of religious." If England gave no helping hand to the young nationalities to which belonged the future, she would find herself in twenty years shut out from the sympathies and alliances and markets of the Continent. /'He vigorously condemned the Crimean War, and took his stand with the few, who tried to save England from that colossal blunder. Not that he objected to war with the oppressor of the Poles. But a war, which might have been a crusade for the downtrodden peoples of the East, had ranged England, once the champion of liberty, on the side of Turkey and Austria. The alliance with the tyrant of Italy and Hungary "took from the war whatever made it sacred in the eyes of God and man." It pledged English backing for the evilest of Continental despotisms. It robbed the war of any principle, and "war is the greatest of crimes, when it is not waged for the benefit of mankind, for the sake of a great truth to enthrone or of a great lie to entomb." He "bowed before" the heroism of the army, "the quiet, silent devotedness, with which the nation accepts all the sacrifices inseparable from a war"; but "the policy of your war," he said, "is absolutely immoral, how can you hope for victory?" How different had it been, had England avoided the dishonouring touch of Austria, and sought her ally in a Polish revolution.

Mazzini's interest in English society and politics was, like everything else except his friendships, turned to the use of his own country. He expected three results from his English propagandism,—to secure for Italy the moral support of English opinion and the English press, to influence the foreign policy of the country in her favour, and to obtain money for his insurrectionary schemes. He worked on the traditional sympathy for Italy, and tried to turn it from its belief in Piedmont to his own revolutionary and democratic programme. He appealed to the anti-Papal feeling of the country, and played on the theme that a free Italy would allow fair play for Protestant missions. With men of the Manchester School he argued that free trade would follow free government; with the working classes he spoke of the common interests of working men the world over. His own friends he constantly enlisted in his schemes, and made large levies on their private purses. "It makes my hair stand on end," said one of them—a well-known politician—afterwards, "to think of what I did at the suggestion of that man." Public opinion he hoped to influence through the Society of the Friends of Italy, founded in the autumn of 1851 by the men, who had promoted the People's International League four years before,—James Stansfeld, Peter Taylor, William Ashurst, William Shaen. Some of the best English

Liberals of the day were on the committee,—William Byles of Bradford, Joseph Cowen, George Dawson, John Forster, W. E. Forster, J. A. Froude, G. J. Holyoake, William Howitt, Douglas Jerrold, Walter Savage Landor, G. H. Lewes, W. J. Linton, David Masson, Edward Miall, Professor Newman. Mazzini generally, if not always, spoke at their annual meetings,—with intense nervousness, for he was not yet sufficient master of English to speak it fluently, and he "could not think without a pen in his hand." "I cannot understand people," he writes, "who can prepare a speech or article walking up and down their room or garden. I could walk about a day without an idea entering my head." His speeches, none the less, seem to have been eloquent and successful, his manner being, as the newspapers reported, "most exciting." The Society suspended work, when the Crimean War broke out, and was re-constituted again at the end of 1856. As far as money went, Mazzini got less than he hoped from his English agitation. A few friends gave generously, but there was little of the response that came to Garibaldi's appeal a few years later. But the Society did much to win English opinion, if not for Mazzini's own special schemes, at all events for the bigger question of Italian liberty. The *Leader*, the *Daily News*, the *Morning Advertiser* opened their columns, and did something to counteract the anti-Italian bias of the *Times*. In 1857 a fairly vigorous agitation, especially in the North and Scotland, carried on the work that Kossuth's meetings had begun, and roused a vehement popular feeling against Austria.

Chapter IX

Mazzini and Cavour

1850-1857.   Aetat 45-52.

The Piedmontese School—Mazzini and Cavour—The French alliance—
Mazzini and Manin—The theory of the dagger—Conspiracies—The
Genoese plot of 1857.

IT is painful to turn from Mazzini in England, the great-hearted friend, the prophetic thinker, the generous worker in the cause of man, to his political action in Italy.   Had he yielded to the advice of some of his friends and left politics at this time for literature, his fame were brighter and his life more fruitful in pure good.   His work for Italy was done ; he had conquered it for more than half his creed.   Half its best men had been nurtured on his writings, had learned from him to believe in independence and unity, though still they spoke of unity in whispers, and he himself knew not how far opinion had advanced. The day of conspiracy had passed ; free Piedmont was slowly marshalling the forces of the nation for another and decisive war.   The republic became impossible on the day, when Victor Emmanuel swore loyalty to the constitution, and thereby proclaimed himself champion of Italian aspirations.   The one thing needful was to rally every section of patriots to

154

the one possible flag. To attack the monarchy now
only hurt the bigger issue, lost sight of the great goal
in mists of schism, brought bitterness and dissension
where discipline was all important for the day of trial.
No one was more insistent than Mazzini on the need
of discipline, but in practice he conditioned it in these
years by being himself leader. One who found it
so difficult to compromise, could hardly follow.

Had Mazzini thought the republic the more important issue, his action would at least have been
consistent. But he had deliberately set unity above
it, and independence from Austria above either. A
saner politician would have been silent on the minor
question. But Mazzini could never long repress his
republican teaching. It was partly that, save in
moments of comparative lucidity, he convinced himself
that Piedmont would never make a cast for unity, that
the Austrians could not be expelled but by a great
rising of the people. Had he gauged Italian sentiment
more accurately, he would have spared himself the error,
would have lost his deep distrust in Piedmont and
its king, his bitter animosity to Cavour, his pitiable
exaggeration of the strength of his own party. But
an exile lives in necessary half-knowledge. The
government of Piedmont, as exclusive and intolerant as
himself, barred from wholesome activity in his own land
the man, who, had he been at Turin in daily contact
with men of other parties, would have been a mighty
force for good ; and to them, more than to Mazzini
himself, belongs the pity of his wasted patriotism.
Not but what in any circumstances Mazzini found it
hard to recognize new facts. The prophet is by nature
inflexible ; and Mazzini's whole creed was a thing of

such passionate intensity, each part had twisted itself so inextricably round the rest, that it cost a wrench to part with any detail. " I may, of course, be mistaken," he wrote of his political creed, " but mine is a matter of deep conviction, and it is impossible for me to modify or alter it."/ He was incapable of taking advice ; if men differed from him, he assailed them bitterly instead of examining the reasons for their dissent.   And the partisan, that was always latent in him, grew till it obscured the statesman.   He who was so insistent that no one had a right to set his own opinions above the people's common sense, was the last to bow to the popular verdict, when it declared against himself. / Henceforth Mazzini was more foe than friend to his own ideals. / Much he still did to stir his countrymen to strenuous and high-thinking patriotism.   Though he aimed beyond their ken, he shot more high than all the politicians.   But in the great march he broke the ranks, and made the task more difficult for men, who, with a patriotism as true and with a saner strategy, had set their faces for the same high goal.

Retirement was however impossible for a man of Mazzini's temperament.   He was too feverishly impatient for his country's salvation to only stand and wait. /Inaction seemed treachery to the cause of righteousness.   Both in public and private life he insisted that " thought and action " must go hand in hand, that a man had no right to confine his energies to literature and decline his part in practical political work.   He criticized intolerantly the men in Italy, who wrote patriotic literature instead of plotting insurrection. "Actions," he said, "are the books of the

masses," especially in a country where the majority
were illiterate. He in fact, like every other patriot,
was maddened by the savage tyranny, with which the
Austrians and the Pope and the King of Naples were
scourging his unhappy country,—"the insolent triumph
of brute force, the exile and death of our brothers in
two-thirds of Europe, the long weeping of their sisters
and mothers, the lying, the espionage, the corruption,
the cry of the oppressed masses, the teaching of those
who fight and die in silence, the shame that makes us
blush for those who submit and sell themselves in
despair." "Such a state of things," he wrote to an
English friend after the Mantuan executions, "cannot
last, must not last. It is far better to die in a supreme
glorious battle, fought under the eye of God with our
national banner unfurled, than to see the best of our
land falling one by one under the axe of the execu-
tioner." It were sin to wait, and he saw no need for
waiting. He was right of course in his belief that a
nation, which had once so nearly won its freedom,
would try for it again. "The dreams of violence," he
said, "are brief, and infallible the triumph of a people,
that hopes and fights and suffers for justice and holy
liberty." He had persuaded himself that the masses
were only waiting for a signal to rise and throw
themselves on Austria. As so often in his logic, the
thing ought to be and therefore must be. He knew
indeed that he could not count on the middle classes
for insurrection. The men, who had been the strength
of Young Italy, had gone over almost in mass to the
Piedmontese School, and he did not spare them his
reproaches. But he hoped in the working men.
While the Moderates hardly noticed them, he saw

what stuff lay in the despised and misunderstood Italian artisans. But he exaggerated his influence with them. "They are mine, devotedly mine, to blindness." Individuals, indeed, among them he won, as he won men of every class, by his simple, noble earnestness. But except in and round Genoa their numbers at this time were few.

It was an impossible policy. It had nearly succeeded in 1848, when Europe was in flames, but Mazzini would not see how radically circumstances had changed. There was no serious hope now that a general movement of European democracy would divide the forces of Austria ; and his efforts to bring together again the democrats of different countries, especially of Italy and Hungary, had no results, at all events till in after years. The resuscitation of Austria, the evidence of her military strength, the Second Empire in France, the resignation of Palmerston, the collapse of the German democrats had killed any early hope of a successful war, even though all the armed strength of the nation, regular armies and volunteers alike, were put into it. It was true that the nation could win its freedom even now, if it sought it at all cost, if it were willing to face the awful sacrifice,—the mowing down of the undisciplined levies, the wasting of the country, — and fight through defeat to victory. But Mazzini's hopes shipwrecked on the fact,—and bitterly he came to recognize it, — that the Italians, like most other peoples, were not a nation of martyr-heroes, that the peasants had little active patriotism, that thousands in other classes cared more for church than country, that even among the rest there was little of the grim

tenacity of Americans or Dutch or of the fierce un-
conquerableness of Greeks and Spaniards.

It was this that gave the Piedmontese party its
justification. Timid and conservative as it often was,
it at all events recognized facts. It saw that this
undisciplined enthusiasm was not business, that in
the present condition of Europe another national
rising meant another and more terrible disaster, that
each little revolt with its miserable ending only
tightened the tyranny and damped the patriots, that
Piedmont's first duty was to preserve its own liberty,
—no light task in itself,—that its next was to gather
round it all the aspirations of the country, discipline them and husband them, till the chance came
again to fight with a probability of victory. The
Piedmontese had learnt the lessons of 1848-49 very
differently from their critic. To them discipline was
the one essential. Never again must dissension
about means paralyze the country in front of the
enemy. And in the interests of union they had
small mercy for democratic theories, they were prepared to be unfair to opponents and crush minorities.
Victor Emmanuel must be the figure-head of the
movement and the Piedmontese statesmen its leaders.
Theoretically, of course, their policy was a smaller
one than Mazzini's. It had little of the poetry and
idealism of the movement, which he had helped to
inspire. There was no majestic vision of a people
rising in its own spontaneous might and deciding
its destinies in a great national pact. It postulated
encroachments on democratic freedom. It was willing
to buy alliances by concessions, that abated the
country's dignity. It veiled the great ideal of Unity,

and sought attainment by slow stages and crooked paths. But, assuming that independence and unity were the great essentials,—and on this the best men of the party were at one with Mazzini,—it was on its main lines the only possible policy. And it was a sense of this, that rallied the great mass of patriots to the flag of Piedmont, and left Mazzini to protest almost alone, a leader without followers.

The antagonism of the two schools was typified in Cavour and Mazzini. They were very different in temperament :—the one an aristocrat by training, a genial hater of theories, an opportunist content to feel his way by little steps, to wait patiently year after year rather than risk failure, making success his object, with small scruple as to means or personal honour, so his country stood to gain ; the other a man of greater nature and culture but less capacity, democrat of democrats, distrusting king and nobles and middle classes, passionate and outspoken in his friendships and his enmities, the uncompromising, inflexible, restless apostle, who would conquer armies by a principle of abstract righteousness, too dazzled by the future to see the mundane obstacles and hard facts about his feet. Cavour had a supercilious contempt for Mazzini and his doctrines ; he probably regarded him as a nuisance, and would have gladly seen him shot. His business was to win Italy, if he could do so without risking overmuch ; but he was minister of a crown and would do nothing to endanger it. He had convinced himself, save at moments of impatient optimism, that only through a French alliance could Austria be driven out. For this he was willing to humour

Louis Napoleon, to stoop to trickery, to be brutal to the republicans. He would use the revolutionaries if he could, but it must be at their own risk and for the greater glory of the monarchy. Cavour, hiding his ideals and working in mists of diplomacy, chose to be misunderstood ; and it is no wonder that Mazzini generally read him on the surface, and refused to see how much their programmes had in common. To him Cavour's slow patient policy came of mere weakness and inconstancy of purpose. He thought of him as a timid diplomatist, half-leagued with the despotisms, more careful of convention than of right, incapable of aspiring to Italy and Rome. It was only late in life, that he re-cognised his statesmanship. He hated him as a truckler to Napoleon ; he thought that he favoured Napoleon's cousin, Lucien Murat, for the throne of Naples, that he held the Emperor's friendship of more account than Italy. He never realised that under the careful statesman lay a bold and eager spirit, that at the fitting moment might be as revolutionary as himself.

Two men of such diverse character could probably have never worked cordially together. But under other circumstances they might have helped and supplemented one another. It was a cruel fate that, owing to Mazzini's exile and the consequent impossibility of mutual understanding, they should have wasted so much in a bitter and unnecessary antagonism. Mazzini no doubt had much provocation for his fixed hostility. He, who had given all for country, was an exile from the land he loved, seeing it only in rare and secret visits, stealing to his mother's grave by night "like a man bent on a crime," his followers persecuted, his apologies suppressed. But he painfully exaggerated the deficiencies of the rival school. When he asked the Piedmontese government, "Are you with Austria or against her?" when he branded the royalists as being, "next to Austria, the great obstacle to Italian freedom," he showed a partisan's unwillingness or incapacity to grasp the facts./ His watch, in Giusti's phrase, had stopped at 1848; and he could not see how radically Cavour and the new King had changed the spirit of Piedmontese policy./ Victor Emmanuel, he confidently asserted, though "better than his ministers," "neither wishes to be nor can be King of Italy"; it was "an absolute impossibility" that he would try, unless compelled, to win Italian freedom. Mazzini was on sounder ground, when he fulminated against the French alliance. Others besides him foresaw the difficulty of reconciling Louis Napoleon's timidity with Italian aspirations, the recurring temptation to duplicity, if Italian statesmen had to quiet his suspicions and fears. He well said that it stained the name of Italy to seek salvation from the man who had crushed the Roman Republic and made the *coup d'état*. But Mazzini never faced the hard fact, that no otherwise could Austria be driven out. And his blindness grew partly out of the sheer personal hatred of the Emperor, which he did not attempt to conceal. / Only in later years he came to see at all, and never fully, that Louis Napoleon, however timidly, wished to remodel Europe on his own principle of nationality. He never understood how real was the Emperor's good-will to Italy, how far his foreign policy outstripped his people's./ He thought he had first-hand information as to Napoleon's schemes, and the first-hand information was always incomplete and misleading. Nor were his antipathies limited to the Emperor. "My antagonism to the French," he writes in 1850, "grows stronger every day." He had a bitter controversy with Louis Blanc and the French socialists. But, strangely, he had no word of condemnation for the French Catholics, who had prompted the expedition to Rome and were ever pulling back Napoleon in his more generous designs. At a later time, at all events, he quite underrated their strength.

Was compromise with Piedmont impossible? /Daniel Manin, the republican Triumvir at Venice in 1849,/ whose rule there stands out with Mazzini's own at Rome as one of the most brilliant pages in the history of the century/founded in these years a National Society, with a unitarian but royalist programme. He recognised with the Piedmontese politicians the need of discipline, and that discipline could only come by accepting Victor Emmanuel as nominal leader. But he conditioned his conversion to royalism by the King's acceptance of Unity. "Make Italy," he wrote to him, "and we are with you ; if not, not." Manin hoped to win Mazzini to his programme. He, like him, had been a republican ; he was a man of noblest private life, of sincerest patriotism ; he was striving earnestly for Unity ; he fretted almost as much as did Mazzini himself at Cavour's slow manœuvring. Why should not Mazzini abandon his impossible dream of the republic, and work together for the bigger end with a man as

democratic as himself?   Mazzini refused./ All that
he would offer was "the neutral flag" of 1848,—
a promise to leave the settlement of the question
between monarchy and republic to a future Constituent of the freed nation. The position was
plausible enough, but there were fatal objections to
it.   It encouraged the federalists to agitate; it must
necessarily alienate the King; it would make discipline more difficult than ever.   And, when the
country, as Mazzini himself began to recognise, was
declaring unmistakably for the monarchy, to keep
the question nominally open was a homage more to
the letter than to the spirit of popular sovereignty.

As a kind of appendix to the controversy, Mazzini
had his famous argument with Manin on "the theory
of the dagger."   In 1856 Manin wrote an open letter,
attacking the theory as "the great enemy of Italy."
He sent his letter to the *Times*, provoking Mazzini's
retort that his "sense of personal dignity and respect
for his country should have prevented him from
writing to such a paper."   Manin did not specifically
mention Mazzini, but the reference was understood,
and Mazzini indignantly replied.   It is hardly necessary to-day to answer the charge that Mazzini encouraged political assassination.   He held indeed that
there were rare occasions when it was right,—"ex-
ceptional moments in the life and history of nations,
not to be judged by normal rules of human justice,
and in which the actors can take their inspiration only
from their conscience and God."   Tyrannicide was
justifiable, when it was the only means, and the
successful means, of staying an intolerable oppression.

It was a commonplace to glorify Judith and Brutus and Charlotte Corday; it was hypocrisy, he said, begging his own postulates, to condemn for the same actions the men who tried to kill Louis Napoleon or Ferdinand of Naples.[1] In every other case he "abominated" political assassination. It is, he says, "a crime, if attempted with the idea of revenge or punishment; a crime when there are other roads to freedom open; culpable and mistaken, when directed against a man, whose tyranny does not descend into the grave with him." When, for instance, Cavour charged him with plotting to kill Victor Emmanuel, he indignantly replied that the King's life was "protected, first by the existence of a constitution, next by the uselessness of the crime." With one exception only, he was loyal to his profession. Young Italy explicitly abandoned the Carbonaro tradition of assassinating traitors, and so far as its founder could control the society, it never sinned against the precept. The forged charge of the French government in 1833 that he ordered the murder of some spies at Rodez was amply exposed, when Sir James Graham repeated it in 1845, though the Paris correspondent of the *Times* was not ashamed to drag the libel up again nineteen years afterwards. When Triumvir at Rome, Mazzini vigorously repressed the assassinations there and at Ancona. He was absolutely ignorant of Orsini's attempt to assassinate Louis Napoleon, though he disdained to defend himself from the suspicion of complicity, partly because he scorned the puny libellers of the press, partly

---

[1] Walter Savage Landor wrote to one of Mazzini's friends, promising £95 for the family "of the first patriot, who asserts the dignity and fulfils the duty of tyrannicide."

because "Europe needed a bugbear to frighten it and his name would do as well as any other." The charges that he was privy to Tibaldi's and Greco's plots against the Emperor were certainly in the latter case, and almost as certainly in the former, inventions of the French police. Late in life, he vigorously discouraged plots to assassinate the Pope and Victor Emmanuel, and stopped another to explode six bombs at a ball given at Venice by the Austrian Viceroy. In one case only—in early life—Mazzini was in some sense an accomplice in an assassination plot. In the midst of the preparations for the Savoy raid, a young Corsican, Antonio Gallenga,[1] who afterwards settled in England and was for some time special correspondent of the *Times* in Italy, came to him with a plan to assassinate Charles Albert in revenge for the Genoese executions. Mazzini tried to dissuade him, but at last persuaded himself that Gallenga was an appointed agent of Providence "to teach despots that their life may depend on the will of a single man." He gave Gallenga the means of travelling to Turin and sent him a dagger; but he seems to have given little more thought to the matter, perhaps concluding on reflection that, as proved to be the case, Gallenga had no stuff in him for the business.[2]

Manin's indictment aimed equally at the use of the knife in popular insurrections. Mazzini's answer here was easier but less ingenuous in its applications. It was cant, he properly replied, to call it no murder, if

[1] *Alias* Luigi Mariotti, writer of Italian grammar books for English schools.
[2] For some of the evidence on these cases, I may refer to my *History of Italian Unity*, II. 385-387. See also Uccellini, *Memorie*, 209-210; Mazzini, *Lettere ad A. Giannelli*, 301, 437. Signor Dagnino tells me from his personal knowledge that in 1864 Mazzini stopped a plot to blow up the Austrian Viceroy of Venetia.

a soldier shot an enemy with his rifle, and murder, if an artisan conspirator stabbed an Austrian soldier with the only weapon he possessed. Unfortunately he weakened his argument by extending this theory of "irregular warfare" to cases, like those of Rossi or Marinovich, where men had been killed treacherously in revolutionary times for political or private vengeance. Perhaps he was defiantly exaggerating, for before this he had strongly reprobated Rossi's murder; probably he did not know the facts of Marinovich's case. It would at all events be very hard to justify him, when he commissioned Orsini to find men to surprise and kill the Austrian officers at Milan as the first step in an insurrection. It was no lower in its ethics than some established rules of war, but it came sadly below his own more noble estimate of the sacredness of human life.

While Mazzini's theories kicked against the pricks, his political work of these years is a pitiable tale of noble effort all in vain, of high purpose spoilt by obstinacy and incapacity. In the autumn of 1850 he founded a National Italian Committee, which claimed to be a kind of legal successor to the Assembly of the Roman Republic. Practically, though not ostensibly, it was a republican organisation. "The manifesto is moderate," Mazzini wrote privately to Italy, "but behind the manifesto am I, which means, I think, the republic." The ambiguity doomed it from the start. The straiter republicans attacked it as departing from the faith. The much vaster host of democrats, who were learning to believe in the Piedmontese monarchy, held carefully aloof. Others revolted at Mazzini's "intolerable dictatorship"; and the charge was half a true one.

He proudly and sincerely replied to the taunt of personal ambition, but now, as always, he exacted an impossible obedience from his fellow-workers. In Italy the society found a certain following; and Mazzini boasted half-seriously to his friends that the republican flag would be flying on the Quirinal next year. But outside some of the Lombard towns the movement had little real strength; its organisation was too loose to be effective; and one by one the exiles on the Committee drifted away, till in 1853 it died a natural death. The same fate befell a "National Loan," which he had started with the ambitious hope of raising an adequate fund for insurrection. He issued bonds, which were to be honoured by the future Italian state. It was to be "the first act of a financial war, which would prove that the few monarchical or aristocratic possessors of big capitals can be matched by the collective power of the small capitals of democracy." Apparently a good many of the bonds were taken up in Italy, but the money they brought in seems to have been soon exhausted in the expenses of agitation and conspiracy.

Up to this time Mazzini had been inclined to postpone insurrection, till, at all events in his own judgment, it had a fair prospect of success. Unluckily at this moment he was approached by a revolutionary society among the artisans at Milan. He was hesitating whether to encourage them to action, when the ruthless execution by the Austrians of some conspirators at Mantua maddened the men, and they decided on revolt whether he supported them or not. He was very anxious about the scheme and far from hopeful, but he was too generous and impatient to refuse help now. He did what he could to find them money and sympathisers, and late in 1852 he went in disguise to Locarno to complete the preparations. The rising was fixed for the Carnival on February 6, and on the eve of it Mazzini was on the frontier at Chiasso, ready to go on to Milan, as soon as the call came. Had the rising been better organized, it had some small chance of success. As it was, Mazzini learnt at Chiasso that it had smoked itself out in a confused and bloody scuffle. The business was disastrous to him, and he came out with reputation badly damaged. The responsibility was fixed on him, and he accepted it, though he had only been drawn into a plan that others made. His friends in Italy had published a two-years-old appeal from Kossuth urging the Hungarian regiments in the garrison to revolt, and whether or not Kossuth authorized its publication now, had made unjustifiable alterations in the wording. Mazzini was responsible, if at all, only in not taking precautions to prevent the issue, but he did not make matters better, when he pleaded that men, who were risking their lives for their country, were " not amenable by strictly punctilious rules of normal times." [1] The fatuousness and mismanagement of the whole business, the pity of the wasted lives, a feeling that these ill-judged risings hindered the cause and damaged it in the eyes of Europe, hastened the stampede from his

[1] Mazzini's and Kossuth's letters on the subject are in the *Daily News* of February 19, March 2 and 4, 1853. See also Mazzini, *Scritti*, VIII. 283-4. He seems to have made a disingenuous use of another proclamation by Kossuth later in the year : see Bianchi, *Vicende del Mazzinianismo*, 85. I hardly think that Mr Stillman's statement in his *Union of Italy*, p. 275, can stand against Kossuth's plain statement in the *Daily News*. Mr Stillman too is wrong as to Mazzini's share in the rising. I am inclined on the whole to think that he was justified in using Agostino's name ; see *Daily News*, February 17 and 20, 1853.

own party.   He still kept a considerable though
reduced hold on the artisans in a few towns of the
North, but among the middle classes his following
shrank to nearly nothing.

Even he almost despaired.   He felt himself "accursed by all," the "scapegoat on whom all the faults of
Israel will be heaped with a curse."   The Piedmontese
press loaded him with shameful scurrility ; and there
seems to have been an attempt to assassinate him.
He fretted with the sense of failure, with something
like remorse at the sufferings of the conspirators under
the Austrians' brutal vengeance.   But instead of taking
the moral of the failure home, he broke into invective
against the Piedmontese, and only plunged more
desperately into schemes of insurrection.   He had
been misled into suspecting an understanding between
France and Piedmont to create French protectorates
in the South and Centre ; and he was eager to checkmate it by forcing on the movement for unity and
a revolutionary war with Austria.   He had two main
plans of operation.   For one, the revolutionising of
South Italy, he could, though anxious for immediate
action, at present only sow the seed.   The other was
to organise guerilla fighting in the Alps and Northern
Apennines and encourage the Lombard cities to revolt.
He had persuaded himself that the fast-maturing
Eastern question gave a favourable chance of attacking
Austria.   Her policy of see-saw between the Western
Powers and Russia had won her the ill-will of both
sides, and she had been obliged to denude her Italian
garrisons to concentrate troops on the Russian frontier.
Mazzini had vague hopes, too, of help from America.
Kossuth's lecturing tour in the States in 1852 had ex-

cited an angry feeling against Austria. The American government was irritated by the unfriendly attitude of France and England, and perhaps had its designs on Cuba; and Mazzini hoped that it would encourage the revolutionary forces in Europe, in order to keep the Powers occupied at home. George N. Sanders, the American Consul in London, gave a dinner to him and Kossuth and Ledru Rollin, and healths were drunk to a future alliance of America with a federation of the free peoples of Europe.[1] Mazzini's hopes were high. He studied military maps with Kossuth and Ledru Rollin at St John's Wood. He went to Paris and Italy in 1854 in disguise, probably spending most of his time at Genoa, and perhaps on his way paying a visit to Giuditta Sidoli, now silver-haired, and sweet and gracious as ever. His movements worried all the police of Italy and France and Switzerland, and his secret journeys had their romance of clever disguises and audacious escapes. A popular rhyme of the time, attributed to Dall' Ongaro, said:—

> Where is Mazzini? Ask the pines
> Upon the Alps and Apennines.
> He is, wherever traitors cower
> In terror for their fatal hour;
> Where'er men wait impatiently
> To give their blood for Italy.

Mazzini wrote home to England that the people were fretting for action, and would have risen already, "had he not been exceptionally prudent and calm"; in two months more he hoped to have sapped the influence of the royalists, and then "the field will be mine." In August he was in the Engadin, arranging for insurrec-

[1] Mr W. R. Thayer has kindly ascertained for me that there is absolutely nothing in Sanders' correspondence in the U.S.A. Bureau of Rolls, that relates either to Mazzini or Kossuth; but Saffi, who tells the story of the dinner, was present at it himself. See Mazzini, *Scritti*, IX. xciv, 60.

tion in the Valtellin and the Como hill country.   But
the Swiss police broke up the conspirators, and Mazzini
narrowly escaped capture as he came by the Julier
diligence to Chur.

His hopes of Austrian isolation were soon dashed.
Austria nominally joined the Western alliance, and
Piedmont followed her into it and sent a contingent to
the Crimea.   He was bitterly disappointed, and relieved
himself in angry criticisms on English and Piedmontese
policy.   Against Piedmont he turned with sheer
passionate bitterness.   Cavour's adhesion to the
alliance puzzled his own followers; and even now it is
not easy to be sure as to its wisdom, still less as to its
morality.   But at all events everyone else recognised
that the Crimea was intended to be "the road to
Lombardy."   Mazzini, blinded by his partisanship, saw
only proof that Cavour's sympathies were more with
the oppressors than the oppressed.

For the moment all seemed to him a hopeless blank.
His soul was "wasting in a decline," and he longed to
find mechanical work to drug the pain, or break into
some desperate action.   "I am dreaming of, raving,
raging about action, physical action," he wrote.   "I
am sick of the world and all its concerns, and want to
protest."   "Literally," he wrote to another friend, "life
weighs on me.   My feeling towards my country, right
or wrong, is intolerable.   If I were younger, I would
be on a mountain to protest, with twenty or thirty
more.   As I am, I can only eat myself away, and
pretend to smile, to avoid torturing others."   Next
year (1856) his hopes suddenly revived.   There
seemed a chance that Cavour would secretly assist an
insurrection against the Duke of Modena in the Carrara

country. Through this and the two following years the premier had intermittent plans to foment a rising there, which would lead to annexation of the borderland, or be twisted into a *casus belli* with Austria and force Louis Napoleon to send his army across the Alps. He allowed Mazzini to visit Genoa, and carried on communications with him there. What were the details of the plot, we have no means of knowing ; but at all events it was impossible to come to terms. "The Piedmontese government," Mazzini wrote to England, "are a plague. I am indirectly in contact with them and trying all sorts of concessions, but it is of no use. My own position is extremely delicate and difficult between their party and the extreme men of our own. I have now sent a sort of ultimatum to them, which will compromise them, if accepted, or leaves me free, if not." When the rupture came, he turned to his plans for revolutionising the South. For two years past he had been industriously connecting the threads of conspiracy, that Crispi and others had laid in Sicily and Naples. He had met Garibaldi in London, and discussed plans with him for an expedition to the island ; and Garibaldi had promised to go, if the Sicilians revolted and Cavour was willing to cooperate. Again there seemed a hope that the premier would secretly assist. Every patriot saw the danger of Napoleon's fitful scheme to put his cousin, Lucien Murat, on the throne of Naples ; and Cavour, though he dared not openly oppose, would gladly see the scheme checkmated, and he had his own plans for adding Sicily to Victor Emmanuel's kingdom. He seems to have promised funds for Mazzini's design, but again from some unexplained cause he drew back. Mazzini refused to give up his scheme, and indeed the Genoese conspirators were too impatient for action to desist, whether he wished it or not. He went to England to raise money for the project, and returned to Genoa to mature it. Carlo Pisacane, his friend and fellow-exile, a Neapolitan duke with socialist theories that little accorded with his own, was to seize a steamer plying between Genoa and Sardinia, and make for Calabria, there to join hands with the insurgents in the South and raise the country in the name of Unity. The plot was linked to a more questionable plan. It was proposed that the conspirators, who stayed behind, should seize the forts at Genoa and Leghorn and obtain munitions to send on to Pisacane. Mazzini realised the peril of the business, the risk of civil war, the certainty that the movement would be understood as one for the republic rather than for unity. But he easily allowed himself to be persuaded into it. It would, he thought, at all events prove the solidarity of North and South, force on a war with Austria, and prevent the French alliance; and he had a hardly avowed hope that the movement might after all make for a republic. So, taking careful precautions to avoid reprisals on the Genoese conservatives, and prevent if possible a conflict with the troops, he threw himself into the mad plot. Pisacane seized the *Cagliari,* and went to his doom. Mazzini, finding that the government had scent of the design on the forts, tried to stop it at the last moment; but it was too late, and the fatuous attempt ended in some street fighting and a little loss of life. The government struck at its fellow-conspirators of a few months back with a severity, that did little credit to its honesty. It deliberately misrepresented the movement as anarchist. Mazzini and five more, who escaped, were sentenced in contumacy to death; others were sent to long terms of imprisonment. Mazzini took refuge in the house of the Marquis Ernesto Pareto, a relative of the minister of 1848, who concealed him successfully, though the police searched his house and probed the mattresses and the Marchioness' wardrobes with their swords. The story went that Mazzini, disguised as a footman, opened the door to the police-officer who proved to be an old school-fellow and probably recognised him. Some days after he walked out of the house without disguise, arm-in-arm with a Genoese lady, asked the sentry for a light for his cigar, and drove away unsuspected to Quarto, where he remained in safe hiding, till the news of Pisacane's disaster reached him.

Chapter **X**

Unity Half Won

1858-1860.   Aetat 53-55

The war of 1859 — At Florence — Plans for the South — Garibaldi's
Expedition—Projected raid into Umbria—At Naples.

MAZZINI returned to England, weary and sad, but
not discouraged, and convinced that success was only
a question of opportunity and management. He
recognised how strongly the tide was setting towards
the royalists, but he still thought he had the working
classes with him. Cavour's double play and the cruel
repression of the Genoese plot left him bitterer than
ever against the monarchy and its men. " I have
never loved you," he wrote in an open letter to the
premier ; " now I despise you." He attacked more
angrily still the fast-cementing alliance with France.
The Emperor was maturing his plans to drive the
Austrians out of Italy. It was not, as Mazzini
thought, mere policy alone that moved him. No
doubt, his waning prestige at home, and the fear
that another Orsini might arise, both had their
influence ; but he was still true in a way to his
nationalist ideals, and since he had sacrificed Poland
to the Russian alliance, he was the more eager to
free Italy and Hungary. Mazzini, through his private

channels of information, was among the first to have
an inkling of the compact between Cavour and the
Emperor at Plombières, but, as usual, his information
was inaccurate.   He believed, quite wrongly, as we
know now, that they had agreed to leave Venetia
to Austria and give Central Italy to Prince Napoleon,
and that Cavour had offered to surrender the parliamentary liberties of Piedmont as the price of Lombardy ; he had no knowledge that Napoleon had
promised that half the Pope's territory should pass
to Victor Emmanuel's crown.

Events moved fast. ⁄In the spring of 1859, thanks
to Cavour's unscrupulous but supremely skilful
diplomacy, war was imminent, and all Italy was
fretting for it.   Cavour was hardy and shrewd enough
to use the revolutionary elements, on whose value
Mazzini had laid insistent stress.   The volunteers
flocked to Piedmont with Garibaldi for their general,
and, except for Mazzini and Crispi and a stranded
handful, the republicans declared definitely for Victor
Emmanuel's leadership.   Even Mazzini was sometimes carried by the tide. He told his English
friends that royalists and republicans were aiming
equally at Unity ; he appealed to the Piedmontese
statesmen to pronounce for the greater policy, and
if the French alliance broke down, he was prepared
to support them.   But he could not reconcile himself
to the hated Emperor's help⁄ Shutting his eyes to
the hard facts, he thought that Piedmont could defeat
Austria with no other allies than the hesitating
revolutionaries of Hungary.   To ask assistance from
a despot blighted the country's self-respect ; to win
its freedom, save by its own unaided strength, dis-

honoured it at the birth; and it were small gain to change the tyranny of Austria for the domineering patronage of France. " I am equally hostile to Austria and to Napoleon," he wrote; " and my double aim is to get rid, if possible, of both." /When war was declared, Cavour and he both said, " the die is cast "; Cavour added, " we have made history," Mazzini " we are beaten."/ But when the fighting began, when, in spite of his previsions, the enthusiasm swept through the land, and for a moment Louis Napoleon was, next to the king and Garibaldi, the hero of his countrymen, he could not hold back. Be it right or wrong, the best must be made of the war; it might yet, in the end, make Italy. Modena and Parma, Romagna and Tuscany had driven out their princes and declared for Victor Emmanuel's rule. While the armies were winning Lombardy and Venetia, he wished to see the popular forces overrun all the Centre and make an end of the Temporal Power. He appealed to his friends at Naples to revolutionise the South, though he urged that they should not annex themselves to Piedmont, while the war lasted. After Solferino he was very hopeful. " The Austrian domination in Italy," he said, " is at an end."

Suddenly came the great betrayal of Villafranca. Louis Napoleon, afraid of defeat in Venetia, afraid of an attack from Prussia, repentant of his promises to Cavour, made peace with Austria, and abandoned Venetia to the enemy and Central Italy to the fugitive princes. Mazzini took credit for prophesying it; and what came of the Emperor's timidity and the real difficulties of the situation, he regarded as the pre-determined treachery of Plombières. Relying again on his imperfect private information, he thought he had discovered an understanding between France and Russia to partition Europe into spheres of influence, and that Villafranca was a prelude to a triple alliance of the three Empires. He fulminated against "the European *coup d'état*"; he appealed to English fears, and preached a league of England, Prussia, and the smaller states in defence of Italian freedom. At home he urged a truce to party feeling and the completing of the work in despite of France and Austria. He voiced the feeling of the country. Cavour had resigned in hot anger at the Emperor's desertion; but his influence was still very powerful, and he and the King and the men, who were at the head of affairs at Florence and Modena, were no less determined than the democrats that at least Central Italy should be saved. All through the autumn their obstinate stand baffled the Emperor's half-hearted veto, and pushed on the feeble men, who now held office at Turin. The key of the position was at Florence, and Ricasoli, the stark Tuscan baron, who was practically dictator there, believed with a faith as fearless as Mazzini's own that Italian Unity, pregnant with mighty issues for the world, was written in the decrees of God. He too detested Napoleon, and was determined not to flinch for all his threats.

Mazzini hurried to Florence, and arrived there early in August. The Piedmontese government, to its shame, had excluded the greatest of living Italians from the amnesty, which it granted at the beginning of the war; but Ricasoli allowed Mazzini to remain un-

molested, on his parole that his presence at Florence
should not be publicly known.   There was not a little
in common between the two men,—both stainless in
their private lives, brave, honest, single-minded patriots.
They were, indeed, too uncompromising to work together ; but they sincerely respected each other, and
Ricasoli had none of the narrowness, that made the
Turin statesmen shrink from contact with a democrat.
Mazzini's policy was the same as it had been during
the war.   The people must make the movement as
far as possible their own.   He addressed to them a
rhapsodical appeal to nerve themselves for the great
work.   "You are called," he said, "to a task like the
tasks of God, the creation of a people."   The free
provinces of the Centre must hold fast to their freedom.
Louis Napoleon, he knew, could not enforce his veto ;
the Powers would accept accomplished facts ; the
danger of an Austrian attack he said little of.   At
heart, though, he knew that the perils were thicker
than he publicly owned, and he confessed in private
letters that "the position was more than difficult,"
that, if the suggested Congress of the Powers met and
declared in favour of the exiled princes, Italy could
only make an ineffectual "protest in action."   He
almost hoped that Napoleon would use force after all,
and that a war with France would come to simplify
the situation.

   With a good deal of hesitation, he was prepared to
support annexation to Piedmont.   He promised to
foment no republican agitation, so long as the royalists
marched towards Unity ; and he wrote the King an
irritating but dignified appeal to have done with the
subserviency to France and bid openly for the crown

of Italy. "The day you speak this language," he
said, "parties will disappear; there will be only two
living forces in Italy,—the People and yourself." He
does not seem however to have really expected to win
him. "The King," he wrote privately in reference to
the letter, "is wavering and weak, but on him I did
not reckon." Victor Emmanuel appears, though, to
have read the appeal and taken it to heart, and
perhaps it had its influence on the events that followed.
Mazzini's supreme aim was to spread the movement
for Unity. If the government would not act, the
people must do the work themselves. He wanted to
make Tuscany and Romagna the base for an invasion
of the Pope's remaining territory; and then—onward
to Naples and the South. The hope was shared by
all the democrats and many of the moderates; but
with Mazzini it meant something even more than
Unity. It meant the triumph of religious liberty at
Rome, the downfall of "the Vicar of the Genius of
Evil," the chance that on the wreck of the Papacy
Rome would send forth the gospel of the new religion.
"The liberty of Rome," he wrote, "is the liberty of
the world. If Rome revolts, she must proclaim the
victory of God over Idols, of eternal Truth over
Falsehood, the inviolability of the human conscience."
He urged his English and German friends to stir
public opinion against the French occupation of Rome,
and put pressure on Napoleon in the name of the
principle of non-intervention.

Meanwhile he sent his agents to prepare a Sicilian
rising, and agitated feverishly for an advance of
Garibaldi and the troops of the Central States into
Umbria, which the Papal volunteers had recovered

from the nationalists.   He had thoughts of leading the invasion himself, but he feared that his name "would frighten the mass of the people," and he humoured Garibaldi by promising to make him the hero of the movement and "abdicating my own individuality, which is the easiest part."   He won Farini, the dictator of Modena, once a member of Young Italy, to countenance the raid.   He tried to win Ricasoli, but Ricasoli, though he had threatened to join hands with Mazzini rather than let Tuscany lose its freedom, knew that the dangers of a forward movement were too great at present, that if the Pope were attacked, the outcry of Catholic Europe would compel Napoleon to withdraw his indispensable, however irritating, patronage, and that Italy would find herself caught in a hopeless single-handed fight with Austria.   His own strong will and the King's common-sense stopped Garibaldi's projects.   Mazzini, ignorant of the real position, underrated the difficulties in the way ; he never realised the strength of Catholic opinion, he thought that Austria was not in a position to fight, or that, if she did, it meant an uprising of all Italy and her eventual defeat.   He charged the King's veto to mere truckling to Napoleon.   But he felt his own powerlessness.   He was incensed by the harshness, with which the government had treated some of his friends, by the intolerance that drove himself to live in hiding.   "To be a prisoner among our own people is too much to bear."   "I have never," he wrote, "felt so wretched and worn out in mind and soul as at certain moments now."   Ricasoli intimated that he must leave Tuscany, and hopeless of doing any good there, he left for Lugano and returned to England at the end of the year.

His ideas had passed to men more competent to execute them. In January Cavour was again prime minister, resolute to have Unity with Rome for the capital, prepared, if the Emperor deserted him, to attack Austria, rouse Hungary in her rear, and, so he hoped in sanguine moments, "go to Vienna." But he knew how heavy was the stake, and he would keep the Emperor's protection if he could. When he found that Napoleon would guarantee the annexation of the free provinces at the price of Nice and Savoy, he sadly and reluctantly consented to the humiliating bargain. Mazzini read him by his despatches, and knew nothing of his real ambitions. He thought that the premier was opposed to Unity, even to the annexation of Tuscany, that he clung to the French alliance to safeguard himself from democracy at home. He was indignant at the cession of Savoy, bartered without reference to the wishes of its people, still more at the desertion of Italian Nice. He was eager to drive from office the man, on whom depended the attainment of his hopes. / He was right, however, in thinking that Cavour could not initiate the revolution in the South, that the government would only follow up what the free lances began ; and he was willing to make the road easier for it, by promising, when revolution broke out in the South, to support annexation to Piedmont and leave Rome alone for the present/ He was persuaded that Austria would not attack, and that the Bourbon army would dissolve or join the insurgents.

The programme seemed so simple, that he hoped to unite all the democrats upon it. But the saner men among them saw that, as usual, Mazzini had underrated the danger. They knew that it meant harder fighting than he supposed, and they dreaded a repetition of his earlier ill-starred risings. They insisted that, if the volunteers went to Sicily, Garibaldi must lead them and Cavour's moral support must be secured. Mazzini was ready to welcome Garibaldi's leadership, though there was no very cordial feeling between them; but he knew how reluctant Garibaldi was to go, and he refused to let the movement hang on any one man's action. Early in March, while Garibaldi was still hesitating,[1] he sent Rosalino Pilo, a young Sicilian noble, to lead the insurgents in the island, spending every available shilling of his own in the preparations. He was terribly overwrought and excited, for he must have realised something of the tremendous danger and responsibility; and he travelled to Lugano to be nearer the scene of action. There he learnt that his long efforts had had their fruit, that the impatience he had done so much to rouse had borne down Garibaldi's doubts, and that he and his Thousand had started for Sicily. "God be praised," he wrote, "Italy is not dead." When the news came of Garibaldi's victory at Calatafimi, "Sicily saves us," he said, "Italy will be."

---

[1] The following letter from Garibaldi has, I believe, not been published: I have translated it.

CAPRERA, *March 27, '60*

DEAR MAZZINI,—I am thinking of leaving for Genoa on April 1, from there I shall go to Nice, where I am summoned by my fellow-citizens, who are afraid of falling into the wolf's mouth. I enclose two lines for McAdam [Mr John McAdam of Glasgow]. If you come, let me know.— Your brother, GIUSEPPE.

P.S.—Mr Adam of Glasgow will send Mr William Ashurst a sum for the Million Rifles Fund; please spend it in the purchase of the rifles in question.—G. GARIBALDI.

On May 7, two days after Garibaldi started, he arrived at Genoa, still compelled to live in hiding, and able to see his friends only by night. Characteristically, he amused himself in leisure moments by taming sparrows, which came to him at meal-times, followed by two hens (" I have always been fond of hens," he writes), "whom I feed after dinner, sometimes with bread and wine to strengthen their constitutions against shocks and adversities." He was not welcomed by the men who had organised the expedition, and he found himself regarded as "a self-intruding man," he who was ever ready to take the risk and give others the honour, who was bracing his frail body only by sheer sense of duty. " God knows," he wrote, " that morally and physically exhausted as I am, everything I do is a real effort." But the suspicion of his motives was inevitable. Absolutely disinterested as he was, ever ready to spend and be spent, he was again playing an ill-informed. and equivocal part, thrusting in his unwise projects among the well-laid schemes of shrewder men ; and those who had organised Garibaldi's movement with consummate skill—Bertani and Medici and Bixio—felt that his independent action might spoil the game.[1] He clung to his insensate prejudice against Cavour, at a time when Cavour,—with whatever lapse of political morality,—was straining every nerve to back Garibaldi and win all Italy. In his persistent distrust of the government and its connections with the Emperor, he wanted to act independently of though not in hostility to the monarchy, and while he urged annexation in Sicily to checkmate the separatists in the island, he was eager to prevent it on the mainland, and reserved his freedom to preach his own doctrines there.

[1] Rival funds for Mazzini and Garibaldi were collected in England and there was some strong feeling between their respective backers.

While Garibaldi snatched victory after victory against tremendous odds in Sicily, he was planning a raid into Papal territory, more or less under his own direction; his volunteers, he hoped, would not only free the rest of Central Italy and attack the Bourbons from the North, but would create an influence, independent alike of Cavour and Garibaldi, which might perhaps in the chapter of accidents upset the monarchy, or at least compel it to break with France.   He did not suspect how perilous the situation was, that it was still only Louis Napoleon's protection, that stood between Italy and a terrible conflict with Austria in the North and Bourbons in the South, with utter disaster as its almost certain sequel.   Ricasoli and, it seems, the King [1] gave some countenance to the raid, for which Mazzini and Bertani were, with Garibaldi's approval, completing the preparations.   But Cavour knew that it meant the forfeiture of the Emperor's friendship, and arranged with Bertani, who was throughout lukewarm for the scheme, terms which would at all events save his own credit with the Emperor.   The force, which had been destined for the Papal coast, sailed to join Garibaldi in Sicily. Mazzini either did not know of the agreement or refused to be bound by it; he went to Florence, where another body of volunteers was waiting in the neighbourhood ready to cross the frontier, and intended to lead them to a desperate attack on Perugia.   Cavour insisted that the men should be disbanded, and

[1] According to a letter from Mazzini to Brofferio, published in *Roma e Venezia*, January 15, 1861, (the full text of which I have not seen), the King seems to have asked for an interview with him, and he had "no shadow of difficulty in principle" to it.

Ricasoli, tempering the premier's orders, persuaded them to go to Garibaldi.

Less than a month after, the Piedmontese declared war against the Pope, and Fanti,—Mazzini's follower once in the days of the Savoy raid,—overran such of the Pope's remaining territory as was not occupied by the French. Garibaldi, victoriously advancing from the South, had entered Naples, and save for Rome and its neighbourhood and a small district held by the remnants of the Bourbon army, all the Centre and the South were free. Austria, frightened by Napoleon's threats, had been a passive spectator, while her allies were crushed. Italian Unity was nearly won, but the splendid consummation was dashed by the dread of civil strife. Garibaldi, careless of obstacles, was impatient to march on to Rome; Cavour knew that that meant war with France and would have it at no cost. Crispi and Bertani were trying to organise the South in an opposition to Cavour and his party, that might easily take a republican colour. Mazzini went to Naples, and warmly backed them. He urged Garibaldi to go on, though by preference to Venice rather than to Rome, for he saw now almost as acutely as Cavour did the danger of a conflict with France. If Garibaldi advances, he wrote to England, "we shall have Unity within five months; if he does not, we shall have slumber, then anarchy, then—a little later—Unity." He appealed to the Neapolitans to save the principle of popular sovereignty by conditioning their annexation to Victor Emmanuel's crown with the stipulation that an Italian National Assembly should meet to draw up a new constitution. The cry was a futile and dangerous one, for the mass of the people

were impatient for annexation on any terms; and
with trouble threatening the young country on every
side, it were madness to throw its future into the
melting-pot of the constitution-mongers. It was easy
to paint Mazzini as an enemy of Unity; and a
Neapolitan mob shouted 'death' under the windows
of the man, who had given everything for them.
Pallavicino, the pro-dictator, Manin's old co-worker
and Garibaldi's friend, courteously appealed to him to
leave. "Even against your wish," he said, "you
divide us." Mazzini refused to waive an Italian's right
to live on Italian soil; and he was molested no more.
Garibaldi indignantly intervened on his behalf; the
King probably protected him. "Leave Mazzini alone,"
he had said, "if we make Italy, he is powerless; if we
cannot, let him do it, and I will be *Monsù Savoia* and
clap my hands for him." But Mazzini was bitterly
pained and weary of it all. "I am worn out morally
and physically," he wrote; "for myself the only really
good thing would be to have unity achieved quickly
through Garibaldi, and one year before dying of
Walham Green[1] or Eastbourne, long silences, a few
affectionate words to smooth the ways, plenty of sea-
gulls, and sad dozing." Early in November, after a
friendly interview with Garibaldi, at which they laid
their schemes for winning Rome and Venice, he left
Naples.

[1] Where Mr Stansfeld had his brewery and sometimes lived.

Chapter XI

For Venice

1861-1866. AETAT 56-61.

Policy after 1860—Disappointment in Italy—Rome and Venice—Attitude towards the monarchy—Life in England—the Greco plot—American and Irish politics—Mazzini and Garibaldi—Overtures from Victor Emmanuel—The war of 1866.

MAZZINI'S remaining life is one of melancholy pathos. He could not rest, till Unity was accomplished. Aged and often very ill and suffering, longing for quiet and literature, he braced his frail body and unhappy soul to the fret and weariness and disillusioning of politics. Could one be sure that it profited country or mankind, one would rest content, knowing that he had chosen the hard path and never flinched. But it was—at all events in the near results—a grievous waste. Those splendid faculties were worn, as he would sometimes own himself, in rolling the stone of Sisyphus. Had he given these years to the book on religion, that he ever kept in mind, to building up "the church of the precursors," he might perhaps have done a thing yet greater than the making of Italy. His political work henceforth was mostly thrown away; for, as he said, his star was the Dog, and his business "to bark, generally without being heard." Gloriously right in his ideals, he marred it all by ignorance of facts. His nearer vision failed in blinding partisanship, in his obdurate hatred of Louis Napoleon and suspicion of the Italian statesmen. He could not see that the royalists were aiming at Unity almost as seriously and more wisely than himself, that Louis Napoleon wished to be his country's friend, and that the Emperor's hesitations and backslidings were concessions to the relentless pressure of Catholic opinion. He could not escape from his own past, he had a feverish, unreasoned craving for a single form of action, he could not see that conspiracy and insurrection, which had their justification and chance of success twenty years ago, had neither now. It is perhaps never easy for one man to be both idealist and statesman,—for Mazzini, with his passion and inflexibility, least of all. He could not leave it to other men to achieve his ideals in their own way. He had a dangerous belief that he had "the instinct of the situation," and would never own in politics that others might have their fragment of the truth. This obstinate rebellion—covert or open—against the verdict of his countrymen,—was it the heroism of the one righteous man, or was it, as one of his old friends called it, "a huge egotistical presumption?" Or was it rather the noble error of one, who, with his mind fixed on the highest, scorns the high? Who shall say, who does best service for humanity, he who seeks the small attainable, or he who 'heaven's success finds or earth's failure?'

Mazzini knew that he had failed in the near results. He was a disappointed man. He had indeed the pride that his utopia had come so near accomplishment. But it had come by another way than that which he had marked for it, it had fallen very short of what he looked for. He had idealised his country in his mighty love, till disillusion was inevitable. "I saw," he wrote, "a great void in Europe, a void of any community of belief or of faith, and therefore of initiative and worship of duty and solemn moral principles, of great ideas and potent action for the classes which produce most and yet which are most wretched ; and I thought that Italy would rise and save Europe, and, soon as it breathed its own new life, would say to itself and others, 'I will fill that void.'" "Little it matters to me," he wrote to "Daniel Stern," "that Italy, a territory of so many square leagues, eats its corn and cabbages cheaper ; little I care for Rome, if a great European initiative is not to issue from it. What I do care for is that Italy shall be great and good, moral and virtuous, that she comes to fulfil a mission in the world." So he had dreamed, and woke to find it but a dream. In bitter exaggeration he reproached his countrymen for being "less than their fathers and their destinies." /In his favourite phrase, new Italy had found its inspiration not in Dante but in Macchiavelli. There was no high principle, no true religion, no sense of freedom's dignity. His criticism was partly a true one. / The feeble statesmen, who succeeded Cavour and Ricasoli, opportunists almost all, some of them mere tricksters, may well have roused his anger and contempt. The country had become the hunting-ground of office-hunters and speculators, who, as Giuditta Sidoli said, "have made Italy and now are eating it." The antagonism of North and South, the jealousy of Piedmont, the brigandage, the financial chaos were symptoms of a dangerous discontent. Few cared

for the great moral hopes, the "living apostolate" of
Italy.   But Mazzini did not understand the value of
the sane, wholesome patriotism, that had made Italy
in its own way, or see how great the step had been,
that had brought the country political and social
freedom.   In his absorption in the political question,
he paid at this time small attention to the social
changes that were going on ; he never alludes to the
great cooperative movement, that was beginning in
Italy in these years.

But beyond all this, Unity was not complete, and
its completion was the one thing necessary.   The
triumph of nationality, the cause of morality and
religion, alike in Italy and Europe, depended, he
believed, on the winning of Rome and Venice.   "I
have to kill myself with work," he wrote, " for Venice,
for Rome, for the republic, in order to make the
instrument."   The winning of Rome meant the downfall of the Papacy, the triumph of liberty of conscience,
the dawn of a new religion.   The winning of Venetia
meant the break-up of the Austrian Empire, and a
great reconstruction of Central and Eastern Europe,
in which Italy would prove her mission as the "guide
of oppressed nationalities."   "Providence," he said, "has
written that the function of initiative is a necessary
condition of the life of Italy.   We cannot live without
a European life ; if we free ourselves, we must free
others.   We must be great or perish."   For Rome
he was willing to wait.   Wiser than Garibaldi, he
saw that any attempt to win it by force meant war
at once with France and Austria, and he knew that
that meant ruin.   His Roman policy was at bottom
that of the Piedmontese statesmen,—to secure the

withdrawal of the French by the force of public opinion. He urged that there should be "a temperate but weighty remonstrance" from parliament, backed by half a million Italian signatures. He prompted petitions in England to ask the government to use its influence in the same direction,—a spur that Lord John Russell hardly needed. But he rightly saw that Venice must take precedence. Italy, he thought, was strong enough to fight Austria alone, and he made extravagant calculations as to their relative military strength. Only there must be no French alliance, no more paltering with the false prophet of nationality. Cavour and his successors, except for brief backslidings, were at one with him in the resolve never to call in again the dangerous help of France. But he would not believe this, and he hoped both to make the French alliance impossible and force the government into war with Austria, by fomenting a rising in Venetia or encouraging volunteers under Garibaldi to attack it. Italy's allies must be the nationalities of the East, which had a common interest with her in breaking up the Austrian Empire,—an idea which he shared with the King and Cavour and others of the Italian statesmen. If Venetia and the Balkan countries rose, Hungary would follow, and "war with Austria would dissolve the Empire in twenty days." With Austria, Turkey would go too, for the two despotisms, he held, must stand or fall together. The Polish rising of 1863 made him still more impatient. His love of "poor, sacred Poland" was strong as in the days of Young Europe. Forgetting that a resuscitated Poland was bound to add its weight to the Catholic and anti-Italian coalition, he reproached his countrymen for

G

their indifference to the people, which had sent its sons to fight for Italy ; and he tried to charter a steamer to take a cargo of arms to a Lithuanian port. He industriously encouraged the pro-Polish movement in England, and talked of organising a Hyde Park meeting.

At home, he was still for some years yet willing to suspend any open republican agitation. He indeed attacked the government with increasing acerbity ; he fretted at its delays, he was irritated by the libels of the royalist press. But though he held the monarchy to be the source of all the trouble, he would not openly declare against it. He kept up a secret republican propagandism in view of future possibilities, but so long as there was any hope that the monarchy would go to Venice and Rome, he would not harass it by a barren agitation. He knew in fact, that, so long as that hope remained, the " ice-wall " of popular timidity made the republic impossible, and he was angrily attacked by the intransigents for his saner view. He was anxious for the present even to postpone any agitation for reform, though he pleaded insistently that, when the work of unity was done, a Constituent Parliament should meet to draw up a " national pact," which was apparently to be an ill-defined constitution, temporarily admitting a democratic monarchy, and defining the social duties of the country and the respective functions of state and local bodies. He had a bold domestic programme, whose chief articles were a universal volunteer system, the nationalisation of railways, mines, church lands, and " some great industrial undertakings," state encouragement for productive cooperative societies, and a reorganisation of local government on a basis of some twelve large "regions" and big, amalgamated communes.

Meanwhile, save for an occasional visit to Switzerland, he was living in England, where he returned after leaving Naples at the end of 1860. Here in new lodgings at 2 Onslow Terrace, Brompton, he returned to the old life of the fifties. The days were spent in the weary round of letter-writing, but it was often a physical torture now, and failing eyesight made it impossible to go on after dark. In the evening he had two hours' reading, then went to the Stansfelds' neighbouring house in Thurlow Square, to return home at eleven and read his letters and the Italian papers. His personal life was more and more a struggle with failing health. Earlier attacks he had conquered by force of will. "Make an effort of will and be well; I have often successfully done so," he wrote once to a friend; and again, "I hear that you are rather unwell. Don't. It is absurd to be ill, while nations are struggling for liberty." He had always scorned medicine and doctors, and had an especial detestation for "that infernal irony of homæopathy, for which Hahnemann must atone somehow, somewhere." But now he had often to succumb to an internal trouble, which brought acute pain and sometimes prostrated him. He no doubt smoked too much, and a few years after this Lloyd Garrison tried in vain to break him off the habit. Rheumatism made him "stiff like an English statesman." He could not eat his landlady's ill-cooked dinners, and hid the untouched food rather than hurt her feelings. Now and again he would feel he had "more than ever the ardour of a young man with all the obstinacy of an old one"; more often he knew that work was killing him, and he had a recurring presentiment that he would not live through each new year. He had financial troubles again to worry him. His small annuity was not enough to meet his heavy doctor's bills, and a royalty, which he had been receiving for the collected edition of his writings, failed through the unwillingness or inability to pay of his Milanese publisher. A subscription was raised for him in Italy, but it was passed on to his Venetian fund, and probably most of the £500, that were collected for him in England in 1866, went to public purposes. Serene and cheerful as ever on the outside, he had moods of great depression. "I am sick of men and things," he wrote, "and long for a desperate peace." "Morally," he writes to "Daniel Stern," with whom he began a steady correspondence at this time, "I am always the same, given up to work without enthusiasm, from a sense of duty ; expecting nothing, hoping for nothing in the scrap of individual life left me ; loving and recognising those I love,[1] not for the joy but for the sorrow they can give me ; believing, as in early youth, in the future I have dreamed of for Italy and the world ; sick at the present, but resigned and calm, if people don't talk too much of materialist pantheism or tactics or happiness or French music." When Lincoln was assassinated, he contrasted sadly with himself the man who died in the knowledge that his cause had triumphed.

His literary work at this time was unimportant, for politics and sickness used up his strength ; but his longings went, as ever, to a life of study. "I should like," he wrote, "to drag myself from library to library, from one monastic archives to another, to unearth

---

[1] *Reconnaissant ceux que j'aime ;* one suspects an omission of *à.*

some lines of a great forgotten thinker, Joachim for instance." Mystical writers, like Joachim and Eckhart, attracted him more strongly than ever; and he seems to have joined an esoteric society in Italy, which had Dante for its spiritual chief. Modern spiritualism, however, only irritated him; "when men have ceased to believe in God," he said, "God pays them out by making them believe in Cagliostro or table-turning."

His admiration of English life was stronger than ever. He held up for Italian imitation its freedom of life and thought, notwithstanding his suspicions that his letters still ran the risk of being tampered with in the English Post-Office. He had words of praise even for the monarchy and aristocracy, but predicted that the growing power of financial magnates would prove the death of both. It was about this time that he became again a prominent figure in English politics. A Calabrian, named Greco, attempted to assassinate Louis Napoleon. Mazzini had had no part in or knowledge of the plot; but he had known Greco in the past, and letters from him were found on the assassin. The French police caught at the opportunity to bring odium on him and inculpate Stansfeld, whose name and address were found in one of his letters. Without any particle of evidence to connect the letters with the plot, the French court condemned Mazzini; and the Tories and Irish in the House of Commons gleefully used the handle given them to discredit his English friend. Stansfeld, who was a member of the government, resigned office rather than embarrass his colleagues, but the insincerity of the attack was as clear as its audacious shamelessness. The incident had its sequel of comedy, when Disraeli, who had been foremost in denouncing the imagined sympathy with assassination, was confronted with a *Revolutionary Epick* of his own youthful days, in which he had blessed "the regicidal steel."

Mazzini keenly watched the American Civil War. He had for many years felt intensely about slavery, and he now gave his sympathy and subscription to the London Emancipation Society, which was enlisting English sympathy for the North. " I believe," he wrote to his friend, Mr W. Malleson, who was its Secretary, "that in these times of ours there are three things, against which a man ought to protest before dying, if he wants to die in peace with his own conscience : slavery—capital punishment—and the actual either narrow or hypocritical condition of the religious question." "Abolition," he wrote to Mr Moncure Conway, "is the religious consecration of your battles." But he was not equally enthusiastic for the Union. In curious inconsistency with his usual preference for big nations, he thought that America was "wide enough for two or three eventual sisterly confederations." When the war was over, he implored the Americans not to impair their victory by refusing the vote to the negroes, though they should see that education went hand in hand with it. Again, as in 1854, he was eager that America should come into world politics, and help to build up the future Europe of nationality and the republic. " You," he said, " have become a leading nation. You may act as such. In the great battle which is fought throughout the world between right and wrong, justice and arbitrary rule, equality and privilege, duty and egotism, republic and monarchy, truth and lies, God and idols, your part is marked ; you must accept it." He hoped that they would upset Napoleon's Mexican scheme, which meant "Imperialism at their own door"; at the time of the suggested Anglo-French intervention, when American feeling was bitter against England, he wrote, "war with England would be a crime and a fault; war for Mexico a holy thing." Shortly before Lincoln's assassination, he and Ledru Rollin and Karl Blind wrote to the President, urging the danger to the Union that threatened from Mexico, and suggesting a cooperation with the democrats of Europe, that would weaken or upset Napoleon. Apparently the plan was that the Americans should invade Mexico, while their unofficial allies stirred a republican movement in France or organised an attack on Rome. Lincoln seems to have listened to the suggestion not unfavourably. When the Northern army disbanded after the war, Mazzini would have liked to see the men go as volunteers to aid the Mexicans, and the government "whisper" that it would follow. "It would have done more than anything towards the fraternisation of North and South, and the negroes would have won then, undisputed, the right to the suffrage."

A few years later, he was much concerned in the fate of the Fenian prisoners. "I am feeling," he writes, "between the unhappy and the furious about the Fenians condemned. To-day, I think, is the Queen's birthday. Does she read a newspaper? Cannot she find a womanly feeling in her heart and ask the Cabinet to commute the punishment? In point of fact, the killing of these men will prove an absolute fault [mistake]. Burke will be the Robert Emmet of 1867. A feeling of revenge will rekindle

the energy of the discouraged Fenians. The dream
will become, through martyrdom, a sort of religion.
But that is not my ground. It is the legal murder
reenacted against a *thought*, a thought which ought to
be refuted, destroyed by thought only. Burke and
others are genuine believers in Irish nationality. I
think they are philosophically and politically wrong ;
but are we to refute a philosophical error with
hanging?" After their reprieve he wrote, "You have
been spared the infamy of Burke's execution. I am
glad of it ; I have a weakness for England, and did
not like the shame for her."

Mazzini's active political work in these years was
given almost wholly to the winning of Venetia.
Before he left Naples in 1860, he and Garibaldi had
agreed to agitate for an attack on either Venetia or
Rome in the following year. But the jealousy, that
was always latent between the two, prevented any
cordial cooperation. The fault was very little on
Mazzini's side. He must have felt it, that Garibaldi,
whose work for the country was so small beside his
own, had eclipsed himself in the nation's imagination ;
but he was ever ready to let him take the honour
and keep himself in the background. Once get
Garibaldi with the volunteers, he said, "and he may
send me to the devil the day after." But Garibaldi
had always some grievance to nurse, and he had not
forgotten the friction at Rome in 1849. Mazzini's
theories irritated him, and he dubbed him "the great
doctrinaire." The most easily led of men, "weak
beyond expression," as Mazzini truly said of him, he
hated it to be thought that he was under anybody's

influence ; and Mazzini complained with cause that "if Garibaldi has to choose between two proposals, he is sure to accept the one that isn't mine." The mischief-makers, who always clustered round the hermit of Caprera, did their best to feed his prejudices. And though the two men were both burning to free Venice and Rome, they had radical differences as to the means. Garibaldi believed in the King ; Mazzini's faith in him was very limited. Garibaldi wanted to have an understanding with the government ; Mazzini generally wished to act independently. He saw that the patriots must concentrate on the freeing of Venice ; Garibaldi was ever running back to his cherished design of marching to Rome, or, if he temporarily abandoned it, he leaned to some knight-errant enterprise in Eastern Europe, where he could attack Austria from the rear.

Meanwhile Minghetti and the less statesmanlike section of the Moderates,—a tepid, craven, weak-principled crew,—wanted to stamp out the democratic agitation ; and it was left comparatively unmolested, thanks only to the bigger outlook of Ricasoli, who had become premier after Cavour's death. Had Ricasoli remained in office, he would have amnestied Mazzini from the sentence of 1857 ; and the greatest of living Italians would have been no longer a felon in his own country. But Ricasoli was driven from office by a cabal ; and Rattazzi, who succeeded him, was too much under bond to Louis Napoleon to pardon the Emperor's enemy. Rattazzi began a double game with Garibaldi, which ended, as Mazzini had predicted, in "a solemn mystification" and the catastrophe of Aspromonte. Mazzini was opposed to the whole foolhardy business, and among his English friends condemned it in strong language; but apparently he helped to collect funds for Garibaldi, and when once Garibaldi took up the cry of "Rome or Death," he thought it his duty to help. The day after the volunteers crossed from Sicily on the tragi-comic march for Rome, he left London to join them. He had got as far as Lugano, when he heard that Italian soldiers had fired on them, and that Garibaldi lay stricken by an Italian bullet. His anguish at the pity of it all brought on delirium. The ghosts of martyr-patriots reproached him, as they had done in 1836; he cried that Garibaldi was dead, and his friends could not quiet his ravings. He recovered quickly, but broke into passionate denunciation of the government, scourging the monarchy as impotent and unwilling to make Italy, and threatening to raise the republican flag again.

The threat was forgotten, as he regained his calmness, and he returned to his old plan of a volunteer movement on Venetia, which the government would be compelled to follow. He was "silently raging at poor, brave Poland being left alone in the field," and hoped that an attack on Austria would save her. It was at this juncture,—in the spring of 1863,—that he received strange overtures for alliance from the King. The two men had always had a certain fascination for each other. Victor Emmanuel shared Mazzini's impatience to win Venetia, his hatred of Austria; he had something of the great agitator's wish to see the nationalities of Eastern Europe free. Both were irritated by the feeble Minghetti ministry, which had come into office after Aspromonte, half-hearted in its nationalist aspirations, dreading the democratic forces, which Cavour would have taken in hand and guided. The fellow-conspirators bargained hard, but, after months of tedious negotiation, they seem to have agreed that Mazzini should foment a rising in Venetia and waive meanwhile any republican movement, that the King should make his government supply arms to the insurgents and eventually declare war, while both would encourage a rising in Hungary or Galicia. It was impossible, however, to give effect to the alliance. The fact of the negotiations leaked out more or less. The Greco plot, though probably few believed that Mazzini was an accomplice, made it difficult for the King to treat with him. The ministers, morbidly afraid of any contact with the revolutionaries, and possibly aware that Mazzini had made their dismissal a condition of his cooperation, remonstrated ; and indeed it shows the King's and Mazzini's small respect for parliamentary government that the personal treaty was attempted at all. The King was irritated at Mazzini's exigencies, and began to transfer his attentions to Garibaldi. Garibaldi at this moment (April 1864) was paying a long promised visit to England, where he had a mythical prestige almost as great as in his own country. As usual he was buffeted by the various influences that sought to capture him. The English Radicals wanted to use him for a series of popular demonstrations ; Palmerston laid his schemes to keep him quiet in the hands of hosts, like the Duke of Sutherland and Charles Seely, the member for Lincoln, who would be responsible for his discreet behaviour. Victor Emmanuel, while still negotiating fitfully with Mazzini, sent his agents to persuade him

to head a rising in Galicia; Mazzini wanted him for
the Venetian movement.   The worthy, puzzled man
tried to please everybody, provided that he appeared
to be managed by nobody.   Mazzini wrote to him to
begin his tour in the provinces at once, before he went
to London; and met him, soon after he arrived, at
Mr Seely's house in the Isle of Wight.   There was a
cordial reconciliation, and Mazzini thought he had won
Garibaldi to his own scheme.   At a breakfast given
by Alexander Herzen, the one rich man among the
exiles, at his house at Teddington, Garibaldi spoke
of Mazzini as the counsellor of his youth and constant
friend.   The incident alarmed the English government,
and their contemptible and dishonourable manœuvres
secured Garibaldi's departure.   Mazzini still supposed
that Garibaldi was faithful to his scheme, and went to
Lugano to forward the preparations for the Venetian
insurrection.

Garibaldi, however, though he had given Mazzini no
hint of his change of mind, had accepted the King's
plan.   The Duke of Sutherland's yacht took him to
Ischia, where he was preparing to sail to the East,
when the secret was given to the world; and the
King, frightened by the publicity, hastily broke from
the plot.   Mazzini, though he tried to persuade Garibaldi
to visit England again and make his abandoned provincial tour (" Newcastle is the best place "), was justly
incensed at him and the King for their want of candour.
He suspected, with good reason, that the ministry had
fallen in with the Galician scheme, for the sake of getting
Garibaldi out of the country and perhaps sending him
to his death.   He was " sick at heart of the equivocal
position," and determined to " go on in a clearer path."
Events helped to bring him back to frank hostility

towards the government. The September Convention, most dishonouring and impolitic of treaties, was concluded, and it seemed to mark, as in the letter it did, a renunciation of the claims to Rome. He passionately denounced the surrender, the " policy of subterfuge and crooked ways," which threatened to founder Italy. " I prefer half a century of slavery to a national lie,' he wrote. He was hoaxed into believing that the government had offered France a large slice of Piedmont to buy her acquiescence in any winning of Venice or Rome. He had a bitter quarrel with Crispi, who was fast sliding down the decline of respectability. Crispi had attacked him in the Chamber, as dividing the country by his republicanism. Mazzini wasted words in retorting on the opportunist, who yesterday had been most intransigent of republicans, and was now parading his new-found faith in the monarchy. He was inclined to break the slender threads, that connected him with the parliamentary Left, "who had laid aside their old democratic ardour to assume the icy demeanour of English members of parliament." But he still hesitated at any complete rupture with the monarchy, so long as any hope remained that the government would attack Austria.

It was doing better than he knew. The outcry at the September Convention had wrecked Minghetti's ministry, and under the brave and honest La Marmora there was some chance of going forward. The negotiations for the Prussian alliance were pushed on, and early in April 1866 the treaty was signed. Mazzini had preached co-operation with Germany in 1851 and 1861, but now he denounced the alliance with " men who represented despotism," an alliance which, he imagined, implied the abandonment of the claims to the Tyrol. He had information, which again was almost certainly inaccurate, as to the arrangement of Biarritz, and "knew from positive information" that Italy had promised to cede Sardinia and part of Piedmont to France, as the price of Napoleon's help. Much, however, as he disliked the diplomacy, still it was a war for Venice, and he urged his followers to join the volunteers. If the war ended in victory, they could then march on to Rome. He had his plan of operations for the war,—to mask the Quadrilateral, and push on with the main body of the army to Vienna, while the volunteers landed in Istria and tried to rouse the Slavs. Whether the plan was original or not, it was almost identical with one, which had been favoured by Ricasoli, now again premier, by Cialdini, one of the two Italian commanders, and probably by Bismarck, and which was rejected, or at least mutilated, only by La Marmora's opposition.

All the world had expected to see the Italians easily victorious. But again, as in 1848, their chance was spoilt by incompetent generalship. The army was defeated at Custozza, the fleet at Lissa ; Garibaldi and the volunteers had little of the spirit of 1860, and were paralysed in the Tyrol. Equally unexpectedly, the Prussians on their side had triumphed swiftly and conclusively ; and Napoleon, afraid that the unforeseen events would nip his schemes, stepped in with a message that Austria had offered to cede Venetia to himself and that he would hand it over to Italy, if peace were made. It was a bitter and humiliating end,— to lay down arms under the shadow of defeat, to abandon the Tyrol and Istria, to have Venetia not by right of conquest but by the condescension of a detested patron. Mazzini did not know how unwillingly the government had bowed to a fate, which the military position made inevitable. To him it seemed mere pusillanimity, pregnant with "dishonour and ruin." "It is my lot," he sadly wrote, "to consume my last days in the grief, supreme to one who really loves, of seeing the thing, one loves most, inferior to its mission."

Chapter XII

The Last Years

The Republican Alliance — Life at Lugano — Mentana — Republican
movement in 1868-70—Intrigue with Bismarck—Imprisonment at
Gaeta, and release—Attack on the International—Death.

IN his ignorance of the facts, he charged it all to
the monarchy. The nation had been sacrificed to the
interests of a dynasty. Defeat and dishonour came of
the equivocations, that sprang from the "primal falsehood" of royalty. The bad government and coercion
(which, in fact, was mild enough), the huge army and
civil service and police, the consequent financial chaos
—all were its fruit. He disclaimed that it was the
republic for its own sake that he wanted now, for its
advent was only the question of a few years more or
less, and its triumph might be left to time. But dishonour was the "gangrene of a nation," and only the
republic could cure that. Only the republic could win
Rome, gather Istria and the Tyrol to the fold, and
stretch a hand to the struggling nationalities of the
East. But, if the republic came, it must be as a great
"moralising education, to change men from serfs to
citizens, and make them conscious of their mission, their
strength and dignity." The republic must not mean

revenge, or spoliation, or repudiation of debt, or violent
anti-clericalism ; and he was already beginning his
crusade against Bakounine and the rough socialism,
which was making some headway in the country.

He had promised that if he resumed his republican
agitation, he would announce it frankly beforehand,
and he did so now. Henceforth he gave it all his
failing strength. Hopeless as their cause probably
was at the best, the republicans had a strength now,
which they had not had for fifteen years. The shame
of Custozza and Lissa lay heavy on the nation, and
the disillusioning had shaken faith in men and institutions. The sense of national dishonour maddened ;
civil war was often on men's lips ; the King's prestige
was foundering under the load of private vice and
military failure. There was a mass of sullen, unformu-
lated discontent, ready to find its way into socialist
or republican channels. And though men were slow
to follow Mazzini into his conspiracies, his long years
of self-sacrificing labour, the mystery that wrapped
the exile and conspirator, had given him a vast,
almost mythical fascination for his countrymen. Forty
thousand persons had signed the petition for his
amnesty. Messina elected him time after time for its
deputy, to have the election quashed as often by the
Moderates in the Chamber. There was an angry
feeling everywhere at the senseless intolerance, and
the deputies of the Left did their best to bring the
majority to reason. "While you are still in time,"
said a recent premier of Italy, " prevent Mazzini from
having to close his eyes in a foreign land."

When at last he was amnestied at the beginning of the
war, he refused to accept it as an act of grace or take
his seat as deputy, and returned to Lugano. Much of

his time henceforth was spent there with his friends, Giuseppe Nathan and his wife Sarah, "the best Italian friend I have, one of the best women I know," who nursed him in the attacks of illness, which came with ever greater frequency. Here he would watch "the beautiful calm-lulling lake, the beautiful, solemn, hopeful-death-teaching sunsets." When he was well, he kept to the habits of his English life, writing all day, delighting his friends in the evening with his brilliant talk. His conspiracies often took him to Genoa, where he lived in hiding in the house of a working family, from whose windows in the Salita di Oregina he had a superb view of the city and the Riviera. He nearly betrayed himself once by shouting from his window at a boy who was torturing a grasshopper. He kept in close touch with his English friends and English life. At Lugano he regularly read "the good, dry Spectator and the would-be wicked, never concluding Saturday Review." He made a custom of always returning to England to spend New Year's Day with the Stansfelds or others of their family, crossing the Alps in mid-winter at the peril of his health. He had painfully aged. His face had sunk and wore a deathly pallor ; the thick, black hair was thin and grey. William Lloyd Garrison, seeing him after an interval of twenty-one years, sadly noted the change, though "the same dark, lustrous eyes" remained, "the same classical features, the same grand intellect, the same lofty and indomi-table spirit, the same combination of true modesty and heroic assertion, of exceeding benignity and inspira-tional power." Work told heavily upon him now. Writing made him giddy, and his characters begin to lose their firmness. He was "living as if in a whirl-wind, something like Paolo without Francesca, tired,

worn out, longing for rest." But he would not slacken.
" I am bound to those, whom I have organised for a
purpose. I must, before I die, proclaim the republic
in Italy."

While he was organising his " Republican Alliance,"
losing himself in the huge work of detail which
all came to so little, the impatience in Italy was
breaking down the precautions of the government.
Ricasoli had been driven from office by his own mala-
droitness and Garibaldi's wild, aimless opposition.
Rattazzi, the intriguer of 1862, came back to power,
and began the double play, that was only too likely
to lead to another Aspromonte. There is no need
here to analyse the obscure and sordid story of his
balancings between the Italian democrats and France.
Garibaldi was impatient to win Rome, and cared comparatively little now whether it were in the name of
monarchy or republic. His plan was to lead a raid,
with or without the connivance of the government,
into the small territory that still belonged to the Pope,
meet and defeat the Papal mercenaries, and enter
Rome. With Mazzini the republic was now a more
vital thing than Unity. Only from a republican
Rome could Italy perform her civilising mission to
the world. " If Rome is to be annexed like the rest,"
he wrote, " I would rather it belonged to the Pope
another three years." He disliked Garibaldi's scheme ;
he was not sanguine of its success ; if it did succeed,
it meant that the monarchy would go to Rome and
the Pope stay there. He wished to see the Romans
rise themselves and pronounce for a republic, confident
that, if they did so, Italy would echo the republican
cry, and the Pope would have to go. Sometimes,

however, despairing of his own party, he was willing to compromise; and when at last Garibaldi started on his raid, and the government backed him, risking hostilities with France rather than have civil war, he forgot everything else in the hope of winning Rome, and urged his followers to join the raiders. Probably, if he had not been prostrated by illness, he would have gone himself. When Garibaldi's incapacity was only too apparent, and the French troops landed again for the defence of Rome, he saw that the volunteers were advancing into a trap, and implored Garibaldi to retire to Naples, raise the flag of revolution, and collect forces for another and more hopeful attack. Garibaldi, marching obstinately to defeat, was in no temper to listen to anybody, to Mazzini least of all. The mischief-makers had persuaded him that Mazzini was tampering with his men. There was no particle of truth in it, but the conviction entered Garibaldi's mind and never left it, while Mazzini lived.

The volunteers went to their doom at Mentana. Rattazzi, who at the last rose above himself and would have marched to Rome but for the King's veto, had resigned some weeks before. Menabrea, who succeeded him, had been compelled by public opinion to occupy a part of the Pope's territory; but when the French landed, he withdrew the troops, rather than face war with France. The country writhed in its rage at the French insult, and naturally turned its resentment against the crown. Juries acquitted republican papers; the press lampooned the King. Some of the deputies gave a secret backing to the republican movement; the Friendly Societies, which had always kept more or less in touch with Mazzini, threw themselves into it. Mazzini had a following among the Freemasons, though not one himself, and among the ex-volunteers. Most ominous feature of it all, republicanism gained a large footing in the rank-and-file of the army. Mazzini pushed on impatiently for Rome and the republic. He knew that the Romans themselves were powerless to rise, now that the French were there, and that a volunteer movement had no better chance. The only plan, that could successfully defy the French and capture Rome, was to seize the government,—its army and navy and arsenals,—and make a national crusade with all the resources of the country. The royalists, he thought, would never break with France or attack the Papacy ; and indeed the criticism was true of the conservative ministry, which now held office. He was equally hopeless of the middle classes, but he was confident that the people would respond. Especially he trusted to the younger generation and the women of Italy ; they alone, he thought, were free from the timid opportunism, which had eaten deep into the rest.

After Mentana he left London again for Lugano to be nearer his work, and was constantly passing backwards and forwards between there and Genoa, finding time among it all to write his great religious apology, the sum of all his teaching, *From the Council to God*.[1] His following at Genoa was considerable now. When he came there secretly, little patrols of working men with concealed arms would watch along the streets between the station and his lodgings to guard his person from seizure by the police. The Committee sat waiting for him, each man armed with his

[1] Otherwise entitled *A Letter to the Oecumenical Council*.

revolver. One of them has described the meeting. " A low knock was heard at the door, and there he was in body and soul, the great magician, who struck the fancy of the people like a mythical hero. Our hearts leaped, and we went reverently to meet that great soul. He advanced with a child's frank courtesy and a divine smile, shaking hands like an Englishman, and addressing each of us by name, as if our names were written on our foreheads. He was not disguised ; he wore cloth shoes, and a capote, and with his middle, upright stature, he looked like a philosopher, straight from his study, who never dreamed of troubling any police in the world." In the spring of 1869 he was eager for action, despite the failure of a plot, discouraged by himself, among the garrison at Milan. The remonstrances of the government procured his banishment from Switzerland, but he was back again in August, going " more sadly than usual, feeling physically and intellectually weaker and unequal to the task." He was suffering continuously, and confessed to his friends that he shrank from the effort. He was obviously going on from sheer inability to stop more than from any hope of success. " My new plan," he wrote gloomily, " may prove a dream like many others."

In the spring of 1870 he came again to Genoa to arrange the details. The plot broke down like the rest, and at the moment everything was overshadowed by the coming Franco-German war. In common with the great majority of his countrymen, outside the court and government, his sympathies were with Germany. A German victory would avenge Mentana and compel the French to withdraw from Rome. In

spite of his denunciation of the Prussian alliance in
1866, he had been for three years past carrying on a
desultory intrigue with Bismarck. About the time of
Mentana he had sent a note to Bismarck through their
go-between. "I do not in the least," it said, "share
Count Bismarck's political views; his method of
unification does not command my sympathy; but I
admire his tenacity and energy and independence
towards the foreigner. I believe in German unity and
desire it as much as that of my own country. I abhor
the Empire and the supremacy it arrogates over
Europe." He saw in the intrigue a chance of pushing
his own schemes, and at the same time of preventing a
Franco-Italian alliance against Germany. He asked
Bismarck to send him arms and money, and promised,
if he had them, to guarantee him against the hostile
combination. Bismarck parleyed with him for a time,
as he had parleyed with Garibaldi; and when war
was imminent, and he knew that Victor Emmanuel
and many of the Italian conservatives were trying
again to commit the country to a French alliance, he
promised that the arms and money should be sent.
Mazzini hastened to accept, promising to attack Rome
with the revolutionary forces, and undertaking to
respect the wish of the country, should a future
Constituent Assembly declare for the monarchy. But
Bismarck had learnt now that the danger of the
hostile alliance had passed, and the promised help
never came. The intrigue marks the last stage in
Mazzini's political decline. That he had asked a
foreign government to assist in what meant civil war,
shows how the long years of conspiracy had distorted
his moral vision.

He had intended to use Bismarck's money for a
new plot, this time in Sicily.   It was a fool's errand,
and his friends tried in vain to dissuade him.   But
the monomania was on him, and he started for the
island in disguise.   As so often before, he had a
traitor in his secrets, a man who with strange inconsistency had nursed him tenderly through an illness,
while he was making a living by betraying his plans
to the French police.[1]   When Mazzini arrived by the
Naples steamer at Palermo, he was arrested.   He was
taken to Gaeta and treated with all possible consideration.   The very gaoler took three minutes to turn the
noisy keys silently, that he might soften the sense of
imprisonment.   Here through the loopholes of the
massive fortress, where the Bourbons had made their
last stand nine years before, he would watch the sea
and sky, as he had done at Savona thirty-nine years
ago.   " The nights," he writes, " are very beautiful ; the
stars shine with a lustre one only sees in Italy.   I
love them like sisters, and link them to the future in a
thousand ways.   If I could choose, I should like to
live in absolute solitude, working at my historical book
or at some other, just from a feeling of duty, and only
wishing to see—for a moment, now and then,—
some one I did not know, some poor woman that I
could help, some working men I could advise, the
doves of Zürich, and nothing else."   He smoked indifferent cigars ; he read bad translations of Shakespeare
and Byron from the prison library, and, for want of
better, Tasso's *Gerusalemme*.   He was planning again
a book on Byron, and asks for Taine's critique of him

---

[1] I have some doubts, though, whether this Wolff is identical with the
Wolff of the journey to Sicily.   See *Lettere ad A. Giannelli*, 503.

in his *Littérature anglaise.* "Taine is a materialist writer, and certainly won't have an idea that squares with mine; but I am intellectually half-asleep and I reckon on the stimulus of contradiction and the irritation which I shall get out of his book. He has enough perverted intellectual power to wake me up."

He was released a few weeks later, after the capture of Rome, but he still refused to accept the amnesty, that he might keep his hands free, "without even the shadow of ungratefulness to anybody—even to a king." His one anxiety for the moment was to escape the popular demonstrations of sympathy, and get to a quiet life among his friends. He passed a restless night at Rome; it was twenty-one years since Margaret Fuller and Giulia Modena had persuaded the ex-Triumvir to save himself and fly. He went to Leghorn to his friends the Rossellis; thence to Genoa, to see his mother's tomb, and fled to escape the ovations, with his old sickness on him. "The only thing really touching to me," he wrote to England, "was in the churchyard—it was late—and the place was quite empty, but a keeper had, it seems, recognised me, and coming out of the gate, some poor people, a priest among them, were drawn up in a line, bowing and almost touching the earth. Not a smile, no attempt at absurd applause, they felt my sadness, and contrived to show they were sharing it." [1] The popular welcome had been dust and ashes to him; "even Swinburne's praise," he wrote from Gaeta, "makes me sad. Who am I, whom he praises?" His ideal was shattered. Rome had "the profanation of a corrupt and dishonoured monarchy," and he knew that the monarchy's

[1] Will not some Italian artist paint the scene?

winning of the capital meant that the republic would
not come in his day. France, not Italy, had proclaimed
the republic, and in a spirit that he hated. His own
party had failed him. "Italy, my Italy," he said, "the
Italy that I have preached, the Italy of our dreams?
Italy, the great, the beautiful, the moral Italy of my
heart? This medley of opportunists and cowards
and little Macchiavellis, that let themselves be dragged
behind the suggestion of the foreigner,—I thought to
call up the soul of Italy, and I only see its corpse."
"Yes, dear," he writes to Mrs Stansfeld, "I love more
deeply than I thought my poor dreamt-of Italy, my
old vision of Savona. I want to see, before dying,
another Italy, the ideal of my soul and life, start up
from her three hundred years' grave : this is only the
phantom, the mockery of Italy. And the thought
haunts me, like the incomplete man in Frankenstein,
seeking for a soul from its maker."

But henceforth he resigns conspiracy. Sometimes
he still hoped for insurrection, still believed that "a
month of action transforms a people more than ten
years of being preached to"; but he knew that
the republic was afar off, that all he could do now
was quietly to educate his countrymen, especially the
working classes. "Tell the working-men of Genoa,"
so he sent his message, "that this is not a time for
demonstrations but self-education. Germany is the only
country that deserves a republic." He helped to organise
the Friendly Societies ; he advocated evening classes for
workmen, circulating popular libraries, the collection of a
fund to assist societies for co-operative production ; he
founded a paper, *Roma del Popolo*, to spread his ideas.
He still hoped to write his popular history on Italy and
a book on national education,—hopes, alas, never ful-

filled. He published *From the Council to God*, and was delighted at the success it met with in its English translation in the Fortnightly. He was keenly interested in the English movements for women's suffrage and against state regulation of vice. But his chief work in these last years was to fight the immature socialism of the time. He was bitterly chagrined by the "invasion of barbarians," which was threatening to conquer the Italian working-classes to socialism or anarchism. The International had passed out of its first stage as an organiser of trade-unionism, and was now the battle-ground between the anarchists under Bakounine and the collectivists, who followed Karl Marx. In its earlier days Mazzini had had some relations with it and Bakounine; he had advised his followers to join it, and had a high opinion of its English leaders, Odger and Cremer, "for their power of intellect and heart and their sincere devotion to the cause." He had tried to make it a political, revolutionary society; and when he found himself defeated by Marx' opposition, he retired. Since then, the International had turned to far other roads of revolution. Mazzini hardly distinguished between the two sections that were fighting for mastery in it, and banned indiscriminately the atheism and anarchism of the one and the socialism of the other. And in fact both were equally alien from his spiritual basis of life, his fervid faith in nationality, his more modest economic programme.[1] But he was careful to show that his criticism came from no lack of social aspiration. "Those, whom you call barbarians," he retorted on the Italian conservatives, who had used the word in a far other sense, "represent an idea,—the inevitable,

[1] See below, pp. 288, 289.

destined rise of the men of Labour." The International, he argued, was the necessary fruit of middle-class indifference to social reform ; and the Assembly at Versailles was more guilty than the Commune. He had, in fact, small liking for the Third Republic. A republic, which had only come for lack of an alternative, which had Thiers for its chief, and made no sign of restoring Nice, was a republic only in form. When he read Renan's *Réforme intellectuelle et morale*, it confirmed him in his distrust of France ; and, almost on his death-bed, he reviewed the book in words of acute disappointment at its spirit.

The long life of fighting was fast closing in weariness and sense of failure. " This life of a machine, that writes and writes and writes for thirty-five years, begins to weigh upon me strangely." He had bitter personal chagrins ; his one surviving sister refused to see him, from religious differences ; Garibaldi would not be reconciled. All through the end of 1871 he was kept alive only by the devoted attention of Bertani, who looked after his patient as well as he had organised the Expedition of the Thousand. He still refused to accept the amnesty, and travelled under an assumed name to Pisa and Genoa and Florence, where he laid a wreath on Ugo Foscolo's tomb, for the bones of his hero had been lately brought from Chiswick to rest in Santa Croce. Giuditta Sidoli, " good, holy, constant Giuditta," died. " Did she die a Christian ? " he enquires ; " any faith, even though imperfect and spoilt by false doctrine, comforts the pillow of the dying better than the dry, thin, gloomy travesty of Science, which is called now-a-days Free Thought or Rationalism."

He knew his own end was not far,. and he was willing it should come. " Strange," he said, " that I see all those I loved go one by one, while I remain, I know not why." His one care was that the work should still go on. "What matter," he wrote, " how many years or months I still live down here? Shall I love you less because I go elsewhere to work? Will you love me less, when you can only love me by working? I often think, that when at last I leave you, you will all work with more faith and ardour, to prevent my having lived in vain." In his last words to the working men of Italy he says, " love and work for this great, unhappy country of ours, called to high destinies, but stayed upon the road by those who cannot, will not know the road. This is the best way that you can have of loving me." One of his last acts was to repay an old loan of half a life-time's standing. In the mild spring of 1872 he was living at a house that belonged to Pellegrino Rosselli, son-in-law of his old friends, the Nathans of Lugano, in the Via Maddalena at Pisa. People would watch the white-haired stranger, who went by the name of Brown, taking his daily walk, with the affectionate eyes and a kind word for every child. Early in March he was taken very ill and sank rapidly. On the 10th he died. His last conscious words were—" Believe in God? Yes, I do believe in God." He was buried, where he had always wished to lie, beside his mother, in the cemetery of Staglieno outside Genoa. There, in the words of Carducci's epitaph, rests

L'UOMO
CHE TUTTO SACRIFICÒ
CHE AMÒ TANTO
E MOLTO COMPATÌ E NON ODIÒ MAI.

Chapter XIII

Religion

Religion essential to society—Paramouncy of the spiritual—Criticism of Christianity ; Catholicism ; Protestantism—Christ's teaching :—its truths and imperfections—The doctrines of the new faith:—God ; Progress ; Immortality—The criteria of Truth :—the conscience ; tradition—Humanity—The need of unity ; authority ; church and state ; the new church.

MAZZINI'S life was one piece of almost perfect consistency and continuity. Save in minor points of policy, it had no turnings, no conversions, no recantations. Alike in theory and practice, it goes on its straight, undeviating course from his youthful literary essays to the full-bodied doctrine of *The Duties of Man* and *From the Council to God*, from the first days of Young Italy to those of the Republican Alliance. And its magnificent unity comes of this, that all was dominated by a scheme of thought, that controlled and correlated each sphere of human action. Supremely he achieved the harmony of life, which he never wearied of extolling. He was politician, philosopher, religious reformer, literary critic ; and every side of life completes the others in a perfect synthesis. At the centre of it all, controlling, illuminating, energizing, stands his religious faith. To him religion was "the eternal, essential, indwelling element of life," "the breath of humanity, its soul and life and consciousness and outward symbol," hallowing men's thoughts and actions, ennobling, consoling, fortifying, the inspiring principle of brotherhood and social service./ Deep in the conscience of each man, inseparable from life, lies the religious sense,—the sense of the Infinite and Imperishable, the aspiration to the Unknown and Invisible, the innate desire to apprehend God in his intellect and love. "If ever you have," he once said, "a strange moment of religious feeling, of supreme resignation, of quiet love of humanity, of a calm insight of duty, kneel down thankful, and treasure within yourself the feeling suddenly arisen. It is the feeling of life." And with the sense of the Divine, there comes to man the yearning to reach after the divine perfection and the importunate searching for the way. In every age, men have asked "to know, or at least to surmise, something of the starting-point and goal of mundane existence"; and religion comes to teach "the general principles that rule humanity, to sanction the link that makes men brothers in the consciousness of that one origin, one mission, one common aim."/ Man makes that mission and that aim his guiding star in all his strivings for the good ; and in every branch of his activity he steers his course by his knowledge of God. "From the general formula, that men call religion, issues a rule of education, a basis of human brotherhood, a policy, a social economy, an art." It is impossible to keep it out of politics. It is there "in all questions of the franchise, of the condition of the masses, of nationality,"—all intimately linked with the religious thought of the time, all part of God's providential scheme for man. "I do not know," he says, "speaking historically, a single great conquest of the human spirit, a single important step for the perfecting of human society, which has not had its roots in a strong religious faith." / "No true society exists without a common faith and common purpose ; politics are the application, religion gives the principle." Where this common faith is not, the mere will of the majority means permanent instability and the oppression of the rest ; "without God, you can coerce, but you cannot persuade ; you may be tyrants in your turn, but you cannot be educators or apostles." /

Without religion, then,—deep, heartfelt, vitalising religion,—there can be no true community. / Materialism had been tried, and had failed ;—failed because it was "an individualist, cold, calculating doctrine, that slowly, infallibly extinguished every spark of high thinking or free life, that first plunged men into the worship of success, then made them slaves of triumphant violence and the accomplished fact." It killed enthusiasm in the individual ; it killed true greatness in a nation. / Bare ethics had been tried, "but no morality can endure or bring forth life, without a heaven and a dogma to support it." "No, man needs more than simple ethics ; he craves to solve his doubts, to slake his thirsting for a future ; he wants to know whence he comes and whither he goes." Men had tried philosophy, and indeed philosophy, that took humanity and not the individual for its study, was "the scienc₁ of the law of life" ; but by itself it was a barren rock where life could find no . resting-place. "Heresy i₁ sacred," but only as the transient stage between ₴ lower and a higher faith. Philosophy can "analys₴ and anatomise and dissect," but it has no breath o₴

life to "decree duty or push men to deeds by giving
ethics a new strength and grandeur." The needs of
the age are less intellectual than spiritual. "What
we want, what the people want, what the age is
crying for, that it may find an issue from this slough
of selfishness and doubt and negation, is a faith, a
faith in which our souls may cease to err in search
of individual ends, may march together in the knowledge of one origin, one law, one goal." And such a
faith, and only such a faith, will give the solid, strong
convictions and the energy and unity, by which alone
society can be healed./ "Any strong faith, that rises on
the wreck of the old, exhausted creeds, will transform
the existing social order, since every strong belief must
needs apply itself to every branch of human activity ;
because always, in every age, earth has sought conformity with the heaven in which it believed ; because
all Humanity repeats under different formulas and in
different degrees the words of the Lord's Prayer of
Christendom : Thy kingdom come on earth as it is
in heaven."/

Where shall this faith be found,—this living,
vitalising faith, for which the age is groping, for want
of which its aspiration and its efforts are in vain ?
Does Christianity supply it ? / Mazzini asked the
question reverently and tenderly. Religion, he says, is
above and independent of creeds, but every creed is
acred, for each has added to man's knowledge of God
nd of himself. / However incomplete a faith, so it be
ı faith indeed, it helps to hallow life. He felt his
piritual kinship more with Catholic priest and Pro-
estant pastor, who lighted earth with broken rays of
he divine, than with the sceptic, who would shut

out God and immortality, enthusiasm and love. Reverently, then, he tested Christianity. For the superstructures, indeed, that Catholics and Protestants had built upon the Christianity of Christ, he felt respect and sympathy, but little love. He had his special grievances against the Papacy for the evil work it had done in his own country, and he hated it, as only an Italian of his day could hate it. He held it to be irrevocably doomed: doomed, since the Reformation took the North from it ;—doomed, "because it has betrayed its mission to protect the weak, because for three centuries and a half it has committed fornication with the princes of this world, because at the bidding of every evil and unbelieving government it has crucified Jesus afresh in the name of egoism,"—doomed, because it stood apart from the great humanitarian movements of the century, the freeing of Greece and Italy, the emancipation of the blacks ;—doomed for the root sin, of which these were but consequences, that it had become "a phantasm of religion," "without faith or power or mission." It had missed the meaning of Christ's teaching ; it had sinned against the Holy Spirit, and there was no forgiveness for it. "God will provide for the abominated idolatry, God, who breaks all idols that were and are and shall be." Sometimes he was confident, that, before the century was out, the Papacy would be extinct. And yet, in spite of all, he respected what had been a great fact in the history of religion. Like every strong belief, it had in its time done high service for humanity, it had had its share of the noble and sublime and potent. "I remember it all and bow myself before your past." And die though it must, he would it should die nobly, "like the sun in the great ocean," rejoicing that God's great design bade it make place for a more perfect faith.

For Protestantism his feeling was colder both in its sympathies and antipathies. His Catholic training, his craving for formal unity, made it difficult for him to read it sympathetically; and he saw it chiefly in its defects,—its exaggeration of the individual, its rejection of tradition, its sectarianism, its "indefinite dismembering of the common thought." He recognised somewhat, though imperfectly, the political and social work, which was indissolubly bound up with Puritanism; "'God and the People,'" he said in one of his letters to English working men, "were the inspirers of your Cromwell." As Catholicism had one side of the truth in its respect for tradition, so Protestantism had the other in its assertion of individual interpretation, and in this it had apprehended the essence of Christianity more truly than Catholicism had done. But though Protestants were slowly learning the value of tradition, the preeminence of Humanity over man, they still magnified the individual, till their creed had become a doctrine of material and spiritual selfishness, which must logically develop into pure materialism. He charged it with inspiring the inhumanity and anarchy of the *laissez-faire* economy. It had made the salvation of the individual soul the end of life; and thus it had sundered religion from society, and dwarfed the all-embracing plan of God to the puny borders of a loveless pietism.

But when Mazzini passes from Catholicism and Protestantism to Christ, his attitude is one of infinite reverence and love. His close knowledge of the

Gospels, his native kinship with their spirit, had brought him very near the mind of Christ, and he spoke of Him in beautiful and tender words. Christ's "was the soul most full of love, of holiest virtue, most inspired by God and by the Future, that men have ever hailed upon this earth." He "came for all ; he spoke to all and for all. He lifted up the People and died for it." " I love Jesus," he once wrote in a private letter, "as the man who has loved the most all mankind, servants and masters, rich and poor, Brahmins and Helots or Parias." " In Jesus," so he wrote to the Oecumenical Council, "we worship the Founder of an age that freed the individual, the Apostle of the unity of law,—that law which he understood more fully than did any of the generations before him,—the Prophet of the equality of souls : and we bow ourselves before him, as the man who among all we know of loved the most, whose life, an unexampled harmony between thought and practice, proclaimed the holy doctrine of sacrifice, henceforth to be the everlasting foundation of all religion and all virtue ; but we do not cancel the woman-born in God, we do not raise him where we cannot hope to join him ; we would love him as the brother who was better than us all, not worship him and fear him as pitiless judge and intolerant tyrant of the future." In Christ's teaching he found many of the moral and social truths that were dearest to him. " Does not every word of the Gospel breathe the spirit of liberty and equality, of that war with evil and injustice and falsehood, that inspires our work ? " The cross was the symbol of " the one true immortal virtue, the sacrifice of self for others." " Unity of faith, love for one another, human brotherhood, activity in well-doing, the doctrine of sacrifice, the doctrine of equality, the abolition of aristocracy, the perfecting of the individual, liberty,—all are summed up in Christ's words, 'Thou shalt love the Lord thy God and thy neighbour as thyself, and 'Whosoever will be chief among you, let him be your servant.'" Christ's teaching had inspired each struggle for truth from the Crusades to Lepanto, had destroyed feudalism, was destroying now the aristocracy of blood; Poles and Greeks had marched to freedom's battles under the flag of Jesus and His mother. And, above all, Christ gave the promise of indefinite religious progress,—a promise, which closed the mouths of those who would arbitrarily pin men to a fixed doctrine. 'The Spirit of truth shall abide with you for ever, . . . and shall teach you all things.' "On the eve of his accepted sacrifice, when his mighty love for his brethren lit up the darkness of the future, he had sight of the continuous revelation of the Spirit through humanity." This was the 'eternal gospel' of the mystics of the middle ages; and Christ's promise stood true to-day. "God forgive you," he wrote to a Catholic friend, "you do not understand Christ,—Christ who died that humanity may some day free itself to rise to God by its own strength."

He paused anxiously before he declared himself no Christian. His temperament and outlook on life were essentially Christian; he tried to read new meanings into Christian doctrines; words of Christian prayer came naturally to his lips; Christmas Day was "sacred" to him. Several times in early life he cherished schemes of reform within the church; for some years he doubted how far religious development could be built on Christian foundations, whether the new church would be " an application of Christianity " or " a religion to succeed " it. At all events Christian ethics would remain. " The morality of Christ is eternal ; humanity will add to it, but will not take from it one word." And for long yet Christianity would abide, the greatest of the creeds. " This will reach you on Christmas Day," he wrote to an English friend. " I am not a Christian, I belong to what I believe to be a still purer and higher Faith ; but its time has not yet come ; and until that day the Christian manifestation remains the most sacred re-velation of the ever-onward progressing spirit of mankind."

But that its doctrine and its cult must some day pass, that its ethics needed supplementing, he had convinced himself, at all events as early as his Swiss days. He wasted little time in attacking particular articles of the Christian faith, for analytical criticism was always hateful to him. But he thought it had certain essential imperfections, because of which it failed, and was bound to fail to content the present reach of human knowledge or inspire men's activities. He charged it, firstly, with not sanctifying the things of earth. The church taught that the world was evil, life here an expiation, heaven the soul's true home. At one time he appealed against the church to Christ's own teaching, to texts that spoke of God's will being done on earth, of power given to Christ in earth, of the promise that the meek should inherit the earth. In later life he qualified this reading of the gospel. Jesus, "a soul blessed with such mighty love and perfect harmony between thought and action," could not fail to realise the harmony of earth and heaven. But "while he stood and stands alone, supreme over all other great religious reformers in everything that concerns the heart and affections, his intellectual grasp did not extend beyond the requirements of a single epoch." At the time in which he lived, he "saw no possible mission for the sake of the brethren whom he loved, save by moral regeneration, by creating a country of freemen and equals in heaven. He wished to show mankind how it could find salvation and redemption in spite of and in opposition to the world." Great Christian statesmen and thinkers of a later time, —Gregory VII. and Thomas Aquinas,—had tried to bring the temporal under the spiritual law. But they had failed, and the normal Christianity of the day was fatally divorced from religion and politics and art and science. It left the bigger part of life without God's law to guide it. It told men to renounce the world, when their duty was to live in it and battle in it and better it.

Christianity again came short, because it left out of ken the collective life of the race. The conception was an impossible one at the time in which Christ lived ; and its absence maimed men's knowledge of God, and shortened their power to attain to the Divine Ideal. Christianity pointed, indeed, to "salvation, that is perfection"; but it recognised no instrument beyond "the weak, unequal, isolated, ineffective strength of the individual." Mazzini's criticism came to this : Christianity tells each man to perfect himself by his own strength and God's; but his spiritual growth is conditioned by the growth of the men around him, and therefore his own perfecting depends on the progress of the race, the common search for good, that links all men together and the generations to one another. Mazzini always regarded the French Revolution as the political expression, the "daughter" of Christianity, and there the depreciation of the race, the exaggeration of the individual had borne their necessary fruit of moral selfishness and social anarchy. Yet again, though Christ had promised the continuous teaching of his Spirit, ever leading to new truth, the doctrine of redemption was inconsistent with any theory of progress. There was no Fall; man had begun at the bottom and had been tending upwards ever since. Salvation was for men, not from a single, isolated act, but from the slow, unceasing, inevitable working of the providential scheme. The individual came nearer the divine, not by faith in Christ's sacrifice, but by his own works, by sacrifice of self, by faith in the "ideal that every man is called to incarnate in himself." And because of these imperfections in its theory of life, Christianity had ceased to be a vitalising force. For some it had become an ethical system, for others a philosophy, while men needed a religion. Politics and art and science had gone their own ways. Christian morality knew not patriotism. Charity was its only remedy for social wrongs, and charity was impotent to stop the springs of poverty. Men gave lip-service to Christ's teaching, but it had no binding influence on their lives. It offered no solution for their perplexities; it was no longer a faith that could move mountains or remould the modern world. Its day had gone, and all the efforts of neo-Christians or Christian Socialists or Old Catholics to make it answer to modern needs were bound to fail, as the neo-Platonists had failed in their day to galvanise paganism. " Jesus warned you, when on earth," he said to "the Anglo-Saxon Christian Socialists," "that you cannot put new wine into old bottles."

Such was Mazzini's criticism of Christianity, not always consistent with itself, sometimes confounding Christ's thought with others' perversions of it, sometimes failing to recognise how many-sided a phenomenon is Christianity, sometimes inaccurately tracing its actual results in history and modern life. His attitude towards it may be summed up thus. He retained its belief in the omnipotence of the spiritual ; its faith in God and in His providential working ; its supreme veneration for the character and moral teaching of Jesus ; its insistence on moral perfection and not material interest as the end of life ; its call to love and sacrifice of self ; its belief in immortality ; its aspiration to the Church Universal. He rejected the divinity of Christ, the doctrine of a mediator, the antagonism between matter and spirit and the consequent neglect of the things of earth ; its inability to grasp God's law of progress ; its non-acceptance (though the Church had partially recognised it) of Humanity as the interpreter of that law.

But the new faith, which was to grow out of and supplement Christianity, must have its doctrines too, its positive basis of belief. " There is no life in the void. Life is faith in something, a system of secure beliefs, grounded on an immutable foundation, which defines the end, the destiny of man, and embraces all his faculties to point them to that end." Mankind, he said, is weary of negations, of the hustling conflict

of opinions. " We must prepare for it an abode for
the day of rest,—something on earth, where it may
lay its weary head,—something in heaven on which
its eyes may stay,—a tent to shield it from the storm,
a spring to quench its thirst in the vast unbounded
desert where it travels." / Dogma is essential ; it is
ever " sovereign over practical morality," for " morality
is only its consequence, its application, its translation
into practice." By dogma he meant " a body of ideas,
which, starting from a fixed point, embraces all human
faculties and employs them for the conquest of a positive, practical end, which is for the good of the majority ;
the exposition of a principle and its consequences in
relation to life's manifestation and operations in the
moral and the industrial world, both for the individual
and for society." / The thinker apprehends it, science
and society prepare the medium for its adoption, the
best and wisest incarnate it in their lives, then it
" enters the soul of the many and becomes a religious
axiom." In other words it is an ethical and political
system, so based on the eternal verities of life, so
penetrated (by the spiritual sense of the race,) that
it ceases to be a cold and abstract code, and takes
the warmth and colour of religion, compelling men's
souls and pushing them irresistibly to social duty.

What then is the body of doctrine for the Church
of the future, as Mazzini conceived it ? / First, as the
root of all, belief in God./" the author of all existence,
the living, absolute thought, of which our world is a
ray and the universe an incarnation " ; " a sphere
inviolable, eternal, supreme over all humanity, independent of chance or error or blind and interrupted
operation." /God, then, exists objectively, as maker

and ruler of the universe. Man discovers God; he does not create Him. /In his criticism of Renan, Mazzini attacks any theory of the subjectivity of the Divine. Pantheism (that is, the "materialist pantheism" of Spinoza, not the "spiritual pantheism" of St Paul and Wordsworth and Shelley) confounds subject and object, good and evil, and leaves no place for Providence or human liberty ; it is a "philosophy of the squirrel in the cage," condemning mankind to go for ever rotating in a circle. Deism is a "sordid" creed, which relegates God to heaven and ignores his ever-operating life in creation. / Mazzini gives no clue how he would have reconciled an all-creating Deity,— author therefore of good and evil,—with a beneficent and loving Providence.

/ He finds the proofs of an actual, objective God, first, in man himself, in the universal intuition of the Divine / "God exists. God lives in our conscience, in the conscience of Humanity, in the Universe around us. Our conscience calls to him in our most solemn moments of sorrow and joy. He who would deny God before a starry night, before the graves of his dearest ones, before the martyr's scaffold, is a very wretched or a very guilty man." [The fact that we aspire to the best and infinite proves that there is a best and infinite, that is God.] And, next, the fact of existence bears witness to an intelligent creator. "God exists because we exist." "Call it God or what you like," he once said, "there is life which we have not created, but which is given." "The Universe displays him in its order and harmony, in the intelligent design shown in its working and its law." And this law is "one and immutable." "Everything is preordained"; "God and law are identical terms"; "'chance' has no meaning, and was only invented to express man's ignorance." "There can be no miracle, nothing supernatural, no possible violation of the laws that rule the Universe"; though he realised how big is the unknown of nature, and his rejection of the supernatural did not prevent him from being a mystic. But God is not only intellect but love, not only Lord but Educator. His law embraces Humanity as well as nature, the moral as well as the physical world. He manifests himself "in the intelligent design, that regulates the life of Humanity" and leads man ever upwards towards perfection. "Everything, from the grain of sand to the plant, from the plant to Man, has its own law ; how then can Humanity be without its law ?"

Mazzini seems to have recognised the difficulty of reconciling the oneness and eternity of law with an ever-active Providence, which concerned itself, for instance, with present-day problems of democracy and nationality. He found a solution in making the law consist in an inevitable tendency to progress, both in the material and, still more, in the spiritual world. The law of Progress, which perhaps he developed from Lessing, is "a supreme formula of the creative activity, eternal, omnipotent, universal as itself." His 'Progress' is not equivalent to 'evolution.' He formulated it, of course, before Darwin's day ; so far as I know, he never refers to Darwinism, and probably never studied it. If he had, it would certainly have been to condemn it. But he would have attacked it, not from the scientific side, but on à priori grounds. Progress, he would have said, rules the material world, but it rules

it through the spiritual, by virtue of an inherent God-\
implanted tendency and the operation of the human\
will. He would have rejected as derogatory to the
divine idea an evolution, which results from the
struggle of unthinking and non-moral forces. He
condemned unsparingly, as we shall see, the explana-
tion of social facts by the bare brute struggle of
individuals or the development of material phenomena.
/Progress is essentially a moral phenomenon, and postulates the search, not for self, but for self-sacrifice. / It
is " the slow, but necessary, inevitable development of
every germ of good, of every holy idea." Sometimes,
indeed, he is trapped by the ambiguity of ' self-realisation,' and speaks of " the instinct and necessity, which
urges every living being to the fuller development of
all the germs, the faculties, the forces, the life within
it." But it is clear that he is always really thinking
of the development of good alone. God's plan "slowly,
progressively makes man divine." Whither Humanity
ultimately goes, we know not ; but we know there is
no limit to the march ; and every age, every religion,
each new philosophy enlarges its apprehension of the
end.

He curiously dovetails personal immortality into the
doctrine. For the individual soul the process of perfecting goes on beyond the limits of this world. Life
" here-down " (as he called it in English) is so short, so
full of imperfection, that the soul cannot in its earthly
pilgrimage climb the ladder that leads to God. And
yet intuition and tradition tell us that the ideal will
be reached some day, somewhere ; in words, that
almost suggest that he had read the parallel passage
in Wordsworth, he speaks of memory as the conscious-

ness of the soul's progress up from earlier existences ;
love would be a mockery, if it did not last beyond the
grave ; the unity of the race implies a link between
the living and the dead ; science teaches there is no
death but only transformation. He held passionately
to his faith in immortality, and he believed that the
dear ones he had lost were watching over him and
bringing his best aspirations. The individual soul, he
thought, progresses through a series of re-incarnations,
each leading it to a more perfect development, and
the rapidity of its advance depends on its own purification. [And as the individual has his progress through
a series of existences, so collective man progresses
ever through the human generations.] " No, God
eternal, thy word is not all spoken, thy thought not
yet revealed in all its fulness. It still creates, and
will create· through long ages · beyond the grasp of
human reckoning. The ages, that are past, have
revealed but fragments to us. Our mission is not
finished. We hardly know its source, we do not know
its final end ; time and our discoveries only extend its
borders. From age to age it ascends to destinies
unknown to us, seeking its own law, of which we read
but a few lines. From initiative to initiative, through
the series of thy progressive incarnations, it purifies
and extends the formula of Sacrifice ; it feels for its
own way ; it learns thy faith, eternally progressive."
If once we recognised this progressive evolution of
religion and morals, there would be no room for pure
scepticism ; we should see that an expired form of
faith is not wrong but imperfect, that it needs not
destroying but supplementing. " Every religion instils ·
into the human soul one more drop of the universal life."

But does not this mean fatalism,—the same fatalism, with which he charged the Christian doctrine of redemption, the fatalism, with which he would have charged the evolutionists, had he known them? If the progress of humanity is preordained, what need for man to use his puny powers? Mazzini met the difficulty thus. True, evil cannot permanently triumph, God's progress must go on; but its quicker or slower realisation is in our hands. " The slow unfolding of history proceeds under the continuous action of two factors, the work of individuals and the providential scheme. [Time and space are ours; we can quicken progress or retard it, we cannot stop it."] And this, because progress, being essentially a moral phenomenon, must be realised in the world of thought and will, before it can be translated into practice. Mazzini did not seriously concern himself with the metaphysics of determinism; he took the common-sense position that the will is free; "no philosophic sophisms," he said, " can cancel the testimony of remorse and martyrdom." It depends on a man's choice of good or evil, whether he approaches nearer the ideal in himself, and therefore whether, so far as his influence lies, progress is realised in society. Thus, in his strained and inconclusive argument, [God's providential working is reconciled both with human free will and the oneness of law.]

Progress, then!—onwards to the great Ideal, the ideal which "stands in God, outside and independent of ourselves," which as yet we know but darkly, but which every generation sees more clearly; fixed, therefore, and "absolute in the Divine Idea," but gradually revealed to man, "approached" but never " reached " in this life, ever provisional and shifting for us as knowledge grows. / The world is no mere necessary sequence of material phenomena, but a spiritual stream, that, swift or sluggish be its course, flows irresistibly to God. / The existing fact is not the. law ; choice between good and evil, heroism, sacrifice are not illusions ; conscience, the intuition of the ideal, the power of will, and moral force are ultimate and mastering spiritual facts. The divine design controls it all, and man has liberty to help God's plan. And he who knows this, knows that "a supreme power guards the road, by which believers journey towards their goal," and he will be "bold with God through God." The crusaders' cry 'God wills it' is for him, and his are the courage and consistency and power of sacrifice, that come to those who know they battle on the side of God. / It was this conviction that Mazzini wished his followers to have, when he pleaded that Young Italy should be as a religion. For "political parties fall and die ; religious parties never die till they have conquered." /

/ But how shall man search for the ideal, how learn the providential design ? Mazzini has his answer clear : "tradition and conscience,"[1] or, as we may translate them, experience and intuition, "are the two wings given to the human soul to reach to truth." First, then, the individual consciousness and that in a two-fold sense. / Truth is truth only to the individual, when he apprehends it for himself. / Sometimes Mazzini speaks as if he accepted the whole Protestant doctrine of individual judgment, and in a sense he does.

---

[1] *Conscienza* ; in Mazzini's use of the word, it covers both 'consciousness' and 'conscience.' Mazzini himself translated it by 'conscience' (see below, p. 362), where 'consciousness' would be more accurate.

Each man must prove by his own consciousness every interpretation of God's law, whether it be true or not. But this gift of judgment only comes by righteousness. "In moments of holy thought something of the great flood of man's knowledge of God's law may come to every man." To learn it, he must "purify himself from low passion, from every guilty inclination, from every idolatrous superstition"; and truth will come "in the most secret aspirations of the soul, in the instincts of itself, that hover round in supreme hours of affection and devotion." But, though Mazzini does not very clearly distinguish, he seems generally to be thinking of something more. It is for the consciousness not only to apprehend and appropriate for the individual truths already known to the race, but sometimes it is its privilege to spell a new line of God's law. Glimpses of new truth may come to the collective intuition of a people. There are times, when "the spirit of God descends upon the gathered multitudes," and *vox populi* is *vox Dei*. /He would deny the right of spiritual discovery to a people enslaved by low, material impulses; but in a nation moved by some great aspiration, when thought strikes thought, and enthusiasm kindles enthusiasm, there truth will probably be found./ But though in such times of faith and struggle the people has its "great collective intuitions," though sometimes "the pale, modest star that God has placed in simple bosoms" comes nearer truth than genius comes, it is normally for the best and wisest to discover truth. Only men of holy lives and genius are God's "born interpreters"; his apostles, those "who love their brethren most and are ready to suffer for their love, and those on whom

God has bestowed surpassing gifts of intellect, provided
that their intellect is virtuous and desires the good." But
even such as these can find truth only by interrogating
the dim silent workings of the people's mind.   Light
comes to no man by his own unaided effort ; and the
solitary thinker may mistake his own conceit for truth.
" Great men can only spring from a great people just
as an oak, however high it may tower above every other
tree in the forest, depends on the soil whence it derives
its nourishment.   The soil must be enriched by countless decaying leaves."

But the untested intuition, whether of man of
genius or people, is by itself no sufficient criterion
of truth.   Every heresy has its martyrs.   There is
a more unerring interpreter of God's law, known
imperfectly to Catholicism, but neglected by Protestantism and the individualist schools of the day,—
the consciousness of the race, checked and corrected
and perfected by each succeeding generation, the
" common consensus of humanity," " the tradition,
not of one school or one religion or one age, but
of all the schools and all religions and all the ages
in their succession," for " no one man or people or
school can presume to discover all the law of God."
The seeker after truth will find it most surely in " the
severe study of the universal tradition, which is life's
manifestation in Humanity."   Humanity (the conception of which he seems to have derived from Vico
and Herder), " the living word of God," " the collective
and continuous being," is " the only interpreter of
God's law."   " Humanity," said a thinker of the last
century,[1] " is a man who is ever learning.   Individuals
die ; but the truth they thought, the good they

[1] Pascal.

wrought, is not lost with them ; Humanity garners
it, and the men who walk over their graves, have
their profit from it. Each of us is born to-day in
an atmosphere of ideas and beliefs, that are the
work of all Humanity before us ; each of us brings
unconsciously some element, more or less valuable,
for the life of Humanity that comes after. The
education of Humanity grows like those Eastern
pyramids, to which each passer-by adds his stone.
We pass, the travellers of a day, called away to complete our individual education elsewhere ; the education
of Humanity shines by flashes in each one of us,
but unveils its full radiance slowly, progressively,
continuously in Humanity. From one task to
another, from one faith to another, step by step
Humanity conquers a clearer vision of its life, its
mission, of God and of his law." And here again
comes strength. " It matters little," he replied to
Carlyle, " that *our* individual powers be of the smallest
amount in relation to the object to be attained ; we
know that the powers of millions of men, our brethren,
will succeed to the work after us, in the same track,
—we know that the object attained, be it when it
may, will be the result of *all* our efforts combined."
But he who would have this strength, must needs
respect Humanity's tradition, must recognise that the
race is more likely to be right than his own poor
intellect. He turned angrily on the " barbarian "
schools, that would sweep away the past, and create
Humanity anew on some arbitrary plan. Humanity
spurns builders of utopias ; and preachers of new
principles, the masses fervent for some new idea,
must prove their beliefs by the infallible test of

tradition. Mazzini hardly recognised how difficult and vague and diverse might be the detailed interpretation of tradition, and he was never very modest in making his own inductions. /He believed that history proves that there are certain "immortal elements of human nature,"—education, fatherland, liberty, association, family, property, religion; and the theorist, who offends any one of these, is in conflict with God's law./ In the conjunction, then, of these two criteria and no otherwise stands the discovery of the truth. Neither suffices without the other; and therefore Catholicism and Protestantism, each of which had apprehended one alone, are incomplete. Tradition by itself leads to stagnation; intuition alone to chance and anarchy. But "where you find the general permanent voice of humanity agreeing with the voice of your conscience, be sure that you hold in your grasp something with absolute truth,—gained and for ever yours."

It will be noted that Mazzini parts himself from the intuitive school, when he admits experience as the surer criterion of truth, when, again, he says that the intellect is necessary to verify the instincts of consciousness. On the other hand he is a pure intuitionist in his conception of the function of genius, for genius meant with him something other far than 'the infinite capacity of taking pains'; it was a God-given, almost mystical faculty, that saw truth by its own natural, unaided light, that possessed her forcibly, not wooed her timidly. He is an intuitionist again when he holds, as obviously he does hold, that it is for the pure in heart to see God, that religious and ethical enquiry depends for its results on the cultivation of the moral sense, and therefore more on the moral than on the intellectual development of the enquirer. And, even when he sides with the opposite school, it does not mean that he trusts to any scientific process of ratiocination. He has more confidence in the unconscious reasoning, by which the race has gathered its experience, and which allows no room for the errors of the solitary thinker. He did not neglect metaphysics, but he was little influenced by them, and he would have sided with ' the vulgar ' against ' the philosophers.'

/ Mazzini's conception of Humanity was essentially related to his craving for religious and moral unity./ Fighter though he **was** ever, and recognising some-what the value of " the holy conflict of ideas," he did not see how much in an imperfect age progress depends upon the clash of creeds and conflict of opinions. He was so weary of debate, so confident that others must come to the same truth that he had. As far as humanity had learnt God's law, all should bow to it ; and he looked to a true national education to generate this unity of faith. As unity was the law of God's universe, so unity was the condition of humanity's advance. Without it " there may be move-ment, but it is not uniform or concentrated." There-fore " the world thirsts for unity," " democracy tends to unity," and every great religion must of necessity strive to be catholic. But now " discord is every-where,"—creeds that curse one another, warring states, class hatreds, party bitterness, the search for truth itself a source of conflict. It is time to end this wasteful strife, and march together, " reverently seek-ing the future city, a new heaven and a new earth, which may unite in one, in love of God and man, in faith in a common aim, all those, who tossed between fears of the present and doubtings of the future, now stray in intellectual and moral anarchy." / " We must found moral unity, the Catholicism of humanity," " the unity of belief that Christ promised for all peoples," " a unity which binds the sects in one sole people of believers, and on the churches and conventicles and chapels raises the great temple, Humanity's Pantheon to God."

The new faith, like the old, must have its visible embodiment. " Sacred," he said, " is the church, but not a false church." At the time of the Roman Republic, a liberal cleric warned the Catholics that " if the church did not march with the people, the people would march without the church, aye, outside it and against it." " Against the church, no ! " Mazzini replied ; " we will march from the church of the past to the church of the future, from the dead church to the living, to the church of freemen and equals. There is room enough for such a church betwixt the Vatican and Capitol." Sometimes he thought that the new church would have its cult, a cult " which would gather believers together in feasts of equality and love," where men of saintly lives would preach plain truths of duty and inspire enthusiasm. And in some undefined way the authority of the church was to be supreme in the state. Gregory VII.'s principles, he says, were right, but erred in the application.[1]

---

[1] In the undated letter, quoted by Signor Donaver in the *Rassegna Nazionale*, Oct. 1, 1890, he speaks of a reformed Catholic church becoming " the guide of the State and not its servant " ; but I think he says rather more than he really felt in order to conciliate an old clerical friend, to whom the letter seems to be addressed.

/ " Religion will be the soul, the thought of the new state." " Power is one ; religion, the law of the spirit, sits in the seat of government ; its interpreters, the temporal power, reduce it to practice." / It is true that till men find a common faith, while the existing church is a church only in name, the state must protect itself by the separation of the two. But the Cavourian ' free church in a free state ' means religious indifference and " an atheist law " ; and a higher order will terminate " the absurd divorce between the temporal and spiritual." / In his later years it seems to have been a fixed idea with him to get some kind of state creed recognised by the Italian parliament. Some day " a few men, reverenced for their doctrine and virtue, their intellect and love and sacrifice of self," would form a " supreme Council " for Europe and America, proclaiming new truths and the common duties of the nations ; while under them would sit national councils to define the several duties of each people. He seems to have expected that at first these councils would have a voluntary basis outside the state, but that eventually they would be recognised by law as the supreme international and national authorities, and, as such would be the authoritative exponents of tradition and control education. And with this reconciliation of the spiritual and temporal the world would find that real authority, of which it stood in need. For authority in itself was a good and not an evil thing ; and on the wreck of the existing phantasms of authority, another would arise, democratic, based on the common will, loving liberty and progress, with virtue to initiate and inspire, the unexhausted fountain of reform, correlating and organising men's various labours for the commonwealth. For such an authority "the world is ever searching, and save in it and through it, it has no life or progress."

That the new religion,—one which in its time must pass too,—would come, he had no doubt. He looked for the day when a Council of the best and wisest (whether or not identical with the supreme European council) would define the articles of the new faith. It might be "a truly Oecumenical Council of virtuous intellects," or it might spring from one free people, which had found brotherhood in the worship of duty and the ideal." It was the dream of his life that this faith would issue forth from Rome,—Rome, the only city to whose authority Europe had bowed, Rome, the seat of the old false religion, whose fall must come ere the new one could arise. But, whatever were the more impatient hopes of earlier years, he came to see that the dawn was yet afar. Long missionary labours must come first. Still, the time, he thought, was ripe at all events for a "church of the precursors," and gladly he would have led its builders. In younger days, when the deliverance of Italy seemed near, he prayed that God would let him give the rest of life to the greater work. Afterwards, when the new Italy delayed its coming, and age and weakness came ere the first task was done, the dream of a missionary call faded slowly away, to be cherished to the end as the great unfulfilled ambition of his life.

Chapter XIV

Duty

Morality depends on an Ideal—Criticism of the theory of Rights and Utilitarianism—Happiness not the end of life—Life is a mission—Work for the sake of Duty—Thought useless without action—Power of the principle of Duty—Duties to self ; family ; country.

ON this religious foundation Mazzini constructed his code of ethics,—Christian, very Christian in its spirit, essentially modern in its application; the noblest morality that has sought to answer to the needs of a democratic society. The law of Progress judges all action by the Ideal, and the sole standard of conduct lies in what a man does that the Ideal may be better realised in himself and others. Without the recognition of such a universal law, demanding their cooperation and conformity, there can be no common rule for men ; life becomes the resultant of clashing interests ; its line of advance, if advance there be, depends upon mere chance. True education is impossible, because there is no consensus on its aim ; we come to value character, as he complained that Carlyle did, not by its goodness, but by its energy and persistence, whether it be to good or evil ends. Everywhere in actual life, the neglect of the Ideal means worship of brute force, cowardly acquiescence in the existing fact, the absence of all striving for a better state. But with the

apprehension of the Ideal and of the Divine law, three
things follow, incentive to progress. Every man has a
rule to guide his individual actions; men of good
will will associate their efforts for a common end; and
they can appeal to a supreme, positive law against
those who break it. " In the consciousness of your law
of life, which is the law of God, stands the foundation
of your morality, the rule of your actions and your
duties, the measure of your responsibility." " If there
be no Mind supreme over all human minds, who can
save us from the caprice of our fellows, should they
chance to be stronger than ourselves? If there be no
law, sacred and inviolable, not created by man, what
standard can we find to judge whether an act be just
or not? In the name of whom or what can we
protest against oppression and inequality? Without
God, we have no other law but Fact."

Mazzini lived too soon to have to meet a school
that denied morality, as that school is developed to-
day. But he found a numerous and powerful school,
that built morality on what he believed to be radically
wrong foundations. The theory of Rights, since the
precursors of the French Revolution popularized it,
had dominated Liberal thought, except for a handful
of thinkers,—Lamennais, Carlyle, Emerson. It had
had, he owned, its temporary value, as the necessary
rebellion against fatalism and immobility and privilege.
" It destroyed the empire of necessity "; it finally
asserted the dignity of the individual, so that " God's
creature might appear, ready to work, radiant with
power and will." " Only, it stopped short of God,"
for the ideal was hidden from it. Its work was to
destroy, and it was unfitted for an age that needed a

constructive code of ethics. Mazzini included Utilitarianism in his condemnation, as a mere variant of the principle. He knew that Bentham repudiated the connection ; but Bentham's criticism, he thought, was aimed at Blackstone and the theorists of an imaginary compact, not at a system, which based itself on the *à priori* claims of the individual. The spirit and the consequences were the same in both schools. Bentham and the French alike appealed to the getting side of man and not the giving ; both thought of the individual in his self-regarding rather than in his social aspect ; neither had an ideal or any imperative binding law for men ; both neglected the strongest impulses to right action,—enthusiasm and love and sense of duty. They supplied no guide for conduct ; they gave no definition of happiness, nor therefore of what men's rights should be, and left each individual to interpret them by his own fancy. They gave no answer to the question, For what are men to use their liberty? though on the answer depended the whole value of rights. Thus happiness, left without a theory of life's purpose to define it, slided easily into the satisfaction of man's lower part. "Any theory of happiness will make men fall, soon or late, into the suicide of the noblest elements of human nature, will make them go, like Faust, to seek life's elixir in the witch's kitchen." Man's material interests must indeed be cared for, but not for their own sake ; they were only instruments to higher ends ; they must be satisfied because, only when men have leisure and education and a decent home, the moral life has room to grow. If they became the end and not the means, they led to torpor of the nation's soul, to the paralysis that comes, when men care for power and money only, and a country measures its greatness by its riches and brute strength. The whole position was a false one. No moral theory could work, that made happiness the end of life. The Utilitarians mistook the incident of the journey for the end. The spiritual side of man,— his social instincts, his yearnings after righteousness, the pure uncalculating love that gives up life for duty, —all were outside their scheme. "Martyrdom! Your theory has no inheritance in it. Jesus escapes your logic ; Socrates, if you are consistent, must seem to you, as Plato did to Bentham, a sublime fool." Why should men die for their fellows, why suffer prison, exile, poverty, if happiness be the end of life? Why should they toil on, knowing they would not see their labour's fruits, to make life better for a future generation?

Thus the theory supplied no principle of moral action. You cannot, he would say, by any theory of rights make men unselfish. He knew that when a man thinks of happiness, he will not be impartial between his own happiness and other men's, that directly he balances his rights against those of his fellows, he will, however unconsciously, weight the scales in his own favour. It was impossible, he thought, on utilitarian principles to make men work for the happiness of the many. The principle at once sets men thinking on the selfish side, and makes them dole their good deeds with a thrifty hand. "You have taught the rich man," he said, "that society was constituted only to assure his rights, and you ask him then to sacrifice them all for the advancement of a class, with which he has no ties either of affection or custom. He refuses. Will you call him bad ? Why should he consent ? He is only logical." Mazzini often quoted the fate of fellow-revolutionists, who began life with generous impatience to fight the wrong, but when failure came and disillusion, could not say farewell to joy, and balanced self and duty, till "scepticism twined its serpent coils around them," and he "saw that saddest of all things, the slow death of a soul." "For God's sake," he wrote to an English friend on the education of his son, "do not teach him any Benthamite theory about happiness either individual or collective. A creed of individual happiness would make him an egotist : a creed of collective happiness will reach the same result soon or late. He will perhaps dream Utopias, fight for them, whilst young ; then, when he will find that he cannot realise rapidly the dream of his soul, he will turn back to himself and try to conquer his own happiness : sink into egotism." Christ taught another way. "When he came and changed the face of the world, he did not speak of rights to the rich, who had no need to win them, nor to the poor, who would perhaps have imitated the rich and abused them. He did not speak of utility or self-interest to a race corrupted by self-interest and utility. He spoke of Duty ; he spoke of Love and Sacrifice and Faith ; he said that he only should be first, who had helped all men by his works. And when these words were whispered in the ear of a dead society, they gave it life, they won the millions, they won the world, and advanced the education of mankind one step onward.

And,—as a final criticism,—the theory of rights solved nothing. Mazzini did not waste argument on the automatic identity of public and private interests. Rights jostled against rights, the happiness of one man or one class against another's. The theory could not reconcile them or make peace between the jarring interests; rather, it made war,—"war not of blood but of gold and trickery; less manly than the other kind of war but equally destructive; a ruthless war, in which the strong inevitably crush the weak and inexperienced." He attacked the whole economy of free contract, which made the workman's condition depend not on equity, but on the mere brute conflict of opposing rights, and resulted, he believed, of necessity in the workman's defeat. What good were rights to men, who were too poor or ignorant to use them? "Why do I speak to you of your duties before I speak to you of your rights?" he said to Italian working men in 1847. Because, he answered, the theory of rights has triumphed for half a century, liberty has increased, wealth has multiplied, but the condition of the people grows steadily worse in almost every country.

Mazzini's criticism was aimed at Bentham; had he read the later Utilitarians, as apparently he never did, he would no doubt have owned that some of his arguments had no application to them. Happiness implies a definition of happiness, and therefore an ideal; and that ideal may be as high as was Mazzini's own. He made a theoretical mistake in not distinguishing between the object and the motive of life; though, apart from this, he would have said that the desire of others' good must be, not, as in the Utilitarian theory, one of life's motives, but *the* motive. But he was always essentially a moralist, whose business was to find a practical, popular, effective rule of conduct. He knew that the search for happiness meant the search for pleasure, and that the search for pleasure ends in "impotence and nothingness"; that the difficulty is not so much to make men know the good, as to make them in actual conduct rate the higher good above the lower; and that they will not do this if happiness is their object, since the average man will then prefer the immediate and easy happiness to the remoter and more difficult, still less will sacrifice his own happiness for that of others. " I should like," he says, " to look for the answer to the problem in a good mother's advice to her child. There you would certainly find utility condemned as a basis of education. Mothers know that, if happiness were made the object of life down here, life almost always would be only too much a bitter irony." As for the individual, so for the many; and to bid the masses seek for pleasure without reference to the higher ends of life, was to lay up bitterness and vanity for them and evil for the nation. And no hedonism, no theory of rights, could supply an operating rule for conduct. Perhaps he underrated the value of the sense of individual rights, and did not see how in an imperfect society, where nobler rules are faint or wanting, it may give strength to human dignity and kill the slave and coward in men. But he knew that it could not make them live and work for others. He had gone through it all in his own experience; he had had unsurpassed opportunities for judging the springs of action in other men, and he knew that there was nothing here to inspire to steady, strenuous social service.

And so he met the theory with an uncompromising

repudiation of it all. "Man has one right only, to be free from obstacles that prevent the unimpeded fulfilment of his duties." Life is no-search for happiness, whether "by railway shares, selfishness, contemplation," or otherwise. "Our aim is not the greatest possible happiness, but, as Carlyle said, the greatest possible nobleness." "Pain and happiness, ill fortune and good are incidents of the journey. When the wind blows and the rain falls, the traveller draws his cloak closer round, presses his hat on his head, and prepares to fight the storm. Anon the storm leaves him, the sunshine breaks the clouds, and warms his frozen limbs; the traveller smiles and blesses God. But do rain or sunshine change his journey's end?" The end was something other far than happiness. Mazzini looked for a principle that would rate the moral above the material, altruism above selfishness, humanity above the individual; something that would reconcile where Rights divided, that would make men reach to an ideal, and by it live and die for others. "We must find an educative principle, to guide men to better things, to teach them constancy in sacrifice, to bind them to their brothers without making them dependant on any one man's theory or on the brute force of the community. This principle is Duty. We must convince men that they, sons of one God, have here on earth to carry out one law,—that each of us must live not to himself but others,—that the end of life is not to have more or less of happiness but to make ourselves and others better,—that to fight injustice and error, everywhere, for our brothers' good, is not a right only but a duty,—duty we may not without sin neglect, duty that lasts long as life." "Life is a mission," the call

that comes to every man to make the ideal real.
"Life was given you by God, that you might use it
for the profit of Humanity; that you might so direct
your individual faculties, that they will develop your
brothers' faculties, that by your work you might add
something to the collective work of bettering men and
finding Truth." Life is a war with evil; "we cannot
root it out down here, but we can wage undying battle
with it, and everlastingly weaken its dominion." To
such God's Providence has called us. The divine plan
needs our conscious efforts to assist it, and the law,
that rules the Universe, becomes a positive binding law
of conduct. Man's bounden duty is everywhere and
in all things to forward the progress of humanity,
which is written in God's law. "The supreme virtue
is sacrifice,—to think, work, fight, suffer, where our lot
lies, not for ourselves but others, for the victory of
good over evil."

God demands the whole of man. Negative, inactive
goodness is nothing by itself. Our duty lies on earth,
among our fellow-men, in the busy, throbbing life
around us, not in some vain selfish search for spiritual
satisfaction. "Rest is immoral. There is here-down
and there ought to be no rest." Our business is to
make men and their surroundings better, not live for
ourselves in self-absorption or æsthetic ecstasy or
solitary thought and prayer. That is none other than
the search for happiness in subtle shape. "The earth
is our workshop; we may not curse it, we must hallow
it." "God has placed you here on earth; he has set
around you millions of beings like yourselves, whose
march keeps pace with yours, whose life finds susten-
ance in your life. He willed to save you from the

perils of solitary existence, and therefore gave you needs, which by yourselves you cannot satisfy,— mastering social instincts, which are only latent in the brute creation and which distinguish you from it. He has placed this world around you,—this world, that you call Matter, glorious in its beauty, teeming with life, life, which, remember, everywhere displays God's finger, but expects your work upon it and multiplies its powers according as your activities are multiplied. He has planted in you inextinguishable sympathies, pity for them that mourn, joy for them that laugh, wrath against the oppressors of God's creatures, the importunate searching for the truth. And you," he is addressing the pietists, " deny and despise those marks of your mission that God has lavished round you, you lay a curse upon his manifestations, when you bid us concentrate our strength in a work of inward purification,—a work imperfect and impossible to the man who is alone." There is no virtue in the cloistered life. There is " nothing worse than depression, nothing more enervating than self-contemplation." " We are here not to contemplate but to transform nature ; and self almost always lies at the bottom of contemplation. The world is not a spectacle, it is a field of battle, where all, who love the Just, the Holy, the Beautiful, must bear their part, be they soldiers or generals, conquerors or martyrs." " Do not analyse," he once wrote ; " do not light Psyche's lamp to examine and anatomise life. Do good around you : preach what you believe to be the truth and act accordingly ; then go through life, looking forward."

Nor will God's servants take thought for their own salvation. " God will not ask us, ' What hast thou done for thy own soul?' but 'What hast thou done for the souls of others, the sister-souls I gave thee?'" "We cannot rise to God save by our brothers' souls, and we must make them better and more pure, even though they ask us not." "When I hear men say, 'There is a just man,' I ask, 'How many souls are saved by him?'" And again, the mere passive love and apprehension of the truth are no fulfilling of God's law. Even the preaching of truth avails not, unless the preacher strive for it in his daily life. "Thought and action," so he never wearied of insisting, must go hand in hand. "What good are ideas," he asked, "unless you incarnate them in deeds?" "It is not enough that thought be grounded on truth; the thinker's life must visibly express it in his acts; there must be an ever living harmony between mind and morals, between the idea and its application." "Every thought, every desire of good, which we do not, come what may, seek to translate into action, is a sin. God thinks in working, and we must, at a distance, copy him." The great men of earth, of whom Jesus was the prototype, were those who wrought as well as thought,—missionaries, politicians, martyrs, as well as poets and philosophers;—such men as Aeschylus and Dante, Pythagoras and Savonarola and Michelangelo,—most of them, he loved to think, Italians. The great nation was that, whose thought was fruitful in great action, which to high ideals linked noble deeds and taught its sons to work and die. "He who sunders faith from works, thought from action, the moral man from the practical or political man, is not in truth religious. He breaks the chain that binds earth and heaven."

Therefore are we called to work, work without ceasing and with all our power, putting behind us fear and thought of self and looking for results or praise of men; work all the more, when evil is strong around us and the way of truth is dark; work, if need be, even unto death. The law of sacrifice, which Christ left us for our heritage, finds its highest, best expression in martyrdom. "Life and death," he replied, when attacked for sending young Italians to their doom in insurrection, "are both sacred: two angels of God, ministering alike to a higher end, the victory of truth and justice." Men may do more by their deaths than by their lives, and the memory of those, who die in the service of their fellows, may inspire generations and win a country's freedom. "It is not enough to follow the instincts of the heart," he wrote to an impulsive youth, "not enough to let the enthusiasm of a good nature impel you to a good deed now and again. This is the career of 'men of impulse,' who are one degree lower than 'men.' The admiration of the Beautiful, the Great, the Divine, that I ask of you, must be constant in every hour, in every act." We may work from love, while it is given us; but when love grows cold and enthusiasm fails and the damp night of doubt and disappointment settles down, "the simple knowledge of duty" must be there, to bid us work and for ever work. "You must do good," he told another, "for the sake of goodness only." Nor may we ask to see our work's results. Results will come to the race, if not to the individual. Men may see little fruit of their labours; the individual's struggles may end in vanity and disappointment. But the race profits from the

seeming waste. The individual, who is left by himself
" face to face with infinity," loses courage, as he
complained that Carlyle did, and slides into " scepticism and misanthropy." But he will not faint, if he
remembers that all Humanity is working to one
end; he will know that it is not success that matters,
but effort in the right direction. " God measures not
our strength but our intentions." " Where you cannot
have victory, salute and bless martyrdom. The angels
of Martyrdom and Victory are brothers, and both
spread their wings above the cradle of your future
life." " You may succeed or not," he wrote to a
parliamentary candidate;[1] " that is not the vital
question. The question is to work manfully; to
stand on the ground of a principle, whilst almost
everybody makes life a thing of tactics and com-
promises."

But, when a man has listened to the call of God,
and purged his soul of self, and given himself to duty,
—sober, persistent, fearless duty,—his is the power
that nothing else can give. For duty " borrows from
the Divine nature a spark of its omnipotence." Men
will not die for rights; they will for duty. They will
not give up all that makes life pleasant, brave toil and
danger and opprobrium, for self-interest; they will do
it for a principle. Only a sense of duty makes a
people fight through all a generation for a freedom,
that only their children can enjoy. Therefore he,
who would rouse men to noble deeds, and lift them to
sacrifice and heroism, whether it be in the small things
of commonplace citizenship or in the fiery trial of a
revolution, must call them in the name of duty. Again

[1] Mr Peter Taylor in the Newcastle election, 1859.

he appealed to the great example. "Jesus sought not to save a dying world by criticism. He did not speak of interests to men whom the worship of interests had poisoned with selfishness. He asserted in God's holy name principles unknown before; and those few principles, which we, eighteen centuries after, are still seeking to translate into facts, changed the face of the world. One spark of faith accomplished what all the sophisms of philosophers had had no glimpse of,—a step forward in the education of mankind."

Mazzini probably never asked himself what was the ultimate sanction of his code; and, if he had been pushed to it, it is not easy to surmise what answer he would have given. He could hardly have found the sanction in the positive commandment of the Deity, for he held that the will of God was revealed only through humanity, and this transfers the sanction to another ground. Nor, even had he been familiar with them, would he have based the principle on evolutionary arguments,—that altruism is necessary to the race, that that community will survive, which contains the greatest number of self-sacrificing individuals. He would have assented to the facts, but he would probably have said that no theory of heredity or race selection can explain the origin of altruism, which is a personal, conscious, self-generated sense, which therefore cannot come from any 'natural,' unconscious source. Nor, again, would he have said, as a Utilitarian might say, that the life of duty is the highest form of happiness, that there is a sense in which altruism and egoism are identical, because he most tastes fruition, who loses himself in love and work for other men. There is a truth in this, that Mazzini

neglected; he sometimes forgot that Christianity was
an Evangel, good tidings of great joy,—that, so long
as love and enthusiasm and the martyr's passion
possess a man, so far as he has attained to the glorious
liberty of the children of God, the life of duty is the
highest happiness. But he knew only too well that
gloom and depression will come, that, when the light
fails, duty becomes a stern taskmaster, and that no
principle of happiness (in any acceptation of the word)
will keep a man always faithful to his mission. And
so he would almost certainly have fallen back on the
conscience, as the ultimate moral sanction. " Life," he
says, "is a march onwards to Self, through collective
Perfecting to the progressive realisation of an Ideal."
Whether he had called it ' self-realisation ' or any less
ambiguous name, he would have come to the position
that a man feels that he owes it to himself to strive
for the best he knows, to ' do his duty for duty's sake,'
that he must justify his thoughts and actions to himself
—his unsophisticated self,—that, if not, he will feel
remorse and guilt. The practical value of any system
of ethics depends on whether it appeals to ' the sanction in the mind itself,' to feelings familiar to the mass
of would-be moral men. To such the direct appeal to
conscience has more weight than all the arguments of
theologians or utilitarians.

In his essay on *The Duties of Man* and elsewhere
Mazzini enumerates the various spheres of duty. A
man's duties begin with himself, not from any self-
regarding motive, but because as is a man's own
worthiness, so is his power to help his country or
mankind. Never was one more passionate for personal

holiness. 'Be good, be good,' is the recurring theme that runs through all his writings and political aspirations. "There is only one end, the *moral* progress of man and humanity." "You must labour all your life," he wrote to a young Italian, "to make your own self a temple to the Ideal, to God." "To draw near to God, purifying our conscience as a temple, sacrificing self for love,—this is our mission. To make ourselves better,—this is the order of the day, which must be the rule and consecration of our work." All his labours for his country had the supreme end in view, that Italian men and women should lead godly lives. "Make yourselves better," he said to Italian working men in words, that show how little of the demagogue there was in him, "this must be the object of your life. Preach virtue, sacrifice, and love to the classes above you ; and be yourselves virtuous and prepared for sacrifice and love. You must educate and perfect yourselves as well as educate and perfect others."

A man's next duties are to his family. Dear, very dear, to him was the life of family, which he in his self-forgetfulness had put aside. "The only pure joys, unmixed with sadness, that it is given men to enjoy on earth, are the joys of Family." Outside it "men may find brief joys and comforts, but not the supreme comfort, the calm as of a peaceful lake, the calm of trustful sleep, the child's sleep on its mother's breast." The family is an eternal element of human life, more durable even than country ; and the true man will make his family the centre of his life, never wandering from it, never neglecting it. True love is "tranquil, resigned, humble," as Dante's love for Beatrice. The wife will be the equal of her husband, she who is "the

reflex for the individual of the loving Providence that
watches over humanity." Mazzini repudiated any
artificial assimilating of the sexes ; but their differing
functions were equally sacred and necessary. There
must be therefore no superiority of man over woman,
no inequality, domestic or political. A man must
make his wife his comrade, not only in his joys and
sorrows, but in his thoughts and work. He must love
his children with "a true, deep, severe love." "Before
Humanity and God children are the most awful
responsibility that a human being can have." "It
depends on us," so he quoted from Lamennais,
"whether our children turn out men or brutes."

But the family, that shuts itself within its own small
circle, betrays its God-appointed function. It was
made to be a school of service for humanity, and teach
men to be citizens. The *égoisme à deux*, that forgets
country and mankind, the "blind, nerveless, unreason-
ing love of children, that is selfishness in the parents
and destruction for them," betray the family's glorious
prerogative. "Few mothers or fathers, in this irreligious
age of ours, and especially among the well-to-do classes,
understand the gravity and sacredness of their educa-
tional duties." Terrible to their country are the fruits
of "the selfishness taught by weak mothers and careless
fathers, who let their children regard life not as a duty
and mission, but as a search for pleasure and a study of
their own well-being." The true parent will teach his
children not only to be good, but to be patriots, loving
their country, honouring its great men ; will teach them
"not hatred of oppressors but an earnest looking forward
to fight oppression," will make them reverent to true
authority, but rebels against false. There is danger,

he says, in Goethe's maxim : ' do the duty that lies nearest thee.' As him, so it may lead others into a moral solitude, where the cry of humanity comes not. It is so easy in happy life of family, in absorption in one's special work, to forget the duties of a citizen, to avoid the fret and stress, may-be the hardships and the danger, of politics and social duty. But it is not enough for men to be " kind towards their friends, affectionate in their families, inoffensive towards the rest of the world." The true man knows that he may not decline responsibility for those, whom God has made his fellow-citizens. And higher still, higher than family or country, stands Humanity ; and no man may do or sanction aught for either, which will hurt the race. Ever before Mazzini stood the vision of the cross, Christ dying for all men, not from utilitarian calculation of the greatest number, but because love embraces all.

Chapter XV

The State

IN politics, as for the individual, the moral law, so Mazzini taught, must reign supreme. "The end of politics is to apply the moral law to the civil organisation of a country." The state exists for the sake of morality ; its one and only final object is to help the moral growth of the men and women within its borders, help it through all the countless influences that society exercises on the individual. Morality is largely determined by environment ; and the state must so fashion the environment, that the moral life may ever flourish more abundantly in it. "You cannot found the brotherhood of Christ, where ignorance and misery, servility and corruption on the one side and culture, riches, power on the other prevent any mutual esteem and love. Men will not understand the virtue of sacrifice, where money is the sole foundation of individual security and independence." How can they train their children to true patriotism, when a debased conception of it rules, and all around them men and women are thinking of their private gain and pleasure ? How train them to perfect honesty, "when

tyranny and espionage compel men to be false or
silent on two-thirds of their opinions ? " How to despise money, " where gold alone buys honours, influence, respect, nay, is all that stands between them and
the caprice and insults of their masters ? " " Take a
man, for instance," he says, writing in the worst days
of working-class depression, " who labours hard from
fourteen to sixteen hours a day to obtain the bare
necessities of existence ; he eats his bacon and potatoes
(when indeed he can get them) in a place which might
rather be called a den than a house ; and then, worn
out, lies down and sleeps ; he is brutalised in a moral
and physical point of view ; he has not ideas but pro-
pensities,—not beliefs but instincts ; he does not read,
he cannot read. How can you come at him, how
kindle the divine spark that is torpid in his soul, how
give the notion of life, of sacred life, to him, who
knows it only by the material labour that crushes
him and by the wages that abase him ? How will
you give him more time and more energy to develop
his faculties except by lessening the number of hours
of labour and increasing his profits ? How, above
all, will you raise his fallen soul aud give him the
consciousness of his duties and his rights, except by
his initiation into citizenship—in other words, the
suffrage ? " Some day it will be otherwise. " When
there is family life and property, education and
political function for all, when through them men
have closer communion with one another, then family
and property and country and humanity will become
more sacred to them all. When Christ's arms, still
stretched upon the martyr's cross, are freed to clasp
humanity in one embrace, when earth has no more

brahmins and pariahs, masters and servants, but only
men, then shall we worship with far other faith and
other love God's holy name."

There are, in the main, three ways, by which the
state can foster the moral life of the citizens. First
of all it must secure liberty ; not that liberty is an end
in itself, but because it is the necessary condition of
morality. There can be no morality without responsibility, no responsibility without liberty to choose
between good and evil, between social service and self-
interest. Liberty is necessary to true progress, for a
progress that is imposed from above and not freely
accepted by the people,—the whole programme of
paternal despotism,—works no change in character,
and therefore is "a soulless form," which cannot live.
Only the freeman, who owns no lord but God, can
attain to his full spiritual stature. "Where liberty is
not, life is reduced to a simple organic function. The
man, who allows his liberty to be violated, betrays his
own nature, and rebels against God's decrees." Thus
there are certain fundamental liberties, which not even
a democracy may legitimately infringe. "No majority,
no force of the community may take from you what
makes you men." These liberties include, save in rare
exceptions, "all that is indispensable to feed life morally
and materially,"—personal liberty, religious liberty, un-
qualified liberty of speech and press, liberty of association, liberty of trade,—all of them liberties, without
which men cannot choose their sphere of duty, without
which society is destined to waste or stagnation.

It will be noticed that Mazzini omits not only
liberty of immoral action, however 'self-regarding,' but
any liberty that has an anti-social tendency. He did

not admit, for instance, any absolute right of property, and, as we shall see, limited the right of bequest, and advocated severe taxation to check great inequalities of fortune. Theoretically he believed that government should possess very wide powers. But on the whole, when we come to the details of his social programme,[1] his position is the Liberal one ; and (always excepting education) he stood against any great extension of state interference. It was not from any love of individualism and free competition ; he hated them as anarchical,—fatal to spiritual unity and true citizenship, fatal to the welfare of the masses. But he wished the higher order to evolve, not from compulsion, which left the moral sense untouched, not by the force of the majority or of a despotism, but through a moral growth, which carried the community willingly and consciously towards a better state. The liberty to do good would become through education the liberty of doing good. This meant, as we shall see, that he allowed no liberty in education, for moral education must be uniform and therefore removed from individual choice. But this encroachment on liberty once made for the sake of a common morality, for the sake of that same morality he desired liberty in most other spheres of civil life.

But liberty is not enough. By itself, it is a mirage for the masses of mankind. " What is liberty of trade for the man without capital or credit ? What are free opportunities of education for him who has no time for study ? " Only Association can make liberty a reality for the masses, or allow new elements of progress to assert themselves, or save the waste that comes of

[1] See below, pp. 292-294.

isolated or conflicting labours. Nay more, association gives the sense of brotherhood, the spiritual strength, that comes from sharing others' work, from merging individual action in a bigger cause. " Association multiplies your strength a hundred fold ; it makes the ideas and progress of other men your own ; it raises, betters, hallows your nature with the affections of the human family and its growing sense of unity." As Progress is the great intellectual discovery of the modern world, so Association is its new-found instrument. Thus association must be dear to the state as individual liberty ; and provided that any particular association is peaceful and public, and respects elementary liberties, and has no immoral end in view, the state must allow it perfect freedom.

Thus the second duty of the state is to encourage association and harmonise it with liberty ; to give society the originating power of the latter, the effective strength of the former. Both are " equally necessary to the end, which is progress," both " essential to the orderly development of society." On any sound theory, the two principles postulate one another. There can be no association except among free men, since true association implies a conscious recognition and acceptance of the object. Liberty is meaningless without association, because the individual, for all his freedom, is powerless unless he combine with others. Mazzini carefully dissociated himself alike from the *laissez-faire* school and a despotic state socialism. The state must encourage combination, but may do nothing to compel it. The members of an association must be unfettered as to its nature and object and methods (always provided that they are legitimate),

must be free to take up or resign their membership.
" Sacred to us is the individual ; sacred is society.
We do not mean to destroy the former for the latter
and found a collective tyranny ; nor do we mean to
admit the rights of the individual independently of
society, and consign ourselves to perpetual anarchy.
We want to balance the operations of liberty and
association in a noble harmony." " The republican
formula is ' everything in liberty through association.' "

Mazzini did not seriously concern himself with the
abstract relations of the individual and society; probably
it seemed to him a meaningless dispute. His theory
admitted no real antagonism between them. A man's
true individuality lies not in self-assertion but in the
recognition of his duty to his fellows. This recognition
necessarily makes friction impossible between himself
and them, and reconciles the individual and society,
liberty and association, in a common national aim.
Liberty then becomes the higher liberty, not the mere
power of refusing evil, but "the power of choosing
between the different ways that lead to good." Association becomes the economical direction of the country's
forces to a known and common end. It is the function
of the state,—a function it alone can execute,—to instil
the sense of duty into all its members and make that
sense of duty work towards a common ideal. This it
must do through national education, and education
thus becomes the state's third and weightiest task. In
Mazzini's conception education goes far beyond the
imparting of knowledge or even the drawing out of
character. It is the inspiration of a national faith, the
moulding of the soul to great principles of life and
duty. It is, next to religion from which it derives, the

great binding and harmonising element in a nation,
merging individual wills in a common consensus, destroying party friction and class struggle and sectarian
faction, and sweeping a united country onward to the
fulfilment of its destinies. If it had been objected that
the result would be destructive of independence and
originality of thought, he would probably have answered
that the same spirit does not prevent diversities of
operations, and that true originality is better promoted
by discipline than by license. Certainly, as his theory
of genius shows, he set a very high value on originality.
Let thought, he would have said, be free and wide as
air, but without community of aim it wastes itself, and
the state must prevent that waste. Thus there is no
true country without a national education, compulsory
and free. Voluntary education has its necessity under
a political or spiritual despotism, but it leads to moral
anarchy, and religious democracy cannot tolerate false
teaching of its children. The country must have " the
moral direction of the young." " It is ridiculous to
allow every citizen the right to teach his own programme, and refuse the nation the right to transmit
its." Once, when discussing the matter with a friend,
the question was put to him, " If two states had arrived
at an equal stage of education, the one by national and
the other by voluntary schools, which would be the
finer nation ? " " But, my dear," he answered, " that is
to be an atheist." The national education must therefore express the national faith and aim, and give " the
moral unity, which is far more important than material
unity." It is not at all clear how he proposed to
ascertain this national faith. For England, he had a
curious proposal ; " you ought," he said to Jowett, " to

ascertain the mind of the people by making enquiries of the clergy and others what they believed, and when you have ascertained the national mind, you should express it in education." In the future Italy he sometimes thought that it would be embodied in a national declaration of principles, drafted by a Constituent Assembly. But more generally he seems to have distrusted the capacity of the democracy to voice the full faith, and he probably reserved it to the spiritual power under the new religion to enunciate its articles.

At all events national education implied above all else moral education, the moral education which is as " a holy communion with all our brothers, with all the generations that lived, and therefore thought and wrought before us." [1] This, he laments, " is anarchy now." If it is left to the parents, it is often neglected or bad ; if to the teachers, clerical or lay, it too frequently instils either superstition or materialism, or at all events it has no uniformity. Mazzini intended to write a book on education ; if he had done so, we should know more of the agencies, through which he proposed to give moral teaching. Bakounine once asked him, what, if he had got his republic, he would do to make the people really free. Mazzini replied, " Establish schools, in which the duties of man, sacrifice, and devotion would be taught." He had a skeleton programme as a basis of citizen training,—" a course of nationality, including a summary picture of the progress of humanity, national history, and a popular statement of the principles which

---

[1] In the letter referred to on p. 246 note, he calls it "religious education," but it is clear that he did not intend the expression in its usual sense.

rule the country's legislation "; but one cannot think
that this gave all he wanted. He probably counted
more on the universities, and especially on the courses
of philosophy ; and this no doubt explains his strong
dislike of professors, whose teaching seemed to smack
of materialism, his indictment of the eclecticism, which
allowed different schools to be represented in the chairs.
He had a particular animus against German professors
and German philosophy. He blamed the appointment
of Germans at Oxford ; he was very angry that Hegel
was taught at the university of Naples. " One fine
day," he wrote, " we will sweep out all that stuff."

What form of government was best calculated to
attain these ends,—to give full play to liberty, to harmonise it with association, to supply a true national
education ? No form, Mazzini replied, is right *per se.*
He held to the full, though probably not recognising
it, the scholastic doctrine of government by grace.
" Sovereignty is not in I nor we but God." " There is
no sovereignty of right in any one ; sovereignty is in
the aim." A government was legitimate in proportion
as it stood for righteousness. " There is no sovereignty
in the individual or society, except in so far as either
conforms itself to the divine plan and law. An individual
is either the best interpreter of God's law and governs
in his name, or he is a usurper to be overthrown. The
simple vote of a majority does not constitute sovereignty,
if it evidently contradicts the supreme moral precepts
or deliberately shuts the road to progress." " The will
of the people is sacred, when it interprets and applies
the moral law ; null and impotent, when it dissociates
itself from the law, and only represents caprice. "

The theory is of course, as in the days of the schoolmen, a tremendous instrument for reform. No institution, no branch of legislature, no church, no prerogative or prescriptive claim has any rights against the Right. Do they or not make for the country's good? By the answer they must stand or fall. The theory is supremely true, and on occasion of highest social value. Its dangers lie in the possibility of mistaken application, and in its tendency to regard the form rather than the spirit of an institution, —a danger especially present to minds like Mazzini's, which are deficient in powers of accurate analysis. An institution, so runs their reasoning, has failed; therefore it is wrong; therefore it must be swept away. Reform is impossible; therefore let there be root-and-branch revolution. It is strange that Mazzini, with his admiration of English habits and dislike of French, did not see how here his logic approximated to the latter. He did not see how plastic institutions are, how it is often better to save the great expenditure of force, that must go to destroy a rooted institution, how it is sometimes easier to change the spirit than the form. In this his political wisdom went astray, and his long profitless crusade against the monarchy is a melancholy illustration of the error.

Thus, then, there is no essential sovereignty in any form of government. But democracy is the form most likely to interpret God's law aright. We must " reverence the people," not because they are the majority, " but because they concentrate in themselves all the faculties of human nature distributed among the several individuals, — faculties of religion and politics, industry and art." In other words, the collective wisdom of the many is likely to excel the wisdom of the few; a democratic state can use the special knowledge of every citizen, and choose the most capable for its administrators; and its judgment is likely to be more four-sided and better informed than that of a state with restricted citizenship. And just as Humanity is the interpreter of God's law, so a people often has an inspiration that seldom comes to individuals, glimpses of the truth that are granted to the multitude in moments of enthusiasm, an instinct that impels it to give power to its best men. He even, inconsistently with his general position, justifies democracy on *à priori* grounds; it is "a potent, undeniable, European fact," and therefore must be a part of God's providential design.

But it is impossible not to feel that all through Mazzini's thought there runs a certain uneasiness about democracy. He accepted it as an inevitable fact; he recognised that at all events it was superior to any government based on privilege; it fitted in with his theory of Humanity and his own passionate sympathies. But he had an intermittent dread that democracy, like theocracy and monarchy, might forget the law of God. He feared that the French Revolution had started it on the wrong road; he had had his disappointments in Italy; in later life he felt the peril that materialist socialism might deflect it from spiritual ends. He advocated universal suffrage, not because of any absolute virtue in it, but as "the starting-point of political education," and he gravely feared that, till national education had created a national consensus, it might easily become a tyranny of the majority. He preferred a system of indirect election. Towards the end of his life he was a keen advocate of women's suffrage, but he was anxious that the agitation for it should be equally an agitation for their own moral growth, a crusade against "their perennial vanity, their worship of ridiculous fashions, their lightness of parties and conversation," their husband-hunting. And this mistrust made him turn to a strong authority, elected and deposable by the people, but with very extended powers, and charged not only to execute the popular mandate, but go in advance of it. "The supreme power in a state must not drag behind the stage of civilisation that informs it; it must rather take the lead in carrying it higher, and, by anticipating the social thought, bring the country up to its own level." It is for republics to make republicans, not republicans republics. He earnestly repudiated the Whig-American theory o government. Anxiously as he guarded personal an religious and commercial liberty, he wished to see th functions of government, at all events in educatio and as a stimulating and suggestive influence, as wid and not as narrow as possible. Distrust of governmen in itself, the whole system of checks and balances, h condemned as weakening the power of the state t promote progress. It is extremely difficult to dis entangle with precision what was his ideal constitution and it may be doubted whether he had worked it ou himself. Though he probably had no very stron liking for parliamentary government, he seems to hav accepted it, and to have wished to give it larg executive powers. But above it, and apparently distinc from the executive, was to be the real "government, the spiritual authority, whose duty it would be t "point to the national ideal," while parliament and the executive "directed the forces of the country" in the road it indicated. But there must be no suspicion of dictatorship, and perfect trust and mutual inspiration must unite the spiritual and temporal authorities.[1]

At all events the ideal government, whatever its precise form, could, he believed, exist only under a republic. The story of his life has shown how passionately he clung to his republican faith; how for it he gave or wasted his best days, how his untamable desire for it tangled his work for Italian Unity. His condemnation of monarchy was partly a theoretical one. The republic was "the most logical form of democracy," the only corollary of liberty and equality; monarchy was founded on inequality, its dynastic interests were not the nation's, and therefore it could never give a country moral unity. Whether absolutist or constitutional, it was a sham, because in modern life it corresponded to no real belief, no essential principle; and because it was a sham, it was the fruitful parent of dishonesty. Quite late in life he somewhat changed his point of attack, and condemned it as possessing no vitality to lead, and therefore impotent to found a strong government. But his indictment, at least in his early years, was drawn mainly from the actual evidence of corruption and misrule in the monarchies of the first half of the century. It may well have seemed impossible then to reconcile monarchy with any national well-being. He made

---

[1] Mazzini's views are perhaps most clearly stated in his speech to the Roman Assembly of March 9, 1849 (before he became Triumvir). See also *Scritti editi e inediti*, XVI. 14. In the second and perhaps the first of these passages *popolo* seems used as equivalent to parliament. In the second, *governo* is obviously not the executive. See also above, p. 247.

little or no exception for constitutional monarchies. Louis Philippe's rule was small argument for the principle; and as late as 1862 he condemned constitutional monarchy as "incompatible with progress," everywhere outside England. For England, in later years, he made an exception; and his judgment here shows that he could view the issue more serenely, when he escaped from his prejudices. "The struggle, which occupies English life," he said in 1870, "is not between the nation and the monarchy, but between the people and the aristocracy, the latter being the one element of the past, that retains and communicates its vitality." In Italy the facts were after 1848 much the same as in England; but here he was blinded by party feeling, and he could never see that what was the real issue in the thirties had gone into the background. His fallacy was a nominalist one. In his early days there had been a vital difference between monarchy and republic. Afterwards the classification became unreal; and the true differentiation lay in various species of parliamentary government, in various relations between parliament and the executive. In his own Italy to-day the republic becomes increasingly a factitious and academic issue, as more vital questions make the true dividing lines in politics.

However mistaken his distinction between republic and monarchy, the republic, as he conceived it, was no mere form of government. "God is my witness," he said, "that I pay no tribute to forms." He had little liking for the republic in the United States, with its weak bond of union, and its system of checks and balances. He refused his blessing to the Third Republic in France. "By the Republic," he told the Roman Assembly in

1849, "we do not mean a mere form of government, a name, a system imposed by a victorious party on its rivals. We mean a principle, a new step forward in education taken by the people, a programme of education to be carried out, a political institution calculated to produce a moral advance ; we mean the system which must develop liberty, equality, association ;—liberty, and consequently every peaceful development of ideas, even when they differ in part from our own ;—equality, and therefore we cannot allow political castes to be substituted for the old castes that have passed away ; association, that is a complete consensus of all the vital forces of the nation, a complete consensus, so far as is possible, of the entire people." For him the republic meant absolute trust between people and government, choice of the most capable and best for office, a veritable national unity, that destroyed party friction and impelled the undivided forces of the country to social legislation. The republic, and it alone, will be the ideal state, God's kingdom realised on earth, "where institutions tend primarily to the bettering of the most numerous and poorest class, where the principle of association is best developed, where the road of progress has no end, as education gradually develops and all elements that make for stagnation and immobility disappear, where, in fine, the whole community, strong, tranquil, happy, peaceful, bound in a solemn concord, stands on earth as in a temple built to virtue and liberty, to progressive civilisation, to the laws that govern the moral world." There, in the people "that knows no caste or privilege, save of genius and virtue, no proletariat or aristocracy of land or finance," in the people "united by the brotherhood of one sole faith, one sole tradition, one sole thought of love," the people that worships principles more than men, that cherishes its past but looks ever forward to its future, resolute to unlock its destinies,—there stands the city of God, " the similitude of that divine society, where all are equal, and there is one love, one happiness for all."

Chapter XVI

Social Theories

MAZZINI'S faith in the republic came largely of his conviction that it was the only effective instrument or social legislation. He was sometimes charged with neglecting social for political reform, with preaching, as Bakounine put it, a "detestable bourgeois patriotism." The charge was true for no time of his life, least for his later years. To him the social question was "the most sacred" as it was "the most hazardous" problem of the age. He was one of the first to insist that the rise of the working classes was the great social phenomenon of the century. Political reform, so he told the Carbonari and the Chartists, had its only sufficiency and justification, when it was the instrument of social reform. This did not quite represent his thought, for he was insistent that questions of political liberty and justice intimately touched man's moral development; but he held with equal earnestness that the social question had its independent and undying importance. "There is no such thing," he wrote, "as a purely political or purely social revolution; every true revolution has its political and social character alike."

All his passionate sympathy went out to the disinherited. Compassion, says one who knew him,

shone in his face and vibrated in his voice, whe
he spoke of the masses and their hardships.   H
felt intensely for a lot, which in the '40s an·
'50s he believed was growing steadily worse.   Indig
nantly he spoke of the workman's "poverty-stricker
cribbed, precarious life, closing in infirm and squali·
and unassisted old age."   "The workman has n·
freedom of contract," he replied to the old economist:
"he is a slave ; he has no alternative but hunger o
the pay, however small it be, that his employer offer
him.   And his pay is a *wage* ; a wage often in
sufficient for his daily needs, almost always unequal t·
the value of his work.   His hands can multiply th·
employer's capital three fold, four fold, but not so hi
own pay.   Hence his incapacity to save ; hence th·
unrelieved, irreparable misery of commercial crises.
And even without crises, " his life is poisoned by ·
sense of uncertainty and constant dread ; and old age
—brought on prematurely by heavy and often un
healthy work,—awaits him, threatening, implacable.
His " destiny is that of accursed races,—to live an·
suffer, curse and die."   " A life of poverty and a death
bed in a hospital,—that is what society in this nine
teenth century provides for two-thirds of its member
in almost every country, eighteen hundred years an·
more since a Holy One, that men hail as divine
proclaimed that all are equals and brothers and son·
of God."
   But he was no pessimist, at all events in later years
when he knew the workman better, and saw that, ir
spite of all, he was advancing and gave promise o
infinite further advance.   The day of deliverance wa:
near.   The workman's emancipation was inevitable

written in the decrees of Providence. The labour question was the acknowledged problem of the time, its solution "the social faith of all men now who love and know." "The upward movement of the artisan classes in our towns," he wrote towards the end of life, "dates back now for more than a century ; slow but tenacious in its progress, advancing from decade to decade by a law of increasing momentum, and in these last twenty years growing, visibly for all, in intensity and expansion, and acquiring, as it goes, real power and self-consciousness." It all was "leading up to a great revolution, an impulse given by Providence, nevermore to recede, till it has reached its end." And he gloried in it. Whatever fears he may have had for the working of democracy, he had none for the labour movement. The rise of the working classes was "as a flowing tide, that the divine breath has stirred" ; and he watched it "not with fear, but with the loving reverence, with which one watches a great providential act."

But just because his faith and love were great, he was not afraid to point "the men of labour" to the heights. It was his familiar precept of the moral aim. "Material improvements," he told them, "are essential, and we will fight to win them ; not because men have no other interest than to be well housed and clothed, but because your moral development is stopped, while you are, as you are to-day, engaged in a continual fight with poverty." So too in his rather scanty references to political economy, he insists that its teaching must always have reference to a moral ideal. Economics must be "the expression not of the human appetite but of man's industrial mission." Otherwise, they "substitute the problem of humanity's kitchen for the problem of humanity," and teach selfishness for individuals and classes and industrial warfare. It was not only that economic progress must aim consistently at personal morality, at making better husbands, fathers, neighbours, that it must be pure of any spirit of bitterness or revenge or aught that sins against the brotherhood of man. Besides all this, it must not be allowed to maim the working man's powers and duties as a citizen, must never be purchased by the sacrifice of political liberty or manliness He pointed for his moral to France in 1849 and 1850, when the French artisans sold their political rights to Louis Napoleon for the promise of a labour policy. 'Bread and amusements,' he reminded them were ever the offer of despots. Outside liberty and strenuous political interest there was no salvation economic or other. The true man will think not only of his class but of his country, and not of his own country only, but of the sufferings and rights of men the whole world over. If the working classes forgot their political duties, thought lightly of political reform, connived at an unjust foreign policy, they sacrificed one of their nature's noblest functions, and built their own economic progress on the sand. And he believed that, France notwithstanding, the people always knew this in their hearts. The Chartists, he pointed out, with their bare, imperfect political programme, had more followers than all the French Socialists. "The last of those you call political agitators," he told the latter, "will always have more influence with the people than all your utopias; because at the root of every political question the people

ıs at least a glimpse of something that appeals to its
ıul, something that gives it self-consciousness and raises
s trampled dignity." " The working men of Italy
ıught like heroes at Milan and Brescia, in Sicily and
: Rome, not for a rise of wages, but for the honour of
ıe Italian name, for the free life of their nation. The
orking men of Paris fought and won in 1848, not
:cause of a financial crisis or their own poverty, but
:cause the monarchy dragged France's glory and
ıty in the mud, because it refused French citizens a
ee press, and free right of meeting and association."
 It was from this standpoint that he attacked Social-
m. We need not concern ourselves with his strictures
ı the expired schools of the early French Socialists,
· with his very crude criticism of Louis Blanc,—
iticism, which he would hardly have made in later
ïe, and which is certainly inconsistent with his own
ıcial schemes. We can neglect, too, much of his
:tack on the economic side of collectivism, which he
:ver really understood. It is more to the point to
ısume a greater knowledge of modern Socialism than
: possessed, and see what is his essential relationship
ı it. He had not a few ideas in common with the
[arxite school. His own industrial ideal contained,
ıough he knew it not, the germs of the socialist
ımmunity. He looked as earnestly and confidently
ı they do to the death of capitalism, and built his
ıpes on the development of association ; he recognised
ith them the inevitable historic evolution of the
orkers, and that it is the march of the humble,
ıknown multitude, and not the hero, which deter-
ıines the world's progress ; he hailed the time, when
ısses would be no more, and all be equals in rights

and opportunities, and he believed that this equality
could never be reached under a capitalist system.

But in root principles he differed from the strict
Marxites almost as essentially as he himself supposed.
While with him moral and spiritual phenomena are the
fundamental facts, Marx builds his system on material
phenomena. For the collectivist, man is chiefly the product of his economic surroundings ; for Mazzini, the
social and industrial environment is only "the manifestation of the moral and intellectual condition of humanity
at a given period, and above all of its faith." For the
one, history is the sequence of economic cause and effect,
and the growth of mind and morals is the secondary
consequence of economic facts ; with the other, the
economic facts, though not neglected, are subordinated,
religion is the master principle of human progress, and
religious systems are the milestones that mark the
road. The two schools are absolutely antagonistic in
their conception of the ideal. Marx and his followers
would discover it by the right interpretation of the
drift of facts ; if indeed we can call it an ideal, what is
accepted merely as a necessary tendency, and when
right and wrong are judged by the fact, not the fact
by right and wrong. Mazzini understood to the full
the value of facts as conditioning the ideal, as pointing
out how far it was attainable at the moment, nay, as in
some degree indicating the ideal itself. But to him
right and wrong had no dependance on the existing
fact ; facts tended to approximate to the ideal, because
the ideal was sovereign, and Providence guided them
towards it ; and it was man's free privilege and
bounden duty to help the work of Providence, and be
lord of facts. Mazzini did not kick against the pricks

of economic evolution ; he took modern industrialism as it is, and never wished to thwart the natural tendencies of industrial discovery. But he claimed that man has power to turn them to good or evil,—a good or evil that has reference not to them but to a moral end.

Hence their teaching has differed widely in its practical consequences. Marx deduced from his economic studies a confident and detailed prophecy of economic development. It was a faith, whose assurance and optimism gives it a mighty power to sway men, so long as faith stays unquestioned. But economic dogmas, especially of the prophetic kind, are apt to be shaken by the rough wind of facts ; and it has been the fate of Marx' system to be line by line explained away by its commentators. If it still retains its influence,—and, indeed, it is a potent influence,—it is because it has quieted scepticism by shedding much of its founder's doctrine, and because it finds and has more or less always found expression in a political programme, such as Mazzini preached, aiming at high ends of liberty and justice. Mazzini, so confident often in his religious and political horoscopes, here chose a humbler part. He insisted indeed on one broad economic principle,—association, and he pointed to certain reforms of immediate practicability. But he resolutely refused to forecast the economic future. Humanity, he would repeat, goes on its own way, and laughs at the man, who finds " the secret of the world under his pillow." " I think," he wrote, ' that our problem is not so much to define the forms of future progress, as to place the individual under such conditions as make it easy for him to understand

K

and fulfil it." He created no great party of the proletariat; it was his as useful function to fertilise the moral soil, to inspire all classes with a deeper sense of social obligation, and thus to ease the road for social progress, whatever particular shape the circumstances of the time might counsel it to take.

The two men differ again radically in their influence on class relations. To Mazzini 'the struggle of classes,' however peaceful and legal in its form, would have been a hateful idea. It is true he sternly rebuked the short-sighted folly of the richer classes, and he would find excuses for wild acts or theories of proletariat protest. But he set his face resolutely against class hatred, against dreams of violence and revenge against social revolutions which worked hardship to the individual. Hopeless as he was of enlisting the upper classes, at least in Italy, on the side of social reform, he set his hopes on the middle classes; and from the days of the *Apostolato Popolare* down to the last years of life, he preached insistently that middle and working classes must stand together in the social movement. The whole theory of Duty looked to the harmonising of motives, not to the brute struggle of opposing social forces. The collectivist takes the social discord for granted, and bids the workers trust to themselves alone and win their ends by force, however much force may be disguised behind the vote. Each principle has its time; the socialist mistake has been to elevate to a principle, what is the sad necessity of an uninspired age.

It remains to examine Mazzini's own programme of social reconstruction. He lays down certain economic ixioms. First, private property must remain, however much the State should try to equalise fortunes through taxation. Mazzini endorses the familiar argument from expediency, — the necessity of property to stimulate labour and encourage invention. But his apology for it is in the main an *à priori* one. " Property," he says, " when it is the result of labour, represents the activity of the body, as thought represents the activity of the soul ; it is the visible sign of our part in the transformation of the material world, as our ideas and our rights to liberty and inviolability of conscience are the signs of our part in the transformation of the moral world. The man who works and produces has a right to the fruits of his own labour ; in this resides the right of property."[1] There is a flavour of Ricardo and Marx in this, and it is easy to see a socialist application, unintended by the writer. Next, the new social organisation must not be the work of compulsion. He saw that voluntary working-class organisation was an essential preliminary to any lasting social advance ; and, as we shall see, his own schemes pivot on voluntary societies for cooperative production. And lastly, schemes of economic change must always aim at increasing productiveness. He knew that there could be no serious improvement in the workman's condition, unless the national production were increased ; and he seems to have dimly

[1] He was once arguing with Sir James Stansfeld as to the possibility of communism. Stansfeld said, " Why should not all property be vested in society ? " Mazzini replied, " Because that is nonsense. Society abstractedly is nothing, really a collection of individuals. Individuals do the work, therefore individuals get the property ; they may give it away if they like, but the right to it is in themselves." The spirit of the argument is curiously inconsistent with his usual position.

realised that the two things must mutually react, an
rise in the workman's income increasing the deman
for commodities and thereby stimulating productior
and this increase of production in its turn encouragin
a further increase of the workman's pay.

When we come to the particulars of his economi
programme, we find fertility and boldness of sugges
tion, but small attempt to work out the details. H
was constitutionally unfitted to be an economist; h
lacked the necessary precision of thought and accurac
of analysis. He rather despised economic study, a
all events when it came from books. A real know
ledge of the economic question is to be found, he say
"in the workshops and the homes of the artisans,
rather than in "statistics and documents, which ar
sometimes erroneous, always incomplete, compiled a
they are either by officials, whose tendency is t
conceal the evil, or by private individuals, whos
tendency is to exaggerate it." He trusted to a know
ledge of the workman's thoughts and aspiration
gleaned from close and affectionate intercourse, mor
than to any inquiry into the outside facts of h
life.

His suggestions were many. Among the mor
commonplace were free trade in land, legislation t
protect tenants, arbitration between capital and labou
national insurance (apparently to be compulsory), th
regulation by the state of "that den of robbers," th
Stock Exchange. At one time he wished the state t
guarantee work for everybody, but as he does n
mention the proposal later than 1849, it may t
assumed that he relinquished it. For Italy, he su
gested a great scheme of home colonisation on h

unreclaimed lands ; and it is a curious instance of his
want of accurate enquiry, that in his advocacy of it he
took no account of the all-important factor of malaria.
It is curious, too, that, like many Italians at the
opposite pole of thought, he disliked emigration, and
would gladly have checked what has proved to be one
of the chief sources of Italian development. All these,
however, were minor suggestions. His programme
rested mainly on two proposals,—a radical reform
of taxation, and the gradual supersession of capitalism
by voluntary cooperative societies of workmen. His
canons of taxation are shortly stated and may be
shortly summarised. Economy in collection, free
trade, no taxes on food, the smallest possible inci-
dence on industry were his fiscal maxims ; and he
wished to carry them out by abolishing all indirect
taxation and, apparently too, all special taxes on
land, and substituting a single tax on income, to
be graduated and, it would seem, severely graduated.
He also proposed that in all cases of persons dying
without heirs within the fourth degree, estates should
lapse to the state.

He looked for more radical change to his scheme
of cooperative production, a scheme which appears
in its main outlines as early as 1833, but which he
worked out in more detail in the last ten years
of his life. It was a special application of the same
principle of Association, which he had carried into
other branches of social and political activity. He
proposed that a great national capital should be
accumulated for the purpose. Church lands, railways,
mines, and " some great industrial enterprises," which
he never specified, were to be nationalised, whether

or not with compensation does not appear. At one time he wished to confiscate in Italy the estates of those, who fought against the nationalist cause,—a proposal strangely out of harmony with his usual tolerance. The income from these sources, from the rents of reclaimed lands and existing national and communal estates, and from properties which lapsed to the state, would form the "National Fund" or "tax of democracy." At one time he destined part of the fund to education, another part to assist any European democracy struggling for its rights. But its main, and perhaps in his later idea its only purpose was to assist the spread of voluntary societies for cooperative production, industrial and agricultural. Any such society, that could prove its members honesty and capacity, might claim to have its capital advanced from the Fund. The loans were to be at 1 or 1½ per cent., and were to be made through special banks administered by the Communal Councils. Nothing is said as to the repayment of the loans, but as he contemplated the extension of the societies, till they ultimately covered the whole field of industry, we may assume that the loans were to be repaid and passed on to new societies. The societies were apparently to be left absolutely free as to the management of their business, the sale of produce, and the disposal of their net income. To assist their credit, they were to have the right to deposit any unsold produce in national magazines, and receive in exchange negotiable notes which, it seems to follow, would have been legal tender. The societies were also to be admitted on equal terms with private firms to contract for government work ; this latter was perhaps the first suggestion

a system, which is now working in Italy with some
ccess.

Such were Mazzini's sketchy but suggestive economic
hemes,—schemes which, he believed, would ultimately
stroy both poverty and capitalism, without hardship
individuals or danger to liberty, leavening the social
orality with the God-given principle of association.
e seems to have never asked himself what would be
e ultimate destiny of his co-operative scheme; had
: done so, he must have seen that, by however
fferent a road, it was bound to end in collectivism.
will be recognized now that his plan was in all
sentials identical with latter-day socialism, as put
it by its best exponents, and it may be claimed that
the world of ideas Mazzini more than Marx is its
ther. That his scheme would soon come into work-
g, he had little doubt, at all events in Italy. For in
s social plans, as in all else, his own Italy was ever
permost in mind. He knew, when few others knew
the patience and common-sense and idealism of the
alian artisan, and he proudly counted on him to let
aly lead the nations in the solution of the labour
lestion.

Chapter XVII

Nationality

THE law of Duty, man's bounden service to humanity, goes on beyond the individual and the state to be the rule of international relations. Man's end, so runs Mazzini's argument, is to serve the progress of humanity. But the individual, in his isolated impotence, would shrink from the immensity of the burden. And for most men, humanity excites no effective sense of obligation; they will give for country what they will not give for the wider and remoter circle of mankind. The cosmopolitan, who talks of duty to humanity and neglects the nation, is as one who bids men climb a ladder and takes away the rungs. Therefore Providence, once again applying the law of association, has placed the individual among men of like feelings and aspirations, that serving his country he may serve humanity, that through the nation and its common strength he may have power to help the progress of the world. Thus a nation is a God-appointed instrument for the welfare of the race, and in this alone its moral

296

essence lies. "Nationality is sacred to me," he says, "because I see in it the instrument of labour for the good and progress of all men." "Countries are the workshops of humanity"; "a nation is a living task, her life is not her own, but a force and a function in the universal Providential scheme." "Humanity is a great army, marching to the conquest of unknown lands, against enemies both strong and cunning. The peoples are its corps, each with its special operation to carry out, and the common victory depends on the exactness, with which they execute the different operations."

This "division of European labour" is essential to the progress of Europe, and, through it, of the world. But each group of humanity's workmen, if it is to be efficient, must be organised, not by coercion, but by free acceptance of their obligations; they must be impelled by duty and the sense of a great common work to do. Each nation must be a living, homogeneous entity, with its own faith and consciousness of self. Europe, in Mazzini's lifetime, had little of this. He condemned its existing divisions as answering to no principle, since for the most part they were agglomerations of territory, made in the interests of a royal dynasty or in the name of some artificial principle, as the balance of power; and therefore they were powerless to inspire a common national effort for an intelligent and useful end. Factitious and immoral ends filled up the void; unsatisfied national yearnings burst imperiously through diplomatic schemes of peace; there was little of the burning love of independence, that alone safeguarded from designs of aggressive empire, from France in the past, from Russia in the present. The map of Europe must be drawn afresh, and states be made conterminous with nationalities.

What, then, are the inherent, essential marks of nationality? Are race and geographical features, language and literature, customs and traditions? None of these, Mazzini replied, are more than secondary elements, race least of all. Wiser and juster than Bismarck and his school, he saw that race, even if it were discoverable, has small connection with the facts of to-day. He did not investigate the dark problem of race characteristics, he did not even ask whether race affinities are among the physical causes that create a national feeling. But, none the less, his argument is indestructible against the theory that makes race the chief base of nationality. He was saved from ethnological fancies by his sensible conclusion, that races are too intimately compounded to be a cause of national character. "There is not a single spot in Europe," he declared, "where an unmixed race can be detected." "France, the most powerful nationality of the modern world, is a mixture of Germans, Celts, and Romans." There is one aspect however of the race question, that he did not sufficiently recognise. However imaginary the original ethnological basis of a country may be and generally is, yet some races have been fixed for several centuries, and this has generated a belief in a common racial origin, which, however false historically, may none the less, when supported by a common language, become an important and sometimes a dominant factor in creating a sense of nationality.

He gave his fancy play in determining the in-

fluence of geography. He loved geographical study,
and as usual sought for a spiritual purpose underlying
the physical facts. "By the courses of the great
rivers, by the lines of the high mountains, and other
geographical features God has marked the natural
borders of the nations." "Nationalities," he said,
"appear to me to have been traced long ago by the
finger of Providence on the map of Europe"; and
Italy, for instance, had her "sublime, irrefutable
boundary marks." He left this transcendentalism for
safer ground, when he came to language and literature,
and recognised what potent factors they had been in
the making of nations. The importance of language
was sufficiently obvious. Literature had sometimes,
as in the case of his own Italy, remained the one
surviving sign of nationality, when all else was lost.
He knew how great had been the influence of Dante
in forming the national sense of his own country;
how much the Polish poets of the century had done
to feed the Slav national spirit; how intimate is the
power of national melodies; what the common possession of a great poet may do to knit a people. He
realised too, though perhaps insufficiently, how history
has helped to form nations; how a common government draws a people together in common loyalty or
common revolt; how war may be a welding influence;
how men, living for generations under the same law,
acquire from it common habits and customs and
traditions.

All these, however, are but the formative elements
of nationality; they are not its essence. Mazzini's
clear democratic faith kept him from confusing the
justification of the fact with its causes. Nationality

was independent of any of them. Centuries of divided government had not destroyed the national sense of Italy; Switzerland was a nation for all its diversity of languages; difference of tongues did not prevent Poland and Lithuania from sharing the same national aspirations; Alsace belonged to France, however German it might be by race and history. Nationality is a sentiment, a moral phenomenon, which may be generated by material causes, but exists by virtue of moral facts. On any theory of freedom or democracy it can have no positive, meaning basis but the popular will; and it is a parody of nationality that unites by coercion. " Nationalities can be founded only for and upon and by the people "; and it follows that when the inhabitants of a territory desire to be a nation, provided that behind their desire there lies a moral purpose, they have the right to be one. This, despite slight and rare inconsistencies, he made the broad clear principle of modern, democratic nationality, a principle " invincible as conscience," whose triumph no hostility of kings or statesmen, no artificial counterfeits can permanently hinder.

Still, he held, the mere fact of the popular will is not enough. Nationality, like every political phenomenon, must have a moral aim to justify it. A mere momentary reaction against misgovernment, for instance, gave no sufficient claim to independence. " In questions of nationality, as in every other question, the end alone is sovereign "; and a true nation must have its moral intention, its clear and understood mission to accomplish for itself and for humanity, its conscious part in realising the divine idea on earth. It is only in its homage to the moral law, that a nation finds its "baptism and consecration." "A community of men drawn together by a selfish principle for a purely material purpose is not thereby a nation. To constitute a nation, its informing principle and purpose and right must be grounded on eternal bases. The purpose must be essentially a moral one, since a material interest by itself is by its nature finite, and can therefore form no basis of perpetual union." "Country is not a territory; territory is only its base; country is the idea that rises on that base, the thought of love that draws together all the sons of that territory."

This love is patriotism. "O my brothers," he says, "love your country. Country is our house, the house that God has given us, setting therein a populous family, to love us and be loved by us, to understand us and be understood by us better and more readily than others are." It was by such burning patriotism he saved his country and was first to practise it himself. But he detested the sentimental and emotional patriot. His patriotism was a silent, manly thing, that hated display and braggart talk; it was as a steady spiritual flame, that never roared to heaven and never sank to ashes. He tested it by its fruit in the individual life. No ill-living man was true patriot. "Let country," he said, "be incarnated in each one of you; each one of you feel and make himself responsible for his brothers; each of you so act that in yourselves men may respect and love your country." "Where the citizen does not know that he must give lustre to his country, not borrow lustre from it, that country may be strong but never happy." Real patriotism will not fear to speak the truth. "Flattery will never save a country, nor proud words make us less abject." "The honour of a country depends much more on removing its faults than on boasting of its qualities." One can imagine what would have been his scorn for the degenerate imperialism of latter days. The patriot's supreme desire is that his country's true honour may be untarnished; he thinks more of duty than of victory. His own Roman Republic, that glorious and illuminating example of patriotism, had small hope of success, but its honour stood entire, and therefore morally it triumphed. Success, empire, military glory may be a country's lot; so may failure and defeat and poverty; neither this nor that fate touches its real being. True national dignity and glory lie in right doing, and humiliation comes only from public dishonour and a mendacious diplomacy. "You must keep your country pure of selfishness," was his maxim of patriotism for Italian working men.

Patriotism, then, is intense regard for a country's moral greatness; and it expresses itself in that sense of national duty, which he held to be the only justification of a country's national existence. This duty has two objects, the community itself and all humanity. We have seen what he conceived to be a nation's duty to its members; there is no true country, he said, without a national education, or where men starve for want of work. Here we are more concerned with that forwardness to serve humanity, which he made the other mark of the true nation. "National life and international life should be two manifestations of the same principle, the love of good." Above the separate nations stands the European brotherhood, the late-born child of Christianity. Sir Thomas More, he says first formulated the new law of peace; literature and trade and travel are ever drawing the nations together by "a law of moral gravitation"[1]; the French Revolution echoed through the democracies of Europe; the struggle with Napoleon renewed the common understanding of the nations. The cause of the people is the same the whole world over, and the democracies must join hands to fight the battle of them all, as he had tried to make them do, when he founded Young Europe. Humanitarian movements,—the abolition of the slave trade, the cause of Greece and Italy,—were European. "There exists then in Europe a harmony of needs and wishes, a common thought, a universal mind, which directs the nations by convergent paths to the same goal." No country may be isolated, economically or intellectually; and it is a poor and counterfeit patriotism, that despises other countries. That way lies destruction. "A nation's growth depends on the trust that other peoples place in it"; a country guided by a moral principle "finds everything open readily to it from markets to political alliances," but one that stands for an unjust policy has mistrust and jealousy for its portion.

Hence the country, that does injury to another, sins against itself. "I hate," he said, "the monopolist, usurping nation, that sees its own strength and greatness only in the weakness and poverty of others." That is a poor and stunted people, whose foreign policy is "one of aggrandisement and selfishness, whether it seeks them basely or buys glory at other

---

[1] The first address of the People's International League, from which these words are quoted, was written by W. J. Linton, but was based on Mazzini's rough draft.

men's expense." Countries, that cherish liberty at home and outrage it abroad, "are fated to expiate their error through long years of isolation and oppression and anarchy." So far he preached familiar doctrine, but he carried it into regions of his own. International duty does not stop at non-aggression. Every country has its positive duty to humanity ; and while evil is enthroned, and right can hardly hold its own, and the eternal battle rages round, it may not stand aside in cowardly forgetfulness. Mazzini abhorred the doctrine of non-intervention—the principle that no country may interfere in the domestic matters of another,— a doctrine which the Americans and Canning introduced for the protection of freedom, but which less hardy statesmen in France and England had perverted to excuse their own faint-heartedness. If the principle had been generally accepted, if it had meant for instance that France could not intervene at Rome or Russia restore despotism in Hungary, it might have worked successfully. But practically it meant that "intervention was all on the wrong side," that only England observed the principle, and therefore the one Great Power, which in some degree stood for liberty, tied its own hands, while the Powers that stood for despotism worked "their unhallowed ends when, where, and how they thought fit" over three-fourths of Europe. As Mazzini pointed out, the theory took for granted a system based on nationality; and where nationality was non-existent, as in Italy and South-Eastern Europe, it had no rightful application. At the best it was a "poor and incomplete" doctrine. A country has its "bonds of international duty," obligatory in proportion to its strength. "The

absolute doctrine of non-intervention in politics corresponds to indifference in religion ; it is a masked
atheism, a negation of all belief, of every general
principle, of any mission of a nation in humanity's
behalf." "Neutrality in a war of principles is mere
passive existence, forgetfulness of all that makes a
people sacred, the negation of the common law of
nations, political atheism. On one side," he was speaking to Englishmen in 1859, "stands the flag of liberty
and right, of the true and good ; on the other the flag
of tyranny and ambition, of the false and evil. And
you, a free nation and strong, you who profess belief
in truth and justice, would you say, 'Between evil and
good we will remain neutral, impassive spectators'?
It is the word of Cain. No people, that chooses to
teach that policy, may dare to call itself Christian, for
it is practically a people of atheists or cowards. Sooner
or later a tremendous expiation will visit the cowardly
desertion of the duty which God lays on peoples as on
individuals." "Can it be that England," he wrote
twelve years earlier, "the England of the Reformation,
the England of Elizabeth and of Cromwell, self-centred
in immoral indifference, gives up Europe to the dictatorship of force?"

Hence he was no believer in peace at any price.
Sternly, indeed, he condemned war, when it was not
fought for a right principle ; it was "fratricide," if not
imperative in the interests of the race. But it was
"sacred as peace, when the triumph of good is to be
its issue." He attacked the Manchester School for
perverting the sense of human solidarity. "Peace,"
he wrote to the Geneva Congress of 1867, "cannot
become a law of human society, except by passing

through the struggle, which will ground life and association on foundations of justice and liberty, on the wreck of every power which exists not for a principle but for a dynastic interest." Europe, he held, could not have lasting peace, till Austria and Turkey made way for the nationalities, which they held down; it would ever be perturbed by fears of Russian aggression, till Poland was restored to be its bulwark; and only war could free the Poles and Southern Slavs. "When you have substituted justice for tyranny, truth for falsehood, duty for selfish interests, the republic for monarchy, then you will have peace, but not till then."

Mazzini, unluckily, was not content with the broad human principle that a country must use its strength for right and freedom everywhere. He appended a theory, which has its germ of truth, but defies definition, and is easily twisted to save a special argument. Each nation had, he thought, some distinct and specialised service to render to humanity. "God has written one line of his thought on the cradle of each people." "Special interests, special aptitudes, and before all special functions, a special mission to fulfil, a special work to be done in the cause of the advancement of humanity, seem to me the true, infallible characteristics of nationalities." The theory escapes any exact precision; but it offers a rich field for poetry, and Mazzini's imagination was at home in it. England's function was "industry and colonies," Russia's was the civilisation of Asia, Poland's "the Slav initiative." Germany's mark was thought, France's was action, Italy's thought in unison with action. "While the German walks earth with his sight

lost in the depths of heaven, and the Frenchman's eye
rarely looks aloft but scours earth's surface with its
restless penetrating glance, the Genius, that guards
the destinies of Italy, has been ever wont to pass
swiftly from the ideal to the real, seeking from of old
how earth and heaven may be joined together." We
have seen what curious use he made of this theory of
special missions to rebut Irish claims.

Such were the principles of nationality, and nations
built on them would make the Europe of the future.
Mazzini believed that democracy would tend towards
large nations. He repudiated any love of administrative centralisation and urged the widest local government; but the bigger the nation, the more perfect, he
thought, would be the development of association within
it, and the greater therefore its momentum on the
road of progress. And, as the larger nations would
be approximately equal in territory or population, a
new and natural balance of power would arise to
safeguard peace. This liking for large countries
sometimes nearly led him into inconsistencies with his
own principles, and made him question the national
basis of most small states. He made a confident
forecast of the future European settlement. (He was
writing, of course, prior to 1870.) England and France
(apart from Savoy and Nice) were the only countries,
whose territory marched with their natural borders, and
they alone would remain unchanged. Italy would be
united, and include the border districts and islands
that spoke the Italian tongue, except, apparently, the
Canton of the Ticino. Germany, including the German-
speaking provinces of Austria, would also achieve its
unity, but be divided into two or three "great ad-

ministrative sections." Spain and Portugal would form a single country. Greece would expand over all territories with a Greek-speaking population. Switzerland would be the nucleus of an Alpine Federation, embracing Savoy and the Tyrol. Holland was, apparently, to keep its independence ; Belgium, on the other hand, had no future as a nation, though he does not indicate its destiny. In early life he seems to have thought that Denmark would remain a separate state ; afterwards he believed that the three Scandinavian states were inevitably destined to unity.

The most difficult problem, of course, was that of Eastern Europe. Mazzini evidently thought that, next to the unity of his own country, the Slav movement was the most important question in European politics. Here was a mighty people, awakening to life, proving its power by its literature,—for it, he believed, had produced the only living poetry since Goethe and Byron, —claiming its rightful place in the European commonwealth. Nothing could arrest the self-assertion of the Slavs, but the future of Europe largely depended on the direction which it took. If the other nations hailed it and guided it, it would enrich the life of Europe by the new elements it brought into it ; if it went unfriended and undirected, it would be perverted into "Czarism," and cost Europe twenty years of bloodshed to check Muscovite ambitions. Two things Europe would do well to keep in mind. It was as useless as it was immoral to bolster up Austria and Turkey, for the Slav movement would be inevitably fatal to them both. And Europe must see that the Slavs became a barrier and not a help to Russian designs of domination. This could be done, and done only, by helping the non-Russian Slavs to organise themselves into powerful and independent nations. Czarism owed its strength not to Panslavist aspirations, but to the fact that the Czar was the only hope of the Christian populations of the Balkans. Mazzini's detailed forecast of the Slav national settlement varied from time to time; but his favourite plan was that Russians, Poles, Czechs, and Serbs should form four separate nationalities. In curious and impossible inconsistency with his own principles, he seems to have thought that Hungary and Roumania would be annexed to or federated with one or other of these states; and he looked to a federal union of Serbs and Greeks, with Constantinople, as a free city, for the centre of the federation.

Out of the nationalities would grow "the United States of Europe, the republican alliance of the peoples," "that great European federation, whose task it is to unite in one association all the political families of the old world, destroy the partitions that dynastic rivalries have made, and consolidate and respect nationalities." Mazzini's ken, strange to say, was almost restricted to Europe. He scarcely mentions in this connection the American United States, though sometimes he seems perhaps to imply that they would enter the European commonwealth. He had no inkling that Eastern races might claim their own independent development. His forecast of European colonisation hardly extended beyond Asia and North Africa; he believed that Asia was destined to be "an appendix of Europe," and that the great stream of European colonisation would set towards it, chiefly through the agency of Russia and England. Thus he was concerned with Europe only;

and for the Europe of the future, a federation of harmonious nationalities, he had a splendid prophecy. When nationality had triumphed, "all cause of war would disappear, and in its place arise a spirit of brotherhood aud peaceful emulation on the road of progress." Revolutions would be no more, and "the slow, continuous, normal unfolding of activities and powers" would lead the nations ever onwards. We come again to his vision of a European authority sitting at Rome to give guidance and harmony to the peoples. When the great day arrived, that brought the victory of liberty and nationality, the peoples would assemble their "true General Council." No doubt the Council was the same as that which would define the new religious faith. It would formulate the common national duties of the peoples, and secure their freedom to perform those duties, while the separate national councils defined the special duty of each country.

It would be Italy's glorious function to lead the nations to this unity. France had lost the opportunity in 1815; England, when she isolated herself from the life of Europe by her enslavement to non intervention; the Slav countries were disqualified by their rivalries or obsequiousness to Russia. Italy had her unquestioned titles to the proud hegemony —her geographical position, her character, her traditions, the universal looking for some great thing to come out of her new life. She was "the land destined by God to the great mission of giving moral unity to Europe, and through Europe to Humanity. She would be the armed apostle of nationality, the protectress of oppressed peoples, the instrument to destroy Austria and Turkey and give freedom to

e Slavs. And when this part of her mission was
lfilled, and through her nationality was victorious,
en the gratitude of the peoples, and the divine
)pointment of Providence, and her own essential
:ness for the task, would make Rome the centre of
e cause of peace, the seat of the Diet of the nations,
lfilling Dante's vision, that saw her "helmsman"
' humanity, to steer it to its peace. It was a
)ble dream, much of it, it may be, fantastic and im-
)ssible, and yet, perhaps, with its seed of truth.
he European Federation tarries behind Mazzini's
.ger prophecy, but its coming cannot be delayed
r ever. The triumph of nationality, despite the
il deed of 1870, has advanced with mighty strides
nce his day. And though patriotism has often
red into ignoble paths, and international fraternity
)ne backward, yet the evil creates its own remedy,
ld disarmament becomes an ever more impor-
nate desire. When the nations learn that ar-
tration and disarmament are necessary for their
vn self-preservation, when the European federation
:adually evolves itself, Rome will be the natural
at of the High Court of Europe. Italy, which by
:r plebiscitary origin has given a rule to the
ttionalities,—a country practically without terri-
rial ambitions or colonial empire, the natural
ediator between the two great European alliances,
lth her ancient prestige and service to humanity
give her lustre, has paramount claims to the high
erogative.[1]

[1] M. Novicow in his *Missione d'Italia* has recently expressed the same
lief, almost in Mazzini's words. [But the Tripoli business has changed
. this.—1911.]

Chapter XVIII

Literary Criticism

IF Mazzini's busy life could have spared more time
for literary study, he would probably have been
among the greatest critics of the century ; perhaps
even as it is, he may rank among them.   He misse
in his lack of accurate and detailed study ; but h
has a rare penetration and originality and gift o
embracing synthesis.   It was his ambition at on
time to found an Italian school of criticism, whos
mark should be constructive and sympathetic interpre
tation.   Keenly sensitive though he was to beaut
of expression, he detested mere criticism of form an
the profitless microscopy, that pries for specks in
writer's life or work.   He loved to read a great autho
reverently, hiding rather than exposing his blemishes
penetrating below uncouthnesses of form and casua
lapses to the great informing thoughts, that had thei
lesson for the world.   " At the present day," he wrot
in an optimistic moment, " we neither worship a geniu
blindly, nor outrage him barbarously ; we set ourselve
to understand him, and we learn to love him.   W

312

ard forms as secondary and perishable phenomena ;
idea alone is sacred, as a thing baptised to ever-
ting life, and we try how we may lift the veil that
es it." He compared genius to the fabled tree
Teneriffe, whose branches discharged showers of
eshing water. "Genius is like this tree, and the
ssion of criticism should be to shake the branches.
the present day it more resembles a savage striv-
to hew down the noble tree to the roots."

In his scheme of life the poet had a part of supreme
portance. He regarded literature as a "moral priest-
d." Poetry would "save the world in its despite,"
it was the poet's prerogative to redeem it from
bt and base ideals, to "reveal duties and create
ctions," to lift men up above the trivial things of
to the eternal verities. "We have," he cries in
forties, "exiled poetry from life, and enthusiasm
faith have gone with it, and love, as I understand
, and constancy in sacrifice, and the worship of
t deeds and great men." His own Italy had little of
throbbing national life, in which alone true poetry
ld flourish ; and everywhere an age of faithlessness
bed the poet of his aliment. The time was for the
ic,—the constructive, "philosophic" critic ; he was
"literary educator," and he could at all events be
cursor of the poet of the future, marking the lines on
ch a modern democratic poetry should travel, and
paring a public to understand him. "The critic," he
s, "is unrelated to genius ; but he stands as a link
ween great writers and the masses ; he explores the
ditions and literary needs of the time, and preaches
m to the nations, that they may learn to feel them,
desire and demand them ; in fine, his prophecies pre-

pare a public for the writer :—a more important
matter than some think, for very rarely do writers
appear before their time."

As critic, then, Mazzini points out the deficiencies of
contemporary literature, and the principles which must
take it to a higher stage. True art, he lays down, has
two great perils to avoid. First, there is the "atheist
formula" of 'art for the sake of art' ;—a heresy he
scourged with pontifical anathemas. His attack was
not aimed at perfection of literary form. He loved a
correct and classic diction, and never underrated style
so long as style was not an excuse for poverty of
thought. His criticism went deeper. The artist may
not live his own art-life, divorced from the moving
world around and all its manifold activities, "floating
bubble-like without support," finding his poor inspiration
in his own fancies and caprices. There was no true
individuality in that ; invented though it was to guard
the poet's independence, in reality it made him but
passive mirror of each passing impression. Instead of
liberty, it brought anarchy and "wild, arbitrary in
tellectual display." It robbed art of touch with the
great facts of life, all fruitful relationship to the
struggling, ever learning, ever advancing race. It sen
it wandering lawless, purposeless, like a sick man's
dreams. The poet ceased to be a thinker and
teacher, and sank to a mere empty singer. "What
want," he said, "is not the Artist but the man-Artist
the High-Priest of the Ideal, not the worshipper of his
own Fetishes." Literature must be "the minister of
something greater and more valuable than itself."

He was almost equally condemnatory of realism
especially of realistic presentation of nature. It was

ticism that he brought alike against Monti and Victor
ugo and Wordsworth, that they " depicted but never
insfigured nature," and thus their art was " useless."
ie real is the mantle of the true, but not the true ;
iigh poetry is truth, because you cannot trace out or
alyse its source." The poet is a " miner in the
oral world "; his function is to hew beneath the
mbol, beneath the real, to the idea shut in within ;
estioning nature alike in her beauties and deformi-
is, to find and teach to men " that fragment of God's
ith that must exist there." " One thing I know,"
 says, " that the phenomena of nature on their
oral side and the inner life of man must be the field
 modern literature, that physical nature and man's
ter life will have their place only as symbols of the
st." And nature's lessons must have a practical
ference to man's lot and destiny. Even when
ture was rightly used and interpreted, there might
 too much of it, and he seems to have always given
tural poetry a secondary place. " Poetry," he says,
s not in nature but in man."

This brings us to his conception of true art. It
ist be essentially human, not realistically so, but
efully, practically, didactically. He did not mean
 this that it must confine itself to the obvious, out-
le facts of life. " In every powerful poetic impres-
n the *vague* claims a full quarter, and the vague,
iich must not be confounded with the obscure, is the
ul's own field." But poetry, however much it may
ncern itself with the spiritual and unseen, must have
rect application to the problems of life. " Art lives
 the world's life ; the world's law is art's law." The
et must gather " the great voice of the world and

God," and so interpret it, that men may listen and profit. He must contemplate man both in his individuality and as a social creature, "in his internal and external life, in his place and with his mission in creation." "Poetry,—great, ceaseless, eternal poetry, —exists only in the development, the evolution of life : only there, in life, understood and felt in its universality, can inexhaustible variety be found."

Thus the poet must find his inspiration, not in his own "incomplete, mutilated conceptions," not in the isolated individual, but in the great collective, democratic movements of the people, voicing their dim thoughts and aspirations, "their latent, slumbering, unconscious life." There can be no great poetry to-day, unless the poet identify himself with "the thought fermenting in the breast of the masses and impelling them to action." Poets are the priesthood of the social and political movement, which is the very blood of a modern people ; and there is no place for individualist poetry in a social age. "True and sacred art aims at the perfection of society," and the art of the future will be "principally religious and political." He hated the aimless art, that busies itself with the mere picturesque and sentimental, which idealises ages, whose meaning and moral standard have passed. He applauded Schlegel's thesis that poetry must be "national, that is useful and related to the civil and political situation," no longer heedless of the great movements of to-day, but "standing in the centre and swaying the heart of the social impulse." The poet, who went to fight for Greece and died there, typified "the holy alliance of poetry with the cause of the peoples."

This democratic art must have a practical use by being didactic and prophetic. It is not enough that its heart should beat with the people's life ; it must help the progress of the race by pointing to the future. Though it may " grow among the ruins, art is ever coloured by the rising sun." " There can be no true poetry without a presentiment of the future " ; it is, as said " the extraordinary man," who is the poet of all time,

> The prophetic soul
> Of the wide world, dreaming on things to come.

' Art either sums up the life of a dying age or heralds one about to dawn ; it is no caprice of this or that individual, but a solemn page of history or a prophecy ; most powerful, when as in Dante, and occasionally in Byron, it is both." But there is no gift of prophecy without an ideal, and " literature, like politics, has no secure foundation without its fixed beliefs and principles,"—those beliefs which make the future and to which facts must bow. " The true European writer will be a philosopher, but with the poet's lyre in his hands." " Nature with her thousand voices cries to the poet, ' Soar, thou art King of earth.' And if we try to pen him down to realism, and rob him of his independent lordship over facts, the poets of the past will answer from their graves, ' We were great, because we created.' It is for poetry to take the creations of the philosopher and give them life and colour, to explore the truth that lies below the real and illumine it with the light of genius, to interpret the universal laws that rule over human history."

And the poet must not only lift men to his vision, but send them forth in quest of it. He is not only

prophet but apostle. It is not enough that he should
stimulate thought ; he must " spur men to translate
thought into action." " Contemplative " poets, Wordsworth and Coleridge for instance, are " incomplete.'
" The element of Action is inseparable from poetry
Poetry," he says, " is for me something like the third
person of the Trinity, the Holy Spirit, which is action.'
" In order to be a religious poet," he writes in criticism
of Lamartine, " it is not enough, in my eyes at least
to say ' Lord, Lord ' ; it is necessary to *feel* his holy
law, and to make others feel it in such sort, as that
they shall constantly and calmly act in obedience to
its precepts." Just as religion gives life and power to
philosophy, so it is for art to grasp ideas, translate
them by images and symbols, and make them
passionate beliefs. " Poetry is enthusiasm with wings
of fire, the angel of strong thoughts, the power that
raises men to sacrifice, consumes them, stirs a tumult
of ideas within them, puts in their hands a sword, a
pen, a dagger." " Written poetry, like music per-
formed, should be in some sense a prelude to other
poetry, which the excited soul of the reader composes
silently within itself." It will " teach the young all
that is greatest in self-sacrifice, constancy, silence, the
sense of solitude without despair, long years of torture
or delusion unrevealed and dumb, faith in the things
that are to be, the hourly struggle for that faith
though hope of victory there be none in this life.'
And therefore art must be ever brave and full of
hope, " teaching man not his weakness but his
strength, inspiring him not with faintheartedness but
with energy and vigorous will." Its song must be
always of steadiness and constancy, and " calmness

adiate from the poet's brow, as the spirit of God
adiated from the brow of Moses on the wandering
sraelites." " The artist is either a priest or a more or
ess practised mountebank." Woe to him, if he teach
pasmodic, evanescent effort, or " revolt and impotent
espair, that dies cursing, ere it tries to fight, that
ays ' All things are evil,' because it finds itself unable
o create good." Mazzini has no pity for the poet of
essimism, " whose sense of moral depression and
inguor " will, if he pose as a religious poet, make his
eaders " reject religion and him together."

Poetry, then, the modern poetry of action, being
ssentially related to politics and social life, the poet's
hemes are in the stir and passion of contemporary
vents or in national history. What field for literature
ke the mighty, moving pageant of the democratic
vorld? To watch God's hand guiding the nations to
heir destinies, to probe the eager ferment of a modern
ociety, to interpret all the dim, half-conscious yearn-
ng of the masses,—what inspiration for the poet
ere! " Popular poetry has invaded everything, the
oetry whose epic is revolution, whose satire is revolt.'
Iow strong and living are the giants of the Revolution
eside the nerveless men and women of the quietist
ovel. " Poetry has fled from old Europe to give life
o the young, new, beautiful Europe of the peoples.
.ike the swallow, it has left a crumbling ruin to seek
purer air and a more verdant world. It has fled
om the King's solitary throne to find its abode in the
reat arena of the peoples, in the ranks of martyrs for
he fatherland, on the patriot's scaffold, in the prison
f the brave betrayed." The armies of the Conven-
ion, the guerilla-bands of Spain, the German students

chanting the songs of Körner on the march to battl
the patriot's anguished passion, the dreams of a libert
to be, the world-mission of European civilisation,—
these are the modern poet's themes. "Think you tha
poetry, whose birth was ushered by such deeds a
these, can die ere it has lived? Would you set u
the poor, pale, narrow poetry of individuals, a poetr
of forms, a poetry that lives and dies in the sma
circle of a palace or a chapel or a castle,—would yo
set up this against the grand *social* poetry, solemn an
tranquil and full of hope, which knows none but Go
in heaven and the people upon earth?" An age c
science and industry is no enemy to poetry, for th
elements of poetry are eternal. "I tell you, in thi
Europe there is such life, such poetry in germ, th
poetry of ages, of all the generations, that genius itse
has not yet dared to attempt to develop it." "Her
round you," so he speaks to the poet of the futuri
"here, before your eyes, there is poetry and movemer
and a European people waiting for you."

The poet has another field in history. Mazzir
prophesied a great future for the historical dram
He was inclined to think that drama would be th
accepted form of modern poetry, seeing doubtless tha
drama is the true communion between poet and peopl
the natural vehicle of the artist, who has a message t
deliver. It would be "a kind of popular pulpit,
chair of the philosophy of humanity"; and he looke
forward to the day when the great dramas, such a
those of "divine Schiller," would be produced on th
stage without mutilations or curtailments to a reverer
and patient audience. The function of the historic
dramatist, as indeed he thought it was the function c

prose historian, was not so much to make minute
arch of facts, as to disentangle the lessons hidden
er every page of history, to interpret the law of
ıan duty and the mystery of existence. Like every
:r poet, he must start with a philosophy of life,
;ing all things by his own law, meting out praise
 blame, drawing guidance for the future from the
. The dramatist " may call up the shadows of the
:, but like the Witch of Endor, in order to con-
in them to reveal the future."   His personages
t be types, each with its social significance ; he
t not, as Victor Hugo did, overload them with
vidual traits, till they lose their message for society,
 rather, as Schiller with his Marquis di Posa, so
·create " them, that they may illustrate some general
of life. Mazzini did not see how pale such charac-
would be ; how difficult it was to reconcile them
ı biographical accuracy, how likely therefore they
з to falsify any induction of historical laws.
[is theory of music was a very similar one. Music,
 poetry, he thought, was nought without a moral
ıtion, without practical teaching and power to
ire.   It should be " the purest and most general
most sympathetic expression of a social faith."   He
essly criticised the music of the thirties, imitative,
ıusted, artificial, clever but without creative power.
ıithless and corrupt generation asked for music to
se it; and music had listened and forgotten its
ion.   There was melody and good instrumenta-
but no soul or thought in it. It was " laughter
out peace, weeping without virtue."   Operas had
nity, no great passionate note; they were ingenious
ıics, much of them mere noise and extravagance,

inferior for all their technique to the chants of
medieval Church, when music had a religious work
do.   Rossini had done something ; he had brol
from the old canons and given liberty to music ;
he had the defects of the Romanticist school, he l
freed but could not create ; he had prepared the v
for the music of the future, but it was not his to wi
it.   Mazzini however saw indications that the n
·music was not far off, and its dawn, he believ
would be in Italy.   But Italian melody must v
itself to German harmony.   Italian music was "lyri·
impassioned, volcanic, artistic," but without unity
soul.   German music knew God, but it was mysti
and impersonal, out of touch with everyday hum
life.   It dulled men's impulses to action ; it stir
them, but to no useful end, left the soul full of gr
emotion, but uninspired to perform plain duti
Mazzini was assured that Italy would produce
master, who would unite the strength of both scho
keep the religion of the German school, but poin
to practical, human ends.   At one time he ho
that perhaps Donizetti might live to do this ; af
wards he thought that Meyerbeer was " the
cursor spirit of the music of the future."   He
always thinking of Opera.   When he insists that
music should be in keeping with the subject and
period, when he pleads for the symbolic use of
orchestra, for the wider employment of motives,
the development of the chorus on the model of Gr·
tragedy, for the large use of recitative, for the en
disuse of cadences and flourishes, he is looking
Opera to be the highest form of music, as he lookec

[1] *Cf.* Richard Wagner's Prose Works (Eng. trans.), pp. 122-123.

historical drama to be the highest form of poetry.
>arently he wished to wed them, and looked for the
, when great poets would write librettos for great
.posers.
Iazzini's criticism of music is for its time so fresh,
full of suggestion and prophecy, that it is matter
regret that his knowledge of it was not more
:nsive.   He knew opera and little beyond it;
had some acquaintance with Beethoven, but he
s not seem to have been very strongly attracted
him, or to have made much study of him.   He
ted on Donizetti and Meyerbeer the enthusiasm,
ch should have been reserved for greater men.   It
infortunate that he lived before Wagnerian opera
eared in London.   It would be possible to show in
iil to what a remarkable extent he anticipated
gner's theories.[1]   Wagner, it is true, rejected the
orical drama, because he believed the requirements
irt to be incompatible with historical accuracy.
his main doctrines are the same as Mazzini's,—
ethical intention of music, the intimate relation-
of art to public life, the belief in the people as
fountain of true art, the value of the folk-song, the
nciliation of harmony and melody, the poet and
ician stretching hands to one another and giving
ral will' to music, by uniting 'word' to 'tone'
)pera.   It is permitted to think that, Wagner's
>nality notwithstanding, Mazzini would have re-
iised in him the master of the new music, whose
i he heralded.

.azzini had a favourite classification of poets into

.azzini's *Philosophy of Music* was written in 1836 ; Wagner's *Art.*
f the Future in 1849.

" objective " and " subjective." The objective art
sinks his own beliefs, and merely reflects and transm
external impressions, neither judging them by his ov
conception of right and wrong, nor supplying a
inspiration or rule of action for mankind. The st
jective artist stamps his themes with the imprint
his own individuality ; he sits in the seat of judgme
and measures out praise and blame ; and thus he hel
others to form a moral law, and creates the futu
The former series, men who excite our admiration l:
not our love, passes from the Greek poets, all save ot
through Shakespeare to Goethe ; the latter frc
Aeschylus through Dante and Michelangelo to Byr
and, apparently, Schiller. Dante was Mazzir
highest type of the subjective poet. Something h
already been said of his influence on Mazzini's thoug
—an influence far greater than that of any otl
writer. There are few, indeed, of Mazzini's doctrin
which are not found in germ in the *Convito* or t
De Monarchiâ. Mazzini revered him as the stro
intellect, which took so little from other men and ga
so much ; the hero, whose life was one long fight, w
" wrote for country, conspired for country, held t
pen and sword " ; the patriot, " neither Catholic r
Ghibelline nor Guelf, but Christian and Italian," w
believed in ' the holy Roman people,' and foretold
Italy the spiritual mastery of the world ; the think
who taught the unity and common task of all mɛ
kind ; the one true poet of love, to whom the love
man and woman was a spiritual thing, wherein s
entered not. He contrasted him with Shakespea
" the lord of individuality," the supreme dramat
who created individuals as no man else has creat

ɛm, giving his creatures choice of good and evil, and
rsuing the lesson of their fates, the choice once made,
the end; who in Hamlet had of pure creative
nius made a prophetic type, that belonged to two
ɪturies after him, and had no contemporary
ginal. But Shakespeare was a man who took
ɛ as he found it, untouched by strong moral sym-
thies, without sense of the race or glimpse of
ty or looking to the future; therefore a cynic
d a " sceptic," obsessed by the feeling of life's
thingness, with no illuminating faith in man's
ɛdestined glory.

Mazzini's favourite contrast was between Goethe and
ʹron. For Goethe's intellect he had the profoundest
miration; he seems to have studied Faust carefully,
d had some acquaintance at all events with his other
ɪrks. "Goethe," he says, " is an intellect, that receives,
ιborates, and reproduces every possible form of
man emotion and aspiration. He dwells aloft,
ɪne, a mighty Watcher in the midst of creation,
ʹutinizing with equal penetration and interest the
ɔths of ocean and the calyx of the flower, . . .
ʹing bare in Faust the problem of the age in all its
rible nakedness, . . . the most representative poet
ɪt Europe has produced since Shakespeare." But
ʹat intellect as he is, he misses the highest; for he
ɛs the man in the artist, he has no moral standard
his own, no sense of the unity of life; he is the
ʹt of detail and analysis, " feeling 'everything but
ʹer feeling the whole," living aloof from religion and
itics, a cold spectator of the world-moving deeds
und him, " learning neither to esteem men nor to
ter them, nor even to suffer with them," " without

need of doing or sacred sorrow or any deep and ardent love." "The poet of the bourgeoisie, he counsels calm and contemplation, order and resignation, tells men to fit themselves to their environment, fulfil their little duties, plant themselves comfortably, do good around them, always provided that the risks are not too great, and that they do not disturb the harmony and balance of the faculties of *sight*."

Turn from Goethe, he says, to Byron ; "there is the man himself, who hopes and strives and suffers for the race, as Dante did, and as Aeschylus did before Dante." Like Goethe, he too is "a poet of individu- ality," "a type of power without an aim " ; but, unlike Goethe's, his verse is no mere reflection of other men's thoughts and actions. He stamps his portraitures with his own personality, surveying the world " from a single, comprehensive point of view," and interpreting and judging it by his own inner light ; more deep as Goethe is more vast, seeking the sublime rather than the beautiful, ever a worshipper of force and action. " In Byron the *ego* is revealed in all its pride of power, freedom, and desire, in the uncontrolled plenitude of all its faculties, aspiring to rule the world around him solely for dominion's sake, to exercise upon it the Titanic force of his will." It is this power of will necessarily propelled to seek an outlet in action, that appealed so strongly to Mazzini. Byron bears his part in the political and social conflicts round him, "wandering thròugh the world, sad, gloomy, and un- quiet, wounded and bearing the arrow in his wound " loving and understanding Italy and Rome, dying for a nation's cause in Greece. And Mazzini found in his verse a great social lesson, such as Goethe

ever tried to teach. Consciously or unconsciously
yron foretold the doom of individualism and aristo-
acy. His characters are moulded on "a single type
-the individual ; free, but nothing more than free ;
on souls in iron frames, who climb the alps of the
physical world as well as the alps of thought " ; but all
earing in their faces the stamp of failure, " a gloomy
and ineffaceable sadness." " Gifted with a liberty
they knew not how to use ; with a power and energy
they knew not how to apply ; with a life, whose
purpose and aim they comprehend not ; — they
ag through their useless and convulsed existences.
yron destroys them one after the other. The
nptiness of the life and death of solitary individu-
ity has never been summed up so powerfully as
his pages."

But Byron, no more than Goethe, wrote the poetry
Mazzini's ideal. In a generation without religion or
ty or enthusiasm, amid " English cant and French
vity and Italian stagnation," Byron was driven to
passionate, tumultuous cursings of a false society. But
was a note of rebellion and despair. Neither poet
had the sense of the race, of man redeemed by love
d social service, of the new hope and power that
would come, as men learned to work together for the
mmon end. Mazzini gives no indication that he
er found the art that he looked for. He seems
have thought that some of the modern Slav poetry
me nearest to it. The new English literature does
t appear to have attracted him ; there is no evidence
t he read Browning, and if he had, he would probably
ve condemned him as " objective." Historical drama
s conspicuously failed to do what he expected of it.

The poetry of social problems is still for the most par analytic and destructive. The poet of his vision, th constructive, prophetic, apostolic poet, with his messag for humanity, whose songs will reach the worksho and the cottage and inspire a nation's policy, is ye to come.

Chapter XIX

The Man

oetic temperament—Defects as a thinker—Greatness as a moral teacher—Strength and weakness as a politician—The man.

RLYLE said that Mazzini was " by nature a little ical poet." The implication was contemptuous, but had a bottom of truth. Mazzini, indeed, save for early aspirations to the drama, never dreamed of ng a poet. His conception of the poet's function s so high, the qualities he demanded of him so acting, that, if he ever felt the call, he put it away, doubt, as something to which he could not reach. is doubtful even whether he wrote more than one :m when a youth. He aspired only to be critic, do something to prepare the way for the poet of the are. But he had qualities, that would have made of i a poet of no mean order. There are many passages is writings, which show his deep communion with ure. When he writes of " the vast ocean, dashing, : a wave of eternal poetry, against the barren rocks 3rittany," or describes a sunrise from the Alps,— ie first ray of light trembling on the horizon, vague pale, like a timid, uncertain hope ; then the long of fire cutting the blue heaven, firm and decided i promise,"—truly the consecration and the poet's im are his. His critical essays prove with what

spiritual insight he would have touched the poetry of
man and society. We have seen how marvellous for
an outsider was his presentiment of the future of music.
And his whole intellectual make, alike in strength and
weakness, is that of the artist,—of the artist, that is, as
he conceived him, God's messenger to the heart of man
He had little power of scientific thought, of accurate
reasoning or careful arrangement and analysis of facts
It led to a curious misconception of scientific method
"Science," he says,—"the true, great, fruitful science,—
is as much intuition as experiment." He generalises
with a hazardous confidence. Sometimes he uses words
that are no more than words, to push difficulties into
a corner and stand in front of them. In spite of his
allegiance to " tradition," he generally prefers deductive to inductive reasoning. " Principles prevail over
facts," as he says ; but he often does not see, in spite
of his own cautions, how, without a supreme respect
for facts, a principle may hang not on the eternal
truths, but on the fancy of a solitary brain. His own
scientific studies were small ; save for some acquaintance with astronomy and geography,—the former to
feed his sense of the infinite, the latter for its relationship
to nationality,—he seems to have given no attention
to any branch of science. He accepted without
question the Genesis story of the creation of man
At a time when Darwinism was bringing a sword into
the intellectual world, he lived apparently uninterested
and untouched by it.

The same defect of method appears in his other
studies. Keen as was his interest in social questions
he evidently had no grasp of economic science ; beyond
Adam Smith, it is doubtful whether he read any of

he great economists, and at a later date he entirely
iiled to understand the economic side of Karl Marx.
Iis theories of history, again, so subordinate everything
o his desire to make it didactic, that he regarded re-
earch and accuracy as comparatively unimportant.
Ie thought,—rash man,—that facts had already been
ccumulated in sufficient abundance and certainty.
ireatly indeed he conceived the historian's ultimate
inction—to discover the laws of human progress, and
e " prophet of a higher social end " ; but he slurred
ver the difficulty of reading facts aright, and was ever
rone to let fancy take their place. He would have
iade the historian's method deductive to a dangerous
egree, and had him fill the gaps of history from an
bstract study of human nature ; he apparently ap-
roved the Thucydidean method of invented speeches.

Here and everywhere he was apt to look down on
rudition. He believed that Genius,—a kind of mystic,
iod-inspired faculty, that lived on intuition and not
n painfully acquired knowledge, — discovers at a
lance the secrets of nature and ethics and history.
Where we see only the confused light of the Milky
Vay, they see stars." Though he would have himself
isclaimed the title to genius, he had a supreme con-
dence in his own thought. It was difficult for him
) own an error, and hence he never learnt from his
iistakes. It was true of him, as Renan said of
amennais, that "when a man believes that he possesses
l truth, he naturally disdains the painful, humble path
f research, and regards the investigation of details
; a pure dilettante fancy." This was no doubt the
iief cause why his mind so soon stopped growing.
/e find in his early writings, when he was twenty-

seven or twenty-eight, the germ, and generally the
developed form of every doctrine that he preached
His character developed normally, but not his intellect
Religion, ethics, politics, social theories, literary canons
—all issued forth at once from his early-ripened brain,
and fixed themselves once for all.   He was always
reluctant to enquire for or admit new knowledge.   It
is strange, lover of books though he was, how restricted
sometimes was his range of reading.   His poets were
the poets of his youth and early manhood, and he read
few that wrote after 1840.   Closely as he studied the
Gospels, he seems to have given little or no attention
to exegesis.   In spite of his keen interest in Utilitarianism, there is no trace that he read the later
writers of the school.   Though so long in intimate
touch with English political thought, he does not seem
to have known Burke or Ricardo or the Mills or
Herbert Spencer.

As a thinker, therefore, his defects are great.   His
thought, indeed, always has its value, coming as it
does from a man of very great intellectual power and
large experience of life, one who fearlessly penetrated
to the heart of things, and was therefore in the true
sense original.   Its range is wonderful for one who
led so strenuous a life of action.   Faulty as his
argument often is, obvious as are the gaps, he wrote
comparatively few pages, that are not stamped with
great and stimulating thought.   But his mind was too
loosely organised, too often out of touch with contemporary knowledge.   He has left an imposing and
suggestive system, and yet perhaps it somehow fails to
add greatly to the sum of human knowledge.   But it
is just the qualities, that depreciate him as a thinker

hich make him great as a moral teacher. His want
: logic, his loose use of words hurt not here. The
volved and rushing language, like a tumbling moun-
in stream, becomes a strength. That very rigidity,
at lifelong iteration of a few dominant ideas, carry
rce and conviction, that a more agile intellect were
)werless to give. His warm and palpitating
:neralisations, for all the flaws in their reasoning,
:ar the irrefutable mark of moral reality. He had
at union of real intellectual force and spiritual
rvour, that gives the insight into moral truth, and
arns the secrets of heaven and hell. He was able to
: a great moralist, because in a rare degree he had
mself the moral sense, because the passion for
:hteousness had so penetrated all his being, that he
uld speak and be understood on the deep things of
od, had something in his own soul that found its
ay to other souls. And, above all, he spoke with
thority. Absolute confidence in his own beliefs was
ined to truest personal humility, and made the
ophet. Humblest and least ambitious of men, he
lt his call from God ; and in God's name he was
sertive, dogmatic, sometimes seemingly egotistic.
he spoke authoritatively and intolerantly, it was
at a duty was laid upon him, and woe to him if he
eached it not. His principles were living and
ctorious certainties to him. " If a principle is true,"
: said, " its applications are not only possible but
evitable." And this unquestioning conviction made
m as fearless morally as he was intellectually,—
arless with the supreme bravery of one who never
rinks from duty,—fearless not only for himself but
hers, bridling all the impulsive tenderness within

him, and requiring of his fellow-workers the sam
readiness for sacrifice, which he exacted of himsel
And so his words, aflame from a pure and passior
ate heart, come with the intensity of prophetic powe
Beyond the words of any other man of modern time
they bring counsel and comfort to those who hav
drunk of the misery and stir and hope of the ag
They have the greater virtue, that impels their hearer
to do likewise. Mazzini is one of the small band, wh
have the strength as well as the love of Christ, nc
only the unselfishness that draws, but the convictio
and the power that command, who impose their ow
beliefs and make disciples.

Would he, had he had the opportunity, have don
what he held higher than to teach through books, an
been the missionary of a religion? Had Italy bee
freed in 1848, we may be sure he would have left hi
desk, forsaken politics, and gone about the lanc
preaching faith in God and Progress and Humanit)
Probably no other man, since the Reformation, ha
had such apostolic power. Would his mission hav
found an answer or ended in pitiable collapse? H
would probably have had no better fate than other
who have tried to found new churches. There ma
be room for new faiths, but there is little for nev
churches in the world to-day. But this does no
necessarily mean failure. His church might have bee
empty, his state religion proved a soulless husk ; bu
in the communion of scattered men and women, wh
are groping for the truth, he might have laid a corner
stone of that church, which is neither in this mountaii
nor yet at Jerusalem, which without forms or unity c
doctrine, spreads the unity of spiritual truth. Some

ng, even as it is, he has done for this. His creed
y fail to content the knowledge of to-day, but he
nds a convincing witness to the spiritual, to the
rnal needs of the soul, to religion as the master
t of life, though creeds may fail and systems perish.

How does he rank as a politician? Our estimate
st be a mixed one. As a political thinker he
nds high. He has left a theory of the state, that
priceless because informed by a great moral ideal.
d apart from this, it has its value from his wide
l profound knowledge of modern politics and the
ctical sense that almost always keeps his idealism
touch with facts. His faith in democracy, the
imism which came of his trust in Providence,
 cautious handling of economic tendencies saved
n from the mistakes of Carlyle and Ruskin. His
nviction that the common-sense of the people was
ling out its way independently of any theory or
ool, kept him from the short-lived formulas of the
ividualists. His deeper knowledge of men and
per reading of history gave him a saner and
npleter view than that of the collectivists. None
them, not even Ruskin, can match the warmth and
piration of a conception, that raises politics to be
 instrument of the divine plan,—an instrument
 only to destroy injustice and poverty, but to
leem the highest part of man and bring the rule
brotherhood and unity and social peace. In the
ailed application of his political doctrines he often
led from that same inaccessibility to facts, which
rred him otherwise. His republic missed the
ential; his theories of democratic government are

vague and hardly satisfy. But even here he is th
prophet of one great enduring principle. Amon
the statesmen of the century, he is almost the onl
one, who understood what nationality meant, saw i
essential relationship to democracy, and put it o
an unassailable foundation.   It was this that mac
him teacher of Italian Unity, and therefore maker (
modern Italy.   Whether without him Italy woul
be united to-day, we cannot tell; but at all even
it was he who gave the impulse, his bold vision the
saw that the hard consummation was attainable, an
gave others too the faith to see it.

As a political thinker, then, he is great; as
practical political worker, he largely failed.   True, h
had many of a statesman's qualities.   He often rea
character acutely, though his confidence in me
sometimes deceived him, and again and again he wa
the victim of informers.   He had rare industry an
considerable organising power; though, owing to h
solitary work, he had learned to bury himself too muc
in details,—in the mass of correspondence and th
immense labour he put out to scrape together littl
funds,—and in them he sometimes neglected th
survey of the whole.   Above all, as he proved a
Rome, he had the true statesman's gift of leadershi
and inspiration.   But it is more than doubtful whethe
even under happier circumstances, he would have bee
an effective politician.   His knowledge of huma
nature was more subtle in the abstract than in th
concrete; individuals were to him too much wholl
good or wholly bad, and he did not recognise ho
complex are the motives that sway puzzled humanit
He could rarely take a sane, unprejudiced view of

The Man

ituation. It amazes us that he expected Pio Nono
ɔ respond to his appeal in 1847, and thought that, if
he republic came at Rome in 1870, it would found a
tate religion. His misconception of Piedmontese
olicy throughout the fifties is a yet stronger illustra-
ion of distorted vision. This was one of the reasons
rhy he found it so difficult to compromise. He could
ot distinguish non-essentials from essentials, and it
ʼas nearly as hard for him to give way on the one as
n the other. Compromise in small or great seemed
ɔwardice, and there was no doubt a strain of egotism
ı his obstinacy. It humiliated him to surrender any
etail of the theories, which he preached with such
ndiscriminating confidence.

But one would fain close not with the thinker or the
ıoral teacher or the politician, but the man. Mazzini's
ersonal life was one of a very rare purity and beauty,
ıat stands out in his generation noblest and faith-
ıllest and most inspired. Its only serious flaw lies in
ıose few lapses from public candour, which have been
oted in these pages. Sometimes he was bitter and
ıtolerant, but the provocation was great. In earlier
fe he was often querulous and self-absorbed, but it
ıay be counted to him, that, with his sensitive nature,
e came through loneliness and poverty with his moral
trength unbroken. Except for these, the critic's
ıicroscope can find no specks. Brave, earnest, true,
ʼithout trace of affectation, he bore the stamp of
ʼhitest sincerity. Gentle, affectionate, pure as few
re pure, he was friend and counsellor and inspirer to
ıose who knew him, gripping and subduing them with
ıat wondrous sympathy of his, that came of burning

love of goodness and made the saving of a soul the highest thing in life. That generosity, which made him share purse and clothes with others perhaps less destitute than himself, and give half his scanty income to help a woman and children that he hardly knew, made him lavish out of his busy days time and thought to help struggling souls. Ever intense in his affections, grateful for any act of kindness, yearning for friendship with the yearning of the homeless man, he was one to draw others with bonds of love.

He had a large and loving view of life. Pettiness and malice and jealousy had very little place in it. Passionate though he was for morality, he was, outside his political work and controversies and an occasional touch of cynicism in his talk, a very tolerant man. No person has, he said, "a right to judge a special case without positive data on the nature of the fact." He was angry and impatient with the "cavilling spirit of mediocrity," that takes pleasure in the lapses of "the mighty-souled." Among his friends he never sermonised, and he had no desire to bend their private life to his own pattern. Ever more or less sad himself, he rejoiced in their happiness. "You are a happy mortal," he writes to one of them on his marriage. "I am, notwithstanding my dislike for *happiness*, truly glad that you are so." Never man had more joy in others' home felicity. It was only among his fellow-revolutionists, whom he thought of as partners in his own high call, that he was exacting and sometimes ungenerous, though he pleaded earnestly with them that public work should leave room for the inner life of love and friendship. In his political controversies, it must be confessed, his equanimity deserted him, and he is often intolerant and unfair. He was too ready to

ink that bad politics implied bad morals, and his hatred
f Louis Napoleon and Cavour made him pen pages, that
ne would gladly not remember. But even in politics
e could sometimes do justice to an opponent, who
bviously acted from high convictions ; and he was one
f the few Italian nationalists, who could appreciate
he motives of the Catholic Volunteers.

But his essential greatness lies on the active side.
.bove all else he shines out white in that consuming
ve of humanity, that accepted poverty and weariness
ıd danger, that made him forego home and love,
ımfort and congenial work, and give himself to one
ıng, self-forgetting service for the good of men.
ıuty was no abstract precept with him, but part
f his very being. In adversity and trial he had
:hooled himself to follow her, till disobedience to her
ıll became almost impossible, and he did not wait for
ır to speak but sought her out. It was nearly allied
ı his almost superstitious fear of personal happiness.
hose miserable years in Switzerland and London
rought on him, till melancholy grew to a habit. He
ıst something of it afterwards in the society of his
nglish friends, but it never left him ; and it tinted all
ıs life with the gentle sadness, which is near akin to
ıiritual yearnings and large-hearted love. Sunless and
ıwholesome as it seems at times, after all, as with the
[an of sorrows, it purged him to the same forgetfulness
፡ self. It was no enervating grief; "do not allow
ıurself to be weakened and self-absorbed by your
ouble" was his perennial lesson to friends, who had
st dear ones. His was the "other part of grief, the
ıble part, which makes the soul great and lifts it up."
By dint of repeating to myself," he once wrote to Mrs
arlyle, "that there is no happiness under the moon,

that life is a self-sacrifice meant for some higher an
happier thing ; that to have a few loving beings, or
none, to have a mother watching you from Italy o
from Heaven (it is all the same) ought to be quit
enough to preserve us from falling."   He, to a degre
that few have done, trod self victoriously under; habitu
ally and systematically year by year, untempted b
failure or success, by misery or comparative happines
he denied himself even the little indulgences and re
laxations and declensions from the strait hard patl
by which most good men make their compromis
with the world and flesh.   So remorselessly was dut
law to him, that sometimes work and sacrifice becam
ends in themselves ; and he laboured painfully on i
the path which he had chosen, when it would hav
served his cause better to have rested or turned t
other activities.   And the unbending labour had it
fruit in that wonderful sum of his life's work, that
beyond all the exacting details of his politica
organisation, has left its stamp on modern Europe
has left so vast a body of thought in half th
provinces of the human mind, has its yet riche
legacy in the example of a life given perfectly an
wholly to the cause of men.

He was not the mere conscientious worker only
he lived in the light of a spiritual vision, and tha
light radiated in almost every page he wrote, on ever
man and woman whom he touched.   Besides th
sense of duty he had faith.   " He was," writes a livin
English statesman, " perhaps the most impressiv
person I have ever seen, with a fiery intensity o
faith in his own principles and in their ultimat
triumph, which made him seem inspired ; a man t

ken sleeping souls, and fill them with his own
our." He loved to commune with those of his
n spiritual kin,—Dante, Savonarola, Cromwell,—
n who had the same undoubting faith in the
hteousness of their cause and their fellow-work
h God,—men, it may be, one-sided and intellectu-
, incomplete, but gifted with the power to do great
ıgs and lift up life. And so great principles and
ıleness of aim carried him through a series of
ctical mistakes, and left his life to be a permanent
iching of the race. What if he dreamed dreams,
t for generations yet may be no more than dreams?
ıat if his mental ken reached not to all the know-
ge of the age? What if he marred his work
mistakes and miscalculations? His errors have
sed; his intellectual limitations can be supplied.
; was the rarer and the greater part, to lift men
of the low air of common life up to the heights,
ere thought is larger, and life runs richer, and the
at verities are seen, undimmed by self and sophistry.
e idealist is still mankind's best friend; and he
:s most for the race, who purges its spiritual vision,
l breathes into cold duty, till it becomes a thing
life and passion and power. Greater still is he,
ɔ is not idealist only, but saint and hero, and in
life bears witness to the truth he teaches. Such
ıt and hero and idealist Mazzini was; and while
n and women live, who would be true to themselves
l to their call, who value sacrifice and duty above
ver and success, so long will there be those, who
l love him and be taught by him.

Dear Mr. Mallyson,

The Polish gentleman is entirely unknown to me. Mr. L. Bulewski known to G. A. Taylor, and living I think 22a. Piccadilly, might inform you.

I wrote, of course, to Sardinia. Spezzian is delighted.

Pray, remember me very kindly to Mrs. M. and believe me

faithfully yours

Jos Mazzini

Friday.

FACSIMILE OF MAZZINI'S HANDWRITING.

Appendix A

THE UNPUBLISHED (IN ONE CASE PRIVATELY PUBLISHED) LETTERS AND PAPERS, WRITTEN BY MAZZINI.

1. *Letter to Mr W. E. Hickson, about* 1844.

2. *A Prayer for the Planters,* 1846.

3. *Letter to Mrs Peter Taylor,* 1847.

4. *Letter to Mr Peter Taylor, February* 1854.

5. *Letter to Mr Peter Taylor, October* 1854.

6. *Letter to Mrs Peter Taylor,* 1857.

7. *Two Letters to Mrs Milner-Gibson,* 1859.

8. *Letter to Mr Peter Taylor,* 1860.

9. *Letter to Mrs Peter Taylor,* 1865.

10. *Letter to Mr W. Malleson,* 1865.

11. *Rest. A Paper written for the Pen and Pencil Club,* 1867.

12. *Letter to Mrs Peter Taylor,* 1868.

13. *Letter to Mr William Shaen,* 1870.

LETTER TO Mr W. E. HICKSON, EDITOR OF THE *Westminst.*
Review (probably in 1844).

[This letter gives some details concerning his early life, whic
are not mentioned in his works or in any of the biographies.]

DEAR SIR,—I began to attract the attention of the Governmer
in Italy by my literary writings. I had been pleading warmly th
cause of what was then called Romanticism, and was the right c
progressive life in Literature. Then, as now, all pleading fc
literary liberty, independence, progression, were suspected i
Italy as educating the mind to forbidden tendencies. I publishe
in 1828 a weekly literary paper the "Indicatore Genovese" : :
was, at the end of the year, and though published under the doubl
ecclesiastical and temporal censorship, suppressed. I caused th
paper to be continued at Leghorn under the title of "Indicator
Livornese" ;[1] it was, at the end of the year, suppressed again.
wrote one long article on "a European Literature" in the best o
our reviews, the "Antologia" of Florence. The review was per
secuted and after some time suppressed. In 1830, after th
Revolution of July I was arrested. The accusation was th
spreading of a secret association tending to the overthrow of th
Italian Government. I recollect a fact, well apt to give a summar
of our condition in Italy. My father, Professor of Anatomy in th
Genoese University, went to the Governor of the town, Venanson
enquiring at the cause of my imprisonment. "Your son," he wa
told amongst other things, "is fond of walking every night, alone
sadly pensive, on the outskirts of the town. What on earth ha
he at his age to think about? We don't like young peopl
thinking, without our knowing the subject of their thoughts." /
committee of Senators was appointed, in Turin, to try me. The
found no proofs, and acquitted both me and some friends who ha
been arrested with me. Nevertheless I was sent, in solitary con

[1] This is inaccurate. See Linaker, *Vita di Enrico Mayer*, I. 124-125.

ement, at Savona, in the fortress for five months : and after-
rds, sent in exile, without leave of seeing anybody, except
' parents. There was no duration determined ; but I was
d that my subsequent conduct would shorten or prolong the
ie of my being an exile. I came through Savoy and Switzerland
France, at a time in which the Government of Louis Philippe,
: yet acknowledged by the absolutist Governments, was active
exciting all insurrectional schemes, both in Spain and Italy. I
rged, of course into them.

When the insurrection of 1831 was quenched in the Estates of
: Pope, I established myself at Marseilles, and founded from
;re the new association "la giovine Italia." Of the distinctions
be made between this and the old Carbonari associations, I
,e spoken in four letters that have been printed in the " Monthly
ronicle." They—the fourth especially—I would advise you to
·use : J have not a single copy in my possession and cannot
:n remember the number ; but they must have appeared between
;8 and 1839. The rapidity with which the Association spread
nced the justice of the fundamental views. At the beginning
1832, the organisation was powerful throughout all Italy. As
: of the main features of La Giovine Italia was to not content
:lf as Carbonarism did, with a secret war, but to reach insur-
tion through the open preaching of its belief, an organ was
ablished at Marseilles expounding all the principles of the
;ociation. La Giovine Italia, a review, or rather a collection
political pamphlets springing from the Association, was under
 direction ; and, in fact, the two-thirds of each volume were my
n. The effect was really electric among our youth. From
.rseilles, through the merchant-ships of our country, the
itains of which were almost generally volunteering their
rts, the volumes were smuggled into Italy, where they raised
 enthusiasm of the patriots to such a pitch that it was evident
eneral outbreak would ensue. Then, the persecutions began.
plications were made by all the Italian Governments to the
:nch : the policy of Louis Philippe had already changed, and
 most active co-operation against the Association and me was
·mised. Measures were taken at Marseilles against such of our
les as were living upon the *subsidies*. They were sent away to
 interior. But few as we were, we could, by multiplying our
ivity, front the task. At last, under the pretence of my being

likely to be connected with the republican agitation in Franc
was ordered to leave France. I protested, and claimed
common justice of a trial ; but unsuccessfully. My presence
Marseilles was imperiously required by the interests of
Association ; the writing, publishing, and sending to Italy
correspondencies with the country, for which Marseilles
offering every facility, the interviews with Italian patriots w
flocked to Marseilles for instructions and communicatio
were all resting on me. I decided to stop ; and conceal
myself. During one year I succeeded in baffling all
activity of the French police, and of our own spies.
it was through the most rigorous seclusion you can imagi
During one year, I remember having had only twice,
breath of fresh air in the night, once dressed in woman's ga
the other as a Garde-National. At last things had reach
such a point that a general rising was thought of. I left Fra
and went to Geneva : there to await for the event, and prepare
expedition into Savoy, so as to divide the forces of the enemy a
establish co-operation between the patriots in Italy and th
exiles. How the hopes of an insurrection failed in Italy, t
fourth of my letters in the "Monthly Chronicle" will tell yc
How we too failed, through our military leader, General Ramorir
in the attempt on Savoy—an attempt I thought it our duty
realise, as a practical teaching to our countrymen, that promis(
once given, are to be kept,—would now be too long to say. Bu
tolerably true account of the enterprise is to be found in one
the volumes of "Histoire de Dix Ans" *par* Louis Blanc. Mea
while the attempt, once unsuccessful, drew upon Switzerland a;
à fortiori upon me, the anger of all Governments. Notes we
literally showering upon the poor Swiss Cantons, where we s
journed. The most of us left Switzerland for France or Englan
I with few others remained. Driven away from Geneva, I we
to the Canton de Vaud : driven away from there, to Berr
There, owing to the friendship of some of the members of t
Government, I stopped for some time, keeping a very seclud(
life. At last the insistence of the foreign Embassies prevail(
upon the weakness of the Bernese Government, and I was oblig(
to go to Solothurn. Meanwhile the principles, embodied in o
writings and in our associations had awakened the sympathies
the Swiss patriots. A National Association was founded on

und of brotherhood with our own. The persecutions with
ich the unwilling but weak Swiss Governments were hunting
, excited almost as much indignation as the opening of the
ers here. The weakness of the Cantons had its source in the
iciency of national unity, in the detestable organisation of the
itral Power, on the old *Pacte Federal*, forced by the Allies on
itzerland at the overthrow of Napoleon. I was requested to
te a periodical advocating and unifying under our political
ief, the national feelings. Funds were given. The "Jeune
sse" was established. It appeared twice a week in French and
German, for the course of one year. Through the German
les, and working-men, through the Tyrolese working-men,
her numerous in the Canton of Zürich, through the Italian
ssin, and the frequent contact with Italian people travelling to
. frontier, the spirit of liberty began to spread again in the
intries approaching Switzerland. The terrors of the Govern-
nts re-excited the persecution. They threatened Switzerland
h war. German troops came to the frontier, M. Thiers was
nacing to ruin Swiss commercial resources with a "blocus
metique." We were sent away. The paper suppressed; the
st horrible calumnies spread against us : all exiles left with or
hout compulsion. I decided to remain as long as necessary to
ive to the Swiss people, that they were the slaves of the Foreign
wers, and devoid of all real liberty, of all independence. Dur-
seven months, I went from place to place, from house to house,
ng in places apparently empty, with mats at the windows,
bout even going beyond the room, except when receiving
rices of the house being suspected : then with a guide, I was
ssing the mountains in the night, and going to another shelter.
iile the Governments were raging, I received from all classes
iopulation marks of sympathy that made and still make me
isider Switzerland as a second Fatherland. Ministers [of re-
on] were inviting me to their houses as one of their family. [At]
inchen, a village of a thousand inhabitants, near Solothurn,
en I had spent one year, in an establishment of baths, I was,
:ing the storm, made citizen spontaneously and without expense.
e poor people, good souls of the village, believed that as a
iss citizen, I would be respected ; the grant of course, was not
mitted. Still had I been alone, I would have, hardened as I
s to all privations, kept on resisting ; [but I was not alone] so I

decided to leave and come to England. It was then that I h
a correspondence with the Duke of Montebello, which ended
his sending three passports for us to a place I named; and
January or February 1837 I landed in England

The "Giovine Italia" had six volumes published at differe
times. All that I have ever written concerning politics bears n
name. Before I established the Association I wrote a long lett
to Charles Albert, who had just then come to reign over Piedmor
remembering him of what he had promised and done, when not
king, pointing to him all the dangers of his position, the imposs
bility of keeping down long the spirit of the nation, the system
blood-shedding reaction to which he would soon be bound, and d
the other side, the Possible, the Beautiful, the Grand, the Godlil
that there would be in his putting himself at the head of th
National party; the letter was printed, and signed only "A
Italian." My name was then quite unknown, and would not hav
added the least weight to the considerations; besides, I did n
believe that the "Italian People" would ever spring from under
royal cloak; and I was writing, not my own opinion, but that
many of my countrymen still fond of such a hope. I wanted t
have the true intentions of the man on whom they relied, as muc
as possible unveiled. As soon as the letter reached him, m
"signalement" was given to all the authorities of the coast, so ¿
to have me arrested if ever I attempted to cross the frontic
again. . . . I have been in 1833 condemned to be shot *in t*
back by a military commission sitting in Alessandria, as having le
from without the agitation. Here in London I have exerted, as
will exert, what influence I possess with my countrymen to en
deavour to raise them from the nothingness and worse tha
nothingness in which now they are; from English affairs I hav
kept myself entirely separated; nor sought the help of Englis
people even for our Italian affairs. As to all the present agitatio
I had nothing to do with it, on the beginning. I did not thin
that the time was properly chosen. But, when the patriots of th
interior *decided* that they *would* attempt, nothing of course, wa
left to me than helping them; and so I did, or rather prepared m
to do so, should a rising take place.

It seems to me that the right of an Italian to work out from wha
ever place he finds himself in, the welfare of his country, ought t
be clearly and boldly asserted by an English writer.

Of the hopes I have of the Italian patriots succeeding at a not
:ry remote period, in what they are now struggling for, I cannot
)w speak here. It would prove too long a subject for a letter;
it I am in intention, if I find time for it, of publishing very soon,
Pamphlet on the question, showing how, all weary of slow, legal,
tional progress being interdicted to us, our only hope must lie
insurrection as the starting-point for a national education. If
ere are points upon which you want more notions, be so kind as
write, and meanwhile, with sincere thanks for the interest you
ke in my case, believe me now dear Sir,—

Truly yours,

JOSEPH MAZZINI.

47 Devonshire Street,
Queen Square.

II

A PRAYER TO GOD FOR THE PLANTERS, BY AN EXILE.

[The original is in French. It has probably not been published
fore. It was sent in 1846 to Mr William Shaen in response to
:equest for a paper on the abolition of slavery. It was to have
peared in Lady Blessington's *Keepsake*, presumably in a trans-
ion, but was not published in it. In sending it Mazzini writes :
To write one or two pages on abolitionism is just the same to me
to prove that the sun gives light and warmth ; or to prove an
iom. So that I was during one full hour at a loss what to
ite, till my soul melted away in prayer."]

God of pity, God of peace and love, forgive, oh forgive the
inters. Their sin is great ; but thy mercy is infinite. As of old
)u didst make refreshing waters gush from the desert rock for
: multitude of thy servants, so now make the living spring of
arity gush out in the desert of their souls. Let the angel of
)entance descend and settle on their dying pillow. And be-
:en them and thy justice, at their last hour,—for them and for
ir country, which they dishonour,—may the prayer rise up of
who suffer for thy holy cause, for thy holy truth, for the freedom
the peoples and of the Soul of man.

Their sin is great. They have sinned, they are sinning still
iinst thee and against Humanity, which is the interpreter of thy

law on earth. The Spirit of Evil, which tempted Jesus, thy so
so dear to Genius and to Love, by offering him, when he bega
his divine career, the riches and the thrones of earth, has als
tempted them, men bereft of Genius and of Love, by takin
the semblance of the idol, which is self-interest. They hav
yielded. They are the bondsmen of the senses, and have fo
sworn knowledge and feeling. They have set the slave in th
place of man, the fetish of the sugar-cane in the place of th
holy image. But thou, didst thou not hear thy son, so dear
Genius and to Love, when he prayed for those who slew him
Forgive them, Father, forgive the planters too.

———

Thou hast placed, as symbol of the eye of thy Providenc
one sun in heaven for the earth. Thou hast interwoven in on
mighty harmony, of which human Music, Religion's eldest chil
is but a faint and stammering echo, the worlds, those finite ray
of thy infinite Thought, that move around us, like the scattere
letters of a heavenly alphabet, which we shall know one day. I
this fair physical Universe, which is the garment of the Ide
thou hast everywhere taught Unity, and the bright light of th
teaching shines upon their souls ; but they have veiled the eye
of their souls, they have broken in pieces that which is so fai
and on the wreck of thy Unity they have built a warring Dua
ism : two natures, two laws, two ways of life. Have pity, Lord
forgive, oh forgive the planters.

———

In History, which is thy life, manifesting itself progressively i
time and space, thou hast set in their sight another fount of truth
whence in great waves flows the great thought of Unity, which i
thy whole Law. Thou madest all mankind spring from one Adam
at the teaching of thy providence, more clearly seen from day t
day, thou hast led man, collective, social man, from slavery t
serfdom, from serfdom to wage-earning ; and that nought ma
be wanting to make the progression clear, thou makest now th
nations to desire impatiently that to wage-earning associatio
may succeed. And over these three stages, which are the imag
of thy triune working, hovers the holy voice of Golgotha, *All y
are brothers, for ye are all one in God.* And they have stoppe
their ears to the holy voice of Golgotha, they have shut their eye
to the evolution of Thought in History : they have said : *we ar*

ot *brothers, we are masters and slaves.* They have kept one
age alone of the Great Book, the page that tells of Cain and
.bel, of Violence and Right; and they have said to themselves :
*ere are then two races of men, the race that is accursed, and the
ice that is privileged, and of this last race are we* ; they know
ot that the sign of thy curse is on their own forehead, since it is
y Violence alone that they make slaves of men.   Have pity,
.ord, forgive, oh forgive the planters.

And for the third witness of thy Truth, thou hast put a voice in
ich man's heart, an impulse in each man's conscience, which
iys : *I am free ; free because I am responsible, free because I am
man, made in God's image, inherently possessing in myself the
iwers and aspirations and destinies of all Humanity.* And they
ave denied that this is the voice of all men.   They have shut
iemselves up in their selfish *Ego,* and have said : *this voice is
irs alone,* and they see not, wretched men that they are, that if
iey put a bound to it, they blot it out from all creation, since God
id not create the *planter* but the *man.*   They have sown hate,
nd they will reap revolt : they have denied the God of love, and
iey have provoked the God of vengeance.   Listen not to their
lasphemy, O Lord.   Forgive, oh forgive the planters.

O Lord, open their understandings and soften their hearts.   Let
ie angel, that inspires good thoughts, descend upon them in
ieir dreams by night.   Let them hear through him the cry
f horror that ascends from all Humanity that believes and
ives ;—the sorrowing cry of all who endure and fight for the
ood in Europe, and whose confidence and faith is shaken by
ieir stubborn crime ;—the mocking cry of the princes and kings
f the earth, who, when their subjects are full of turmoil, point to
ie proud republicans of America, who alone of men maintain the
ilotism of pagan ages ;—the long anguish of Jesus, who, because
f them, still suffers on his cross to-day l   And when in the morn-
ig they awake, let their children lay their innocent curly heads
iside their lips, and whisper, inspired by thee : " Father, father,
ee our brother, the black man ; buy and sell no more the son of
ian for thirty pennies ; see, this black man too has a mother and
ttle children like us ; Oh that his old mother could rejoice to see

him proud and free ! that his children could smile on him, fres
and happy, in the morning, as we smile now on you, father."

God of pity, God of peace and love, forgive, oh forgive the planter:
Their sin is great, but thy mercy is infinite. Open in the desei
of their souls the living spring of charity. Let the angel of re
pentance descend and settle on their dying pillow. And betwee
them and thy justice, at their last hour,—for them and for thei
country, which they dishonour,—may the prayer rise up of al
who, like myself, suffer for thy holy cause, for thy holy truth, fc
the freedom of the peoples and of the Soul of man.

JOSEPH MAZZINI.

III

LETTER TO MRS PETER TAYLOR [May 15, 1847].

DEAR MRS TAYLOR,—First of all let me tell you that m
silence before your note has been owing to my having been mo:
unpoetically ill, with head-ache, sore throat, prostration of force:
fever and other things, till I was thinking that Mr Taylor woul
perhaps get rid all at once of me and of the League : howeve
Homœopathy—that is taking nothing—has cured me : then tha
my silence after the note has been owing to a hope in which I hav
been indulging both on Friday evening, and on Saturday, to ca
on you unexpectedly and talk instead of writing. However tha
hope too—the other is Mr Taylor's hope—has vanished : and
find myself having so much to do that I doubt whether I will fin
a moment of freedom this week. So, I write, and hope to b
forgiven for the past.

.   .   .   .   .   .

And now to Poetry. Alas ! After mature consideration, I fin
no *definition* at all ; by *you* it is not needed ; I am sure you hav
the *thing* in your own Soul, and that is better than all definition
one could supply ; for Mr Taylor I fear no definition of min
would do. Suppose I gave a definition that seems to me ver
true, but that I ought to explain in ten pages at least. " Poetry i
the feeling of a former and of a future world "[1] : he would find ou

---

[1] From Byron's Journal.

ıt it belongs to Byron, and would find himself pledged to refuse
Suppose that I gave one of mine ⁚

" Poetry is the Religion of the individual Soul."
" Religion is the Poetry of the collective Soul."

fear that not only he, but perhaps you too, would ask for
ɔlanations which would fill up a lecture, not a note. Suppose
ıt I quoted lines like these :

"A Poet's art ·
Lies in tolerating wholly, and accounting for in part
By his own heart's subtle working, those of every other heart "

would say that that is charity, and nothing else ; *we* would
ɾ that it is incomplete. Suppose that I adopted yours—which,
h due comments and interpretations, I am not far from—that
'oetry is the soul of the Universe," it would not avail. You
ɾe it already, I am sure, and it was declared unsatisfactory.
We must one day or other *talk* about this. I fear vaguely
ıt even *we* do differ in some way respecting the essence of
etry. I suspect that you leave out in your own definition the
ment of *Action*, which seems to me inseparable from it.
etry is for me something like the third person of Trinity, the
ɔly Spirit, which *is* Action. But this amounts to declare
omplete, the poetry, for instance, of Wordsworth, Coleridge,
. Is that a heresy for you ? If so, our definitions will not
ɾee.—ever faithfully yours,

JOS. MAZZINI.

IV

LETTER TO MR PETER TAYLOR [February 16, 1854].

This letter is inserted, because of its historical importance.
ıs, I believe, the earliest existing mention of any scheme for a
ɛnch protectorate in Tuscany. It also antedates by a few
eks the earliest known mention of Garibaldi's scheme for an
ɔedition to Sicily. Mazzini's information respecting Louis
ɔoleon's plans was probably derived from Dr Conneau, but it
s generally inaccurate.]

ᴠIʏ DEAR FRIEND,—I write because I have no time for coming,
ɖ I write, I must avow, to silence conscience, with very little
ɔe.

Do not smile, and say "the man is mad"; but put your he
in your two hands and try to solve this question : "is there a
earthly way of getting one thousand pounds in a very short tin
ten days, a fortnight at the most?"

With you I have no secrets, and I shall state to you summari
the why.

We *must* act: as early as possible in March : in fact as so
as the declaration of war or an action amounting to the san
takes place, we must *act*, because the initiative is everything f
us.

The actual schemes of the French Emperor, assented to l
your cabinet, are these :

A Muratist movement in Naples : reinforcements in Ron
ready to help, as Piedmont would object to the establishme.
of a French dynasty in the South. France offers to patroni;
the King of Piedmont to the North of Italy. Lombardy will l
Piedmontese. But Lombardy and the Venetian territory wou
together with Piedmont form too large, too threatening a stat
Lombardy and Venice shall therefore be divided. Venice lil
Greece will be given up to some foreign prince, or to Austr
again if Austria yields and submits in other respects. Ror
will remain to the Pope. Only as there are provinces s
disaffected that the case is hopeless, from them and Tuscar
a central Dukedom or Princedom will be formed under Frenc
patronage. Sicily will be given—the old scheme of 1848—
the Duke of Genoa, son of the Piedmontese king.

Thus Italy will have two more divisions, Sicily and Venice
new foreign dynasties would be settled there, new interests woul
group themselves around them : a new partition would begi
with high sanction, a new phasis, and we should have to begi
anew our secret work, our clandestine printing, our series c
martyrdoms, as if nothing had been done.

To all this I know only of a [one] remedy : to initiate : to giv
the leadership to the national party. The multitude will follo'
the first who acts ; the very elements prepared by all thes
intrigues will accrue to us if we move first.

And beyond all, to move in the South. We would thus chec
the French scheme before its realisation. As we would, for th
present, leave Rome aside and untouched, we do not damage i
the least the actual position of England with France.

;aribaldi is here : ready to act. Garibaldi's name is all
verful among the Neapolitans, since the Roman affair of
.letri. I want to send him to Sicily, where they are ripe for
urrection and wishing for him as a leader.

)f course another action would simultaneously take place in a
nt of the centre, and I would lead a third operation in the
rth.

'or these two, I have, though very little, still enough of money.
: the first, that is for Garibaldi, I have none, and claiming
from Italy would imply expenses for travellers, risks, the
'eiling of the secret, and *uncertain indefinite* time.

ire there not to be found in England ten persons willing for
sake of Italy and for the sake of baffling schemes of French
nination absolutely antagonistic to English interests, to take
h £100 of our National Loan notes ?[1]—or twenty ready to
e £50 each ?

'his is the problem.

know nobody almost. It must be the work of some English-
n. If any plan could be devised of certain fulfilment, but
uiring longer time, the sum could be perhaps advanced by
ıe person who would keep all that would come in by degrees.

.   .   .   .

ver yours affectionately,   JOSEPH MAZZINI.

ſo friends whom you can trust, you may, under pledge of
ıour, communicate what you think proper.

Feb. 16.   15 Radnor St.
King's Road, Chelsea.

V

LETTER TO MR PETER TAYLOR   [October 26, 1854].

ΛY DEAR FRIEND,—Are you astonished at our inertness ? at
· talking so much and doing so little ? I often think that you
l so. I could explain everything in two hours of conversation ;
: take my word in spite of all, we are ripe for the aim, and
.t ere long we shall reach it. In fact, had I not been ex-

[1] See above, p. 168.

ceptionally prudent and calm, action would have been alrea&#11;
initiated. It would be any day, were it not for Piedmont a&#11;
the "Western Powers." Piedmont is our curse.

First, on account of its enjoying liberty, it is so much wi&#11;
drawn from the field of action; then we have, just as in 184&#11;
a whole world of courtiers, of ministerial agents, of journalis&#11;
and even of clandestine-press-writers, spreading everywhe&#11;
that the King will draw the sword one of these days, that Fran&#11;
and England will cause the revolution to spring up in Naple&#11;
that you will quarrel with Austria about the Principalities, th&#11;
a better opportunity will come, must come, if only we ha&#11;
patience for one month, for two months, for two weeks. The&#11;
was a whole dream-dispelling work to be done before thinkir&#11;
of immediate action. This work is, for the two-thirds, don&#11;
the other third will take, perhaps some two months. The fie&#11;
will be mine then. The people, the working-classes, a&#11;
admirable : they are mine, mine devotedly to blindness.

One thing is out of doubt: any *initiative* will be an Itali&#11;
one : one spark will settle the whole on fire, only, the *initiati*&#11;
MUST be a successful one. This is the source of all my dela&#11;
I feel too certain of success after the first blow being struck f&#11;
my risking uncautiously the first blow.

The English agitation I am trying to spread would be of re&#11;
importance to me, if taking a certain degree of *consistence*, bo&#11;
from the financial point of view and from the moral one. Y&#11;
have not an idea of how proud and stronger my working men &#11;
feel here, when they find themselves noticed, encouraged an&#11;
helped in England. I trust you will do what is in your power&#11;
promote and help.

How are you? How is your wife? Are you ever talking abo&#11;
me? against me? I am well in health, spite of the forced&#11;
sedentary life I lead. I think very often, under these radia&#11;
skies, of the London fogs, and always regretfully. Individual&#11;
speaking, I was evidently intended for an Englishman.

What are you doing at Pinner? What little dogs have yc&#11;
caused to disappear? How many poor hens kept in a state&#11;
bondage, and tied by the leg somewhere, are awaiting for&#11;
revolutionist to untie them? . . . What do you read? What d&#11;
you anticipate for England's politics? Do you smoke muc&#11;
. . . I wish we could have a talk of one hour all together, wit&#11;

ırs and sherry, and then be back where I am wanted. . . .
: your friend,   JOSEPH.

VI

LETTER TO MRS PETER TAYLOR   [March 19, 1857].

hanks, my dear Friend, for your having remembered my
ıe's day [St Joseph's Day]. I don't know why, but every anni-
ıarÿ concerning myself finds me very sad: those friendly
ıperings are checking the tendency.
he box has arrived. You have made out the *only* point of
ıact between Shakespeare and myself, on all the rest we
ıly differ. He was an extraordinary poet: I am not. He
—spite of your interpretations—calm :[1] I am not. He looked
the world from above: I look at it from within and want to
ıe a revolution. He was—if reports are correct—merrily
ıching: I have always before my eyes, like a remorse, the
ıe convulsion with which a poor thrush, shot by me at the age
ıxteen, was twisting with her beak a bit of grass. He was the
ıd of Individuality: all my tendency, if developed, would have
ı a generalising one. He was powerful: I am powerless—
so on, to the end of the chapter.—your friend,
                                           JOSEPH MAZZINI,

VII

TWO LETTERS TO MRS MILNER-GIBSON
(Translated from the French)

ırs Milner-Gibson had just lost a little boy. Mazzini was
ıather to a younger brother.]
                                           [April 15, 1859.]
EAR FRIEND,—What can I say? You believe, as I do, in
 and immortality. It is there that you must find your
fort and strength. Love your boy as if he were alive, for
ıat you will have what will restore him to you in the series
ıistences, which follows this one. Become even better than

---

[1] Query. The word was illegible in the original.

you are by thinking of him, for this will make a bond of lo*
and mutual influence between you and him. Think of him whe
you are doing good. Think of him, when impulses of selfishne*
or human frailty assail you. Be good and strong. Give yot
other children the love he gave them himself. And count o
God. There is immortality to link the mother and the child, an
only forgetfulness can break it. I have heard of his last wor*
and kisses : he loved you to his last moment, love him to your
and believe it, this will have been but the parting for a journey.

This is all I can say. From me to you such commonpla*
words of comfort as the world generally gives would be a kind *
sin. I suffer with your grief. I, who have no home now, kno
what the sorrows of home are,—they leave a scar in the hea*
which never goes, and that is sad, but it is well. Cherish th
scar, it is a pledge of the future. Do not give yourself up *
the barren, cowardly sorrow, called despair. There is no dea*
in the world except forgetfulness. Everything that loves and h*
loved to death meets again. Good-bye, my friend. Think
your health for the sake of your other children. God bless y*
in them,—your friend, JOSEPH.

[This letter was succeeded by the following.]

DEAR FRIEND,—I have received your letters, they are more a*
more sad. You have been ill and you are unhappy. Your vi*
to the Continent will do you good physically, I hope, but as
your moral health, you must cure that yourself. Rouse your so*
which is in danger of being benumbed by sorrow ; you will fi*
at the bottom of it, I don't say happiness, I don't say even hop*
but duty and faith in some affections which do count. For Go*
sake, do not despair : you have dear children to bring up ; y*
can still do good, and you have friends who esteem and love y*
and suffer with your sufferings and find strength in your ow*
Ah me, what the devil should I do myself, if I allowed the litt*
strength, which God has left me, to desert me, as it often threate*
to do. . . . Good-bye. Yours with all my heart, JOSEPH.

VIII

LETTER TO MR PETER TAYLOR [September 11, 1860].

DEAR PETER,—

   .   .   .   .

I have yours of the 29th of Aug. written with an improved
ndwriting, and the article on Lady Byron. It is according to
:, unwise and unjust : unwise, because to praise Lady Byron for
r life's silence and to abuse the very man about whom she has
osen to be silent, is inconsistent : unjust, because it grounds
verdict on the wrongs of one party, without taking into
:ount those of the other. Everybody seems to forget that
.dy Byron did not only leave her husband for ever, going "à la
omenade," but that she did set at him before, lawyers and
ctors to try if she could make him be proved *mad*! I wish—
, I don't—that your wife should set at you Dr E— and Mr
– for such a purpose, only to see what you would do when
covering it, and I wish I had time to write, before dying, a
ok on Byron and abuse all England, a few women excepted,
· the way she treats one of her greatest souls and minds : I
all never write the book nor—it begins to be clear—any other.
Well, I do not go into particulars about our condition here [at
ples]. As a party we are going through that sort of method
ich you called one day a *suicide*, preparing and attempting
ngs which are calling on us calumnies, abuse and persecution,
t which are taken up by the other Party as soon as we are put
t of the field. After having been baffled and most shamefully
in an attempt against the Pope's dominions,[1] they are now, at
ew days' distance, taking up our plan. We shall have to do
: same, soon or late, concerning Rome, and then Venice. And
· *shall*, if life endures. Only, I am worn out, morally and
ysically.
Everything is now resting on Garibaldi : will he go on, without
erruption, in his invading career, or will he not? That is the
estion. If he does, we shall have unity within five months :
istria, spite of the boasted position, will not hold up, if the
oper means—a coup de main in the Tyrol, an insurrection in

---

[1] See above, p 186.

the Venetian mountainous districts, an attack by land, and a landing near Trieste—are adopted. If he does not, we shall have slumber, then anarchy—then—a little later—unity. *That* you may consider as settled, and so far so good. The rest is all wrong. And as for myself don't talk of either prosperity or consciousness of having done, etc. All that is chaff. The only real good thing would be to have unity atchieved [sic] quickly through Garibaldi, and one year, before dying, of Walham Green or Eastbourne, long silences, a few affectionate words to smooth the ways, plenty of sea-gulls, and sad dozing.

Ah! if you had, in England, condescended to see that the *glorious* declaration of non-interference ought to have begun by taking away the French interference in Rome! How many troubles and sacrifices you would have saved us!—ever your truly affectionate and grateful   JOSEPH.

[In another letter to Mr Taylor, dated June 5, 1860, he says :]

Yes, I heard of Lady Byron's death and her last gift. I wish something came out, now that she is dead, to explain the separation mystery. I shall ever regret the burning of the memoirs which was a crime towards Byron ; and I have ever indulged in the dream that a copy should be extant in somebody's hands to come out after the disappearing of the principal actors. I saw Lady Byron twice, and she looked to me a good sharp positive somewhat dry puritanical woman, sad from the past, conscious of not having been altogether right and doing good half for good doing's sake, half for forgetfulness' sake. But I am so thoroughly Byronian, so deeply convinced that he has been wronged by everybody, that my impression cannot be trusted.

IX

LETTER TO MRS PETER TAYLOR   [February 9, 1865]

DEAR CLEMENTIA,—

.   .   .   .

I shall send back the magazine : read the article again : take away all phrases and periphrases : *squeeze* every period ; and then send to me the first idea or view which strikes you as new to yourself. I shall retract.

The whole article amounts to this : repeating fifty times in rather harmonious words that Art is the reproduction of Beauty, etc., etc. Many thanks. Only, what is Beauty? How to discern it? Why is Nature beautiful? Are we to copy, to reproduce Nature? or to add a work of our own, finding out the idea shut in within every symbol? Is Nature anything but the symbolic representation of some truth, which we are to evolve? Or is the drapery of Nature, Nature ? Miss C—— says that the Artist must choose the object which is Beautiful. Is not *every* object more or less so? Is not the grotesque causing the beautiful to shine by contrast? Are the grave-diggers to be suppressed in Hamlet?

Without sifting the nature of Beauty, without giving some definition of it, nobody can attempt to construct a Hierarchy of Art. Miss C. has not even attempted to do so. Still you have been in raptures. Something, therefore, must be in the article. I have not been able to make it out. I beg pardon humbly. That is all I can say.

.   .   .   .   .

—ever affectionately yours,   JOSEPH.

Thursday.

X

LETTER TO MR WILLIAM MALLESON [Nov. 11, 1865].

MY DEAR FRIEND,—I feel ashamed, but I have been over-whelmed by work, not flourishing in health, although better now, and altogether unable to fulfil what I had promised. Then, and after all, I write to say that I cannot fulfil it. I said that I would write about the education of your son. I find that I cannot. I ought to know him, his tendencies, his capabilities, what he has already learned. To give general rules is nothing. He *may* require special ones.

I have mentioned his tendencies. *That* must be your special object. Every man is a *speciality*, is capable of some definite thing. You must try to discover that *special* tendency, and then frame his education accordingly. After a general teaching of those branches which are good for *any* man, direct his studies towards the development of that special tendency which you will have discovered. Education means *drawing out, educere*, what is in the boy : not creating in him what is not. You cannot create.

But one thing is, must be common to all. You must give him a proper notion of what Life is, and of what the world in which he has been put for the fulfilment of a task is.

Life is a duty, a function, a mission. For God's sake, do not teach him any Benthamite theory about happiness either individual or collective. A creed of *individual* happiness would make him an egotist : a creed of collective happiness will reach the same result soon or late. He will perhaps dream Utopias, fight for them, whilst young ; then, when he will find that he cannot realise rapidly the dream of his soul, he will turn back to himself and try to conquer *his* own happiness : sink into egotism.

Teach him that Life has no sense unless being a task :—that happiness may, like sunshine on a traveller, come to him, and he must welcome it and bless God for it ; but that to *look* for it is destroying both the moral man and his duty and most likely the possibility of ever enjoying it :—that to improve himself, morally and intellectually, for the sake of improving his fellow-creatures, is his task :—that he must try to get at Truth and then represent it, in words and deeds, fearlessly and perennially :—that to get at Truth, two *criteria* have been given to him, his own conscience and tradition, the conscience of mankind : — that whenever he will find the inspiration of his own conscience harmonising with that of mankind, sought for not in the history of a single period or of a single people, but of all periods and peoples, then he is sure of having Truth within his grasp :—that the basis of all Truth is the knowledge of the Law of Life, which is indefinite Progression :—that to this Law he must be a servant.

This knowledge of the Law of Progression must be your aim in all your teaching.

Elementary Astronomy, elementary Geology, ought to be taught as soon as possible. Then, universal History, then Languages.

The difficult thing is to get the proper teaching. When I speak, for instance, of Astronomy, I mean a survey of the Universe, of which the Earth is part, grounded on Herschel's theory and tending to prove how everything is the exponent of a Law of Progression, how the Law is one, how every part of the Universe accomplishes a function in the whole. Herschel, Nichol, Guillemin's recently translated " Heavens " are the guides to be chosen.

Languages are easily learned in boyhood. French, German,

and Italian ought to be taught. Two years of study may put the boy in communication with three worlds.

I would not teach any *positive* Religion ; but the great funda- mental Trinity, God, the immortality of the soul, the necessity of a religion as a common link of brotherhood for mankind, grounded on the acknowledgment of the Law of Progression. At a later period he will choose.

Geography of course will be taught. But everything taught in a *general* way and not applied is easily forgot. The best way is to have a collection of good maps and to give him the habit of never reading a historical book or even a tale without following it up on the map. It is the best and most lasting way.

Avoid novels and tales. Give him a taste for historical books and scientific descriptive *illustrated* books of natural history travels, etc.

In one word, a religious conception of life—then a full notion of the world he lives in—then the special branch of activity to which he seems inclined : that is the whole of education for your boy.

Forgive these hurried notes. Apply to me freely for any detail or special suggestion. I shall be most happy to answer. Give my love to Mrs Malleson and to Miss K. M. How are they? How is your father? Where are you all now ?—Ever affection- ately yours,   JOSEPH MAZZINI.

Saturday.

XI

REST.

[Written for the Pen and Pencil Club in April 1867, and privately published in 1877, with other papers written by its members.]

DEAREST FRIEND,—The subject of your meeting of to-morrow is so suggestive that I would gladly join you all, and write an essay on it, if I had health and time. I have neither, and, perhaps, better so. My essay, I candidly avow, would tend to prove that no essay ought to be written on the subject. It has no reality. A sort of intuitive instinct led you to couple "Ghosts and Rest" together.

There is, here down,[1] and there ought to be, no Rest. Life is an *aim* ; an aim which can be *approached*, not *reached*, here down. There is, therefore, no rest. Rest is immoral.

It is not mine now to give a definition of the *aim* ; whatever it is, there is one, there *must* be one. Without it, Life has no sense. It is atheistical ; and moreover an irony and a deception.

I entertain all possible respect for the members of your Club; but I venture to say that any contribution on Rest which will not exhibit at the top a definition of Life will wander sadly between wild arbitrary intellectual display and commonplaces.

Life is no sinecure, no "*recherche du bonheur*" to be secured, as the promulgators of the theory had it, by guillotine, or, as their less energetic followers have it, by railway shares, selfishness, or contemplation. Life is, as Schiller said, "a battle and a march"; a battle for Good against Evil, for Justice against arbitrary privileges, for Liberty against Oppression, for associated Love against Individualism ; a march onwards to Self, through collective Perfecting to the progressive realisation of an Ideal, which is only dawning to our mind and soul. Shall the battle be finally won during life-time? Shall it on Earth? Are we believing in a millennium? Don't we feel that the spiral curve through which we ascend had its beginning elsewhere, and has its end, if any, beyond this terrestrial world of ours. Where is then a possible foundation for your essays and sketches?

Goethe's "Contemplation" has created a multitude of little sects aiming at Rest, where is no rest, falsifying art, the element of which is evolution, not reproduction, transformation, not contemplation, and enervating the soul in self-abdicating Brahmanic attempts. For God's sake let not your Club add one little sect to the fatally existing hundreds !

There is nothing to be looked for in life except the uninterrupted fulfilment of Duty, and, not Rest, but consolation and strengthening from Love. There is, not Rest, but a promise, a shadowing forth of Rest in Love. Only there must be in Love absolute *trust* ; and it is very seldom that this blessing depends [? descends] on us. The child goes to sleep, a dreamless sleep, with unbounded trust, on the mother's bosom ; but *our* sleep is a restless one, agitated by sad dreams and alarms.

You will smile at my lugubrious turn of mind ; but if I was one

---

[1] A favourite expression of Mazzini, as the equivalent of *quaggiù*.

of *your* Artists, I would sketch a man on the scaffold going to die for a great Idea, for the cause of Truth, with his eye looking trustfully on a loving woman, whose finger would trustfully and smilingly point out to him the unbounded. Under the sketch I would write, not Rest, but "a Promise of Rest." Addio : tell me one word about the point of view of your contributors.—ever affectionately yours,   JOSEPH MAZZINI.

XII

LETTER TO MRS PETER TAYLOR [From Lugano,
December 12, 1868.]

DEAR CLEMENTIA,—

.   .   .   .

I am better, although not so much as my friends here suppose. I feel, from various little symptoms, as if I could any week have the complaint back. I may, and hope to be mistaken, however. So, let us accept what instalment is granted, and not think of the future. I might give myself an additional chance, if I could keep absolutely silent and motionless during one month. But I cannot. There is—at least—a possibility of the Republic being proclaimed in Spain ; and if so, we must try to follow, a preparatory very complex work is therefore unavoidable. It is useless to tell me : "if you keep quiet now, you will be able to work better henceforward." The important thing is to work now. Your cabinet[1] is a shameful contrivance. . . . It is an implement good for the conquest of the Irish measure, and soon after, I think, the majority will split into two or three fractions. As to your—quite forgotten—international life, the main thing about which, according to me, you ought to care, Lord Clarendon s policy will be a French and Austrian policy. What does Peter say? Is he still enthusiastic about Gladstone?

.   .   .   .

Your women-emancipating movement is fairly imitated in Italy. We have a central committee of ladies in Naples, and sub-committees here and there, and one or two members of our

[1] The Gladstone Ministry of December 1868.

House pleading for them. All this is very right, and I hope that next year, European events will help this movement; but meanwhile, I should wish very much that, whilst you attack men with their gross injustice, you should teach women to *deserve* their emancipation : nothing is conquered unless *deserved.* The poor working men *have* deserved ; they have for one century fought, bled, acted for *all* the good causes in Europe : the majority of your women still fight almost entirely for a husband to be won by their personal genuine or artificial appearance ; they worship *fashion* more than the Ideal. You ought to write one tract to men and one to them.

Try to be well : give my love to Peter and believe in the deep and lasting affection of   JOSEPH.

XIII

LETTER TO MR WILLIAM SHAEN [From Gaeta, Oct. 12, 1870].

DEAR SHAEN,—I know that a few words from me and from here will please you. You do not forget me, and you have never been forgotten : none is of those whom I loved in England. For many reasons, I cannot write to all my friends, and they know the general state of things concerning me from good, faithful, dear Caroline.[1] I am, physically, tolerably well ; for the rest "fata viam invenient."

I know that you have been and are very active in the "Woman's Emancipation Movement." Every good cause has ever found you ready to help ; and I had no doubt of your coming forward in one which ought to be a matter of simple duty for anyone believing that there is but one God—one Life—one Law of progress through Love, Equality and Association for it. Still, it is comforting to hear of it. The movement has begun and with some degree of power in Italy too : it would rapidly and successfully increase had we not to complete, before all other things, our national edifice.

.   .   .   .

Ever and most affectionately yours,   JOS. MAZZINI.
28/9/70, GAETA.
                    [1] Mrs Stansfeld.

Appendix

This note was written, as you see, long ago : and through some reason or other, it did not go ; and I am able now to add that to-morrow I shall be free, and the day after I shall leave Gaeta. The *amnesty*, of course, I shall refuse to avail myself of I I must be free of doing whatever I think right and without even the shadow of ungratefulness to any body—even to a King. After a few days I shall therefore leave Italy again. It may be that during next month I come—for one month—to see my English friends : I wish and hope so. Meanwhile : live and prosper.— Yours ever, JOSEPH.

12/10/70.

Appendix B

BIBLIOGRAPHY OF MAZZINI'S WRITINGS.

[THE following is a list of the materials, which (with few exceptions) have been used in compiling this volume. It is, I believe, a complete list of writings of any importance by or concerning Mazzini, except some, which contain purely political references. For some of the minor references I wish to acknowledge my indebtedness to Signor Canestrelli's bibliography, published with his translation of von Schack's *Giuseppe Mazzini e l'unità italiana* (Rome, 1892).]

WRITINGS.

The bulk of Mazzini's writings have been collected in *Scritti editi e inediti di Giuseppe Mazzini*, 18 vols. (Milan and Rome, 1861-1891). There is an excellent selection, edited by Madame Mario, as *Scritti scelti di Giuseppe Mazzini* (Florence, 1901).

A good many of Mazzini's less important journalistic articles have not been included in the *Scritti editi e inediti*. There are several more notable omissions :—

Una notte di Rimini, said to be Mazzini's first strictly political writing, republished in Madame Mario's life.

Due adunanze degli accademici pitagorici, and *Di Vittor Hugo e dell' Angelo tiranno*, published in *Il Subalpino*, 1839, and reprinted in Donaver, *Vita di G. Mazzini*.

Byron e Goethe (very important for Mazzini's literary views), published in *Scritti letterari d'un italiano vivente* (Lugano, 1847), republished in Madame Mario's *Scritti scelti*, and badly translated in the *Life and Writings*, vol. ii.

Sulla pittura in Italia, published in *Scritti letterari*.

Macchiavelli, published in ditto.

Victor Hugo, published in *British and Foreign Review*, 1838, and republished in *Life and Writings*, vol. ii.

Lamartine, published in *British and Foreign Review*, 1839, and republished in *Life and Writings*, vol. ii.

Letters on the state and prospects of Italy, published in *Monthly Chronicle*, May-Sept. 1839.

George Sand, published in *Monthly Chronicle*, July 1839; extracts republished in *Life and Writings*, vol. vi.

Thiers, published in *Monthly Chronicle*, July 1839.

Review of C. Balbo's *Vita di Dante*, published in *The European*, Jan. 1840, and translated in A. von Schack, Joseph Mazzini und die italienische Einheit.

Italian Art, published in *Westminster Review*, April 1841. [There is no direct evidence that this was written by Mazzini, but the internal evidence is rather strong. I believe that it was translated into or from the *Révue républicaine*.]

Introduction and notes to Foscolo's edition of the *Divina Commedia* (see above, p. 94).

Pensieri sulla storia d'Italia, published in *l'Educatore* (London, 1843).

Sull' educazione, published in ditto, and republished in *l'Emancipazione* (Rome), Oct. 5, 1872.

A prayer for the planters, published for the first time in this volume, pp. 349-352.

Address of the People's International League, republished in *Life and Writings*, vol. vi. (see above, note to p. 303).

Notes for an answer to the Irish Repealers, published in *Scottish Leader*, July, 1888 (see above, p. 107).

George Sand, published in *People's Journal*; extracts republished in *Life and Writings*, vol. vi.

Non-intervention, published as a tract by the " Friends of Italy," and republished in *Life and Writings*, vol. vi.

Rest, published privately by the Pen and Pencil Club, and republished in this volume, pp. 363-365.

Italy and the Republic, published in *Fortnightly Review*, March 1, 1871.

The Franco-German War and the Commune, published in *Contemporary Review*, April and June, 1871.

[Signor Cagnacci in his *Giuseppe Mazzini e i fratelli Ruffini* publishes a rhapsodical *Aux jeunes italiens* and a short poem *Addio dalle Alpi*, which he believes to be from Mazzini's pen ; he gives, however, no evidence whatever in support of his theory. For Mazzini's supposed youthful poetry see Donaver, *Uomini e libri*, 77, 119, and *Vita di G. Mazzini*, 29 n., 431, and Canestrelli's bibliography, pp. 290, 291, 305, 308-9, 311.]

TRANSLATIONS.

The greater portion of the first seven volumes of the *Scritti editi e inediti*, with some additional matter, was translated into English as *Life and Writings of Joseph Mazzini*, 6 vols. (London, 1870). The *Duties of Man* and *Democracy in Europe* (*alias The Systems and the Democracy*, the early chapters of which were written originally in English) have been translated by Madame Venturi and were published by H. S. King in 1877 and later by Alexander and Shepherd. *From the Pope to the Council* (*alias Letter to the Oecumenical Council*) and *Lamennais* have been translated by Mme. Venturi. *Faith and the Future* and other essays have been translated by Mr T. Okey and published by Dent. Together with *From the Council to God*, *The Duties of Man*, and *To the Italian Working-man*, they have been published by Dent in "Everyman's Library." Various extracts have been collected by the Bishop of Truro and published by Fisher Unwin. There is a volume of translations in the Camelot Classics. Several earlier translations of separate essays have been published.

There are two volumes of a German translation, published by Hoffmann u. Campe (Hamburg, 1868). The Duties of Man and Democracy in Europe are published in French by Charpentier (Paris, 1881).

JOURNALISM.

Mazzini's papers were—

La Giovine Italia. Marseilles and Switzerland. 1832-1836. [Reprinted in the *Biblioteca storica del risorgimento italiano.*]

La Jeune Suisse. Bienne. 1835-1836.

L'Apostolato Popolare. London. 1840-1843.
L'Italia del Popolo. Milan, 1848 ; Rome, 1849 ; Lausanne and Lugano, 1849-1851.
Pensiero ed Azione. London. 1858-1860.
La Roma del Popolo. Rome. 1870-1872.
He contributed largely to—
L'Indicatore Genovese. Genoa. 1828.
L'Indicatore Livornese. Leghorn. 1829.
L'Italiano. Paris. 1836. [7 articles, signed "E. J."]
L'Educatore. London. 1843.
Italia e Popolo. Genoa. 1855-1856.
L'Unità italiana. Genoa. 1860-1865.

LETTERS.

The following collections have been published :—

Giuseppe Mazzini e i fratelli Ruffini, by C. Cagnacci (Porto Maurizio, 1893). Contains his letters to Madame Ruffini (1837-1841), a few letters to A. and G. Ruffini, and extracts from his letters to Elia Benza.

Lettres intimes de Joseph Mazzini, publiées par D. Melegari (Paris, 1895). Contains letters to L. A. Melegari and Madame de Mandrot (mostly 1836-1843).

La Giovine Italia e la giovine Europa (Milan, 1906). Contains letters to L. A. Melegari (chiefly 1833).

Lettere inedite di Giuseppe Mazzini, pubblicate da L. Ordoño de Rosales (Turin, 1898). Contains letters to Gaspare de Rosales (mostly 1834-1836).

Duecento lettere inedite di Giuseppe Mazzini con proemio e note di D. Giuriati (Turin, 1887). Contains letters to G. Lamberti (mostly 1837-1844).

Lettere di G. Mazzini ad A. Giannelli (Prato and Pistoia, 1888-1892) (letters of 1859-1870).

Lettres de Joseph Mazzini à Daniel Stern [Vicomtesse d'Agoult] (Paris, 1873) (letters of 1864-1872).

Corrispondenza inedita di Giuseppe Mazzini con . . . (Milan, 1872). [This is the correspondence in 1863-1864 with Signor Diamilla-Müller, who was the intermediary between Mazzini and Victor Emmanuel. It has been republished in *Politica segreta italiana* (Turin, 1880).]

A very imperfect collection of Mazzini's correspondence is now being published under the editorship of Signor Ernesto Nathan, as *Epistolario di Giuseppe Mazzini* (Florence, 1902). Two volumes only have as yet appeared; their most important feature is Mazzini's correspondence with his mother.

Many letters are also published in the introductions to Mazzini's *Scritti editi e inediti* and in Madame Mario's *Della Viti di G. Mazzini* and *Scritti scelti*; also in Linaker, *La vita e i tempi di E. Mayer* (Florence, 1898) [letters to E. Mayer]; *Nuova Antologia*, Dec. 1, 1884 [letters to Madame Magiotti and E. Mayer]; *Ib.*, May 1 and 16, 1890 [letters to F. Le Monnier]; *Ib.*, May 1, 1907; Del Cerro (*pseud.*), *Un amore di G. Mazzini* (Milan, 1895) [correspondence with Giuditta Sidoli; see above, p. 51]; *Rivista d'Italia*, April, 1902 [letters to N. Fabrizi and others]. Scattered letters may be found in Ramorino, *Précis des derniers événemens de Savoie* (Paris, 1834); *Daily News*, 1853 [see above, p. 169]; Orsini, *Memoirs* (Edinburgh, 1857); *Il risorgimento italiano*, Feb. 11, 1860; *L'unità italiana*, Jan. 15 and 21 and June 3, 1861; *Roma e Venezia*, Jan. 15, 1861; Cironi, *La stampa nazionale italiana* (Prato, 1862); *Lettere edite ed inedite di F. Orsini, G. Mazzini*, etc. (Milan, 1862); *The Shield*, Oct. 1, 1870; Uberti, *Poesie* (Milan, 1871); Moncure Conway, *Mazzini* (London, 1872); *La Gazzetta di Milano*, Jan. 22, 1872; *L'Emancipazione* (Rome), Jan. 24, 1874; La Cecilia, *Memorie storico-politiche* (Rome, 1876); De Monte, *Cronaca del comitato segreto di Napoli* (Naples, 1877); *Quattro lettere a P. Mazzoleni* (Imola, 1881); *Lettera a Filippo Ugoni* (Rovigo, 1887); Donaver, *Uomini e libri* (Genoa, 1888); Carbonelli, *Niccola Mignona* (Naples, 1889); *Fanfulla della Domenica*, April 21 and 28 and May 12, 1889; *Rassegna nazionale*, Oct. 1, 1890; *Rivista della massoneria italiana*, 1890-1891 and 1891-2; *The Century*, Nov. 1891; *Lettere inedite di G. Mazzini a N. Andreini* (Imola, 1897); *Rivista storica del risorgimento italiano*, 1897 and 1900; Saffi, *Ricordi e scritti*, vol. iii. (Florence, 1898); *Giornale d'Italia*, March 23 and April 10, 1902; Lumbroso, *Scaramucce*, pp. 247, 288; Del Cerro in *Rivista Moderna*, 1902; *Secolo*, Aug. 13, 1902; Donaver, *Vita di G. Mazzini* (Florence, 1903); *Corriere della sera*, Aug. 9, 1903, and Aug. 9, 1909; Card. Capecelatro, *Vita della serva di Dio, Paola Frassinetti*; Mrs Fletcher's *Autobiography*; Froude, *Carlyle's Life in London* ; Ireland, *Jane Welsh Carlyle* ; Duncombe's *Life and Correspondence* ; De Amicis, *Cuore* (pages 222 of Ed. 8) ; Quinet, *Œuvres completes*, xi. 32, 423 ; Luzio, *G. Mazzini* (Milan, 1905) ; Gianelli, *Brevi ricordi Mazziniani* (Florence, 1905) ; Essays of Mazzini, translated by T. Okey; Parliamentary Papers, Correspondence affecting affairs of Italy, 1846-1849, i. 223 (probably genuine).

I have also been able to see some 350 unpublished letters,—to Mr and Mrs Peter Taylor (of the greatest value for Mazzini's public and private life ; Mr William Shaen (a large and important collection) ; Mrs Milner-Gibson ; Mr W. Malleson ; Mr W. E. Hickson (when editor of the *Westminster Review*) ; Mr Peter Stuart ; and Miss Galeer.

BIOGRAPHIES.

Mazzini's autobiographical notes in the earlier volumes of the *Scritti editi e inediti* are of course of the highest value. The completest life is Mario, *Della vita di Giuseppe Mazzini* (Milan, 1886), containing a mass of valuable material, but partial and including much extraneous matter. There is a much better study of Mazzini's early life, prefixed to the same authoress' *Scritti scelti.* Saffi's introductions to several volumes of the *Scritti editie e inediti* are most valuable. Donaver's *Vita di G. Mazzini* is useful, especially for the earlier period. There is a short memoir by Madame Venturi (*née* Miss Ashurst) prefixed to the English translation of the Duties of Man. I have seen no other biographies of any value.

NOTICES AND STUDIES.

There is a life-like portrait of Mazzini and much information about his early life in G. Ruffini, *Lorenzo Benoni* (Edinburgh, 1853); a valuable sketch, largely based on conversations with Madame Mazzini, by Mr William Shaen in *The Public Good*, 1851 ; and some useful information in Donaver, *Uomini e libri.* There are studies of more or less value in Cantimori, *Saggio sull' idealismo di G. Mazzini* (Faenza, 1904) ; Linaker, *La Vita italiana nel risorgimento* (Florence, 1899) ; Nencioni, *Saggi critici di letteratura italiana* (Florence, 1898) ; Oxilia, *Giuseppe Mazzini, uomo e letterato* (Florence, 1902); F. Myers in *Fortnightly Review*, 1878 ; De Sanctis, *La letteratura italiana nel secola* XIX. (Naples, 1902); D'Ancona e Bacci, *Manuale della lettaratura italiana*, vol. v.

(Florence, 1901) ; *Mazzini : Conferenze tenute in Genova* (Genova, 1906). There are valuable analyses of Mazzini's economic position in Bozzino, *Il socialismo e la dottrina sociale di Mazzini* (Genoa, 1895), and Bertacchi, *Il pensiero sociale di Giuseppe Mazzini* (Milan, 1900). Hostile studies in Bianchi, *Vicende del Mazzinianismo* (Savona, 1854) and Grüber, *Massoneria e Rivoluzione* (Rome, 1901), the latter of small value.

There are notices in Mrs Carlyle's *Letters and Memorials* ; Carlyle's *Reminiscences* ; Froude, *Carlyle's Life in London* ; *Correspondence of Carlyle and Emerson* ; Mrs Fletcher's *Autobiography* ; W. J Linton, *European Republicans* and *Memories* ; T. S. Cooper, *Autobiography* ; Gabriel Rossetti, *Versified Autobiography* ; Clough, *Prose Remains and Amours de Voyage* ; Margaret Fuller Ossoli, *Memoirs* ; Fagan, *Life of Panizzi* ; Gustavo Modena, *Epistolario* (Rome, 1888) ; Giurati, *Memorie d'emigrazione* (Milan, 1897) ; Badii, *Antologia Mazziniana* (Pitigliano, 1898) ; *Pensiero ed azione nel risorgimento italiano* (Città di Castello, 1898) ; Faldella, *I fratelli Ruffini* (Turin, 1900) ; Lumbroso, *Scaramucce e Avvisaglie* (Frascati, 1902) ; Cironi in *Il Bruscolo*, March 9, 1902 ; Tracts of the Society of the Friends of Italy ; Saffi, *Ricordi e scritti*, vol. iii. ; Felix Moscheles, *Fragments of an Autobiography* ; article by Matilde Blind in *Fortnightly*, May, 1891; articles by Karl Blind in *Fraser's*, August-September, 1882 ; article by Professor Masson in *Macmillan's*, 1871 ; article by Madame Venturi in *The Century*, November, 1891 ; the privately published Life of Miss Catherine Winkworth ; Jowett's Letters ; letter by C. E. Maurice to *The Spectator*, March 6, 1872 ; Barbiera, *Figure e figurine* (Milan, 1899) and *Memorie di un editore* ; Lloyd Garrison's introduction to his edition of some of Mazzini's Essays ; T. S. Cooper, *A Paradise of Martyrs* ; G. J. Holyoake, *Bygones* ; Caroline Fox, *Memories* ; Madame Adams, *Memoirs* ; De Lesseps, *Ma Mission à Rome* ; Rusconi, *Repubblica Romana* ; Diamilla-Müller, *Roma e Venezia* ; Stillman, *Union of Italy* ; Zini, *Storia d'Italia*, Documenti I.

Index

THE TEMPLE PRESS, PRINTERS, LETCHWORTH